Praise for Engaged Healthy, Wealthy & Wise

"This is a defining book about a couple's relationship with wealth – a must-read for inheritors and parents who are potential grantors! Covie weaves together the personal stories of inheritors with research studies that validate her key principles, which are clear, concise, and insightful by themselves. The structure of the book moves smoothly through three stages, from early adulthood to young marrieds to parenthood. Readers can go directly to their current life stage and later move to the other parts of the book to gain insights from the other life stages and family stories."

— SARA HAMILTON, Founder of Family Office Exchange (FOX) and Family Advisor

"If you are or will be an inheritor, or were raised with privilege, then this book is a must for you! Covie covers the journey next gen inheritors experience in their 20s - 50s and offers a clear roadmap – imbued with the wisdom and lessons learned from inheritors (and their partners) she interviewed who have successfully traveled this road. The book offers a guide for how to build confidence in your abilities, how to include your significant other in the journey, and how to truly integrate your experience around wealth with your authentic self."

— RACHEL GERROL, CEO and Co-Founder of NEXUS

"In her reliably honest, compassionate, and courageous style, Covie's latest book, *Engaged Healthy, Wealthy & Wise*, turns many of our industry norms inside-out. With intelligence, curiosity, and balance, she thoughtfully questions the value of our long-held sacred cows, such as the prenuptial agreement and loyalty to family financial eco-systems. Covie invites the rising gen, their families, and their advisors to consider how we (and they) might be more creative in putting these family members back in the driver's seat of their lives, supporting them to make decisions that give them agency and invite their full engagement."

— Kristin Keffeler, MSM, MAPP Family wealth and family enterprise consultant and author of *The Myth of the Silver Spoon: Navigating Family Wealth & Creating an Impactful Life*

"Eight years ago, I applauded *Raised Healthy, Wealthy and Wise* as a breath of fresh air in the typically pessimistic literature about inheritors and their lives. Covie Edwards-Pitt has now done it again with her third book in the series. *Engaged* draws together the voices of yet another thoughtful cohort of inheritors and their partners for more wisdom about life with wealth. From prenups to partnering to parenting, she makes a compelling case for the role of autonomy, unity, self-discipline, and love in prospering with good fortune. It is another wonderful addition to the field in its positive, affirming perspective."

— James Grubman, PhD, Family wealth consultant and author of *Strangers in Paradise: How Families Adapt to Wealth Across Generations*

"I wrote *Life is What You Make It* with the hope of sharing with others the lessons I've learned about how to move beyond the legacy of a parent's success to craft a life of one's own. Covie's wonderful new book *Engaged* provides all who will walk in shoes similar to mine with a compass and roadmap for their journey. And her warm and hopeful writing style leaves the reader feeling that they have an encouraging, wise friend cheering them along on the way."

— Peter Buffett, musician and author of *Life is What You Make It*

"Covie's book has fundamentally changed the way I will approach work with families working through complexities of inherited wealth. She provides fresh and provocative perspective, told through the powerful stories of families, that is simultaneously heart-felt, grounded, and smart. The advice here is brave and impactful!"

— Debbie Bing, President and Principal, CFAR

"*Engaged* is the antidote to the fear and outdated 'wisdom' that keeps couples from pursuing and achieving healthy and loving partnerships. Parents and professional advisors will certainly be moved by the refreshing and inspirational insight captured within."

— Jim Coutré, family office and philanthropy professional

"Every family is changed with each marriage that expands the family footprint. This terrific book takes a countercultural approach, avoiding the typical scare tactics that emphasize risk management and motivate self-preservation, and instead lifting up success stories that illuminate what wealthy families and inheritors can invest in to make marriage work (identity, self-worth, love, and connection) and how doing so can be life-affirming."

— Danielle Oristian York, Executive Director 21/64, Inc

"Given Covie's previous two books, I knew *Engaged Healthy, Wealthy & Wise* would be an important addition to our field. What surprised me, as a professional in the field with 20 years of experience, was how much the book got me thinking about how to help my own children have strong relationships as it relates to wealth, and how we might best welcome their partners fully into our family."

— Dr. Jamie Traeger-Muney, Founder, Wealth Legacy Group

"Once again, Coventry Edwards-Pitt has skillfully and beautifully written about the complexities of wealth, money, family, and relationships. *Engaged Healthy, Wealthy & Wise* provides excellent guidance for wealth inheritors of many different backgrounds told through stories of diverse inheritors. We see ourselves and our clients through the lives of the book's interviewees. This diversity of perspectives and focus on the strength of love, relationships, resilience, and family makes this book one for us all to keep close and use frequently!"

— Audrey L. Jacobs, Principal, The Sarafina Group, Inc.

"I am just thrilled at the prospect of being able to recommend this book to the many, many families and advisors I know will benefit from reading it! Covie breaks new ground, writing for inheritors and their significant others about how to successfully navigate love and family wealth - a major area that comes up again and again, but none has met the challenge of writing about this sensitive topic. The stories Covie shares in the voices of the inheritors and partners she interviewed are eye-opening and upend a number of industry conventions by revealing how strategies the industry often recommends feel to the inheriting generation whose lives they directly impact. And these novel insights are delivered in a positive, hopeful way, with the ultimate focus on solutions and best practices that center on the heart more than the wealth."

— MARIANN MIHAILIDIS, member Advisory Board Family Wealth Alliance, Wise Counsel Research, Qualitative Capital Advisor and Principal of M2 Connections, LLC, trusted advisor to Single Family Office Senior Executives in small peer group Circles

"Covie's first book, *Raised Healthy, Wealthy & Wise* has become a go-to in my canon of suggested books for parents raising children amid wealth. Now, *Engaged Healthy, Wealthy & Wise* provides an option to young couples, and those who advise them, which previously didn't exist. The combination of insights from couples, in their own voices, and Covie's own integration of ideas in the field, makes her new book extraordinarily accessible and valuable."

— SHARNA GOLDSEKER, founder of 21/64 Inc and co-author of *Generation Impact: How Next Gen Donors Are Revolutionizing Giving*

"Edwards-Pitt's true strength is surfacing simple truths in complicated situations. She listens carefully to her subjects and hears the core values that emerge time and again. The clarity of the writing, embroidered with good sense and practical recommendations, is a pleasure to read. She illuminates the ultimate realization that the real wealth of your family is not financial, and your self-worth is not your net worth. A valuable, essential book."

— Joseph W. Reilly Jr., Family Office Advisor, Director of the Inheritance Project

"Covie's book is the navigation we need right now to separate us from the tangled storylines that the much-anticipated intergenerational wealth transfer has created and redirect us with a heart-centered reminder of who we are at our core. It's a breath of fresh air and a must read for anyone working with inheritors and their families."

— Elaine Martyn., Philanthropic Advisor

"Once again Coventry has brought us the voices of a community that is rarely heard from. Inheritors and their partners talking about money and even more rarely how they have integrated it successfully into their lives."

— James (Jay) E. Hughes, Jr., author of *Family Wealth: Keeping it in the Family*; *Family: The Compact Among Generations*; with Keith Whitaker and Susan Massenzio, *The Cycle of the Gift*; with Hartley Goldstone and Keith Whitaker, *Family Trusts*

Engaged Healthy, Wealthy & Wise

Engaged Healthy, Wealthy & Wise

Lessons from inheritors and their significant others on how they have navigated love and family wealth and forged their own joint path

Coventry Edwards-Pitt

Engaged Healthy, Wealthy & Wise by Coventry Edwards-Pitt
Copyright © 2022 Coventry Edwards-Pitt

All rights reserved

ISBN: 979-8-218-07137-0

www.healthywealthywisecollection.com

For more information, email info@healthywealthywisecollection.com

Printed in the United States of America
First Edition

Book design by Kacy Colson

Contents

Acknowledgments	XIII
Introduction	1
SECTION ONE: ON YOUR OWN	
Meet Our Interviewees	11
1: Building the Foundation	15
2: Starting to Emerge	45
SECTION TWO: JUST THE TWO OF US	
Meet Our Interviewees	77
3: Meeting the One	83
4: For Richer or Poorer, Part I: The Problem with Prenups	103
5: For Richer or Poorer, Part II: Taking a Different Approach	129
6: Melding of the Minds	145
SECTION THREE: BEYOND US	
Meet Our Interviewees	175
7: Meeting the Parents: Staying "We" Amid the Rest of the Family	179
8: Becoming the Parents	203
9: Breaking Free	229
10: Fully Engaged	249
SECTION FOUR: APPENDICES	
Relationship movies that will make you think (and hope)	255
Recommended reading	256
Endnotes	259
Notes pages	268

Acknowledgments

A heartfelt thank you to:

- The interviewees—I am grateful for your candor and willingness to share with me how you have navigated the land of love and wealth. The advice I give will forever be shaped by your hard-earned wisdom, and I'm confident your insights will benefit and inspire any who hear them.
- Our clients—It has been so rewarding to walk alongside you, share in your hopes and dreams, and offer counsel on the issues that you care most deeply about. Thank you for your trust and friendship.
- My partners and colleagues at our firm—It's been a joy to share these past (almost 20) years of my professional life with you, to be part of building our firm together, and to collaborate with you on serving our clients. A special thank you to Roy Ballentine for his mentorship over the years and to Roy Ballentine, Drew McMorrow, and the rest of my partners for believing in the importance of this work and allowing me the time to dedicate to its creation.
- The experts I spoke with during my research process—I'm thankful to the industry colleagues (many of whom I'm lucky to count as friends) who generously shared their wisdom with me for this project—Ella Chase, Jim Coutré, Stephanie Ellis-Smith, Kristen Heaney, Annie Hurwitz, Laurie Israel, Audrey Jacobs, Kristin Keffeler, Caroline Krauss, Elaine Martyn, Arden O'Connor, Lani Peterson, Dana Siperstein, Heidi Tallentire, Jennifer Touchet, Jamie Traeger-Muney, Joy B. Webb, and Danielle Oristian York.
- The many industry thought leaders beyond this group whose

work has informed both this book and our practice—Stacy Allred, Patricia Angus, Tim Belber, Charlotte Beyer, Barbara Blouin, Joanie Bronfman, Fredda Herz Brown, Debbie Bing, Robin Catlin, Diana Chambers, Charlie Collier, Sharna Goldseker, Hartley Goldstone, Jeanne Goussev, Jim Grubman, Sara Hamilton, Amy Hart-Clyne, Barbara Hauser, Lee Hausner, Russ Haworth, Jay Hughes, Adrienne Iglehart, Dennis Jaffe, George Kinder, Ross Levin, John Levy, Kathy Lintz, Charles Lowenhaupt, Susan Massenzio, Tom McCullough, Jackie Merrill, Richard Orlando, Dennis Passis, Scott Peppet, Ellen Perry, Joe Reilly, Greg Rogers, Laurent Roux, Myra Salzer, Jeff Savlov, Sue Schwartzman, Jill Shipley, Ruth Steverlynck, Dune Thorne, John A. Warnick, Philippe Weil, Jamie Weiner, Keith Whitaker, Thayer Willis, and David York.

- ❖ The champions—Thank you to the clients, families, community foundations, organizations, and fellow advisors who have invited me to speak or work with them on implementing the lessons in my first two books. Your kind words about how these books impacted you live in my heart and spurred me on as I buckled down to write this one.
- ❖ The friends whose moral support cheered me on—this includes a number of the people already listed above and the members of my WPO group who shared in the journey from the beginning to the end.
- ❖ Janie Doherty—for being a constant lifeline and for the tremendous amount of effort she dedicated to helping me bring this project to life, from scheduling 50 interviews, to wrangling more than a thousand pages of transcripts, to saving articles, to helping me create a filing system to keep all of this voluminous research in order. I truly could not have done this project without you!
- ❖ The book production team—Thank you to colleagues past and present who were part of the book production team: Leah Warren for her help during the interview process, Laura Cantalini for her

assistance with the literature review, Bobby Moffitt for his reactions and insights as an early reader, Akeiva Ellis for her review of Section One, Carly Augeri for managing much of our firm's marketing function on her own while I was absorbed with this project, and Ashley Cochrane for her book marketing wizardry and for juggling the many vendors and steps involved in getting the book from manuscript to printed copy. Thanks too to Lisa Kirk for copyediting, Kacy Colson for the book's interior design, Colleen Picciotti at Dyad Photography for her help with the cover photo, and Alexander Duckworth from POP for the jacket design.

- ❖ My family—Thank you to my mother, whose struggle with dementia has illuminated for me the things that really matter in life. I appreciate daily all that you did to help me launch independently and confidently into life. Thank you to my father, who I know would read this avidly and have a plethora of comments (and groan-worthy puns) if he were still with us. Thanks to my brother and his wife for keeping our father's sense of humor alive and for all you do to carry forward our family's memories. Thanks too to my in-laws for always helping me feel incredibly welcome in your loving family.

- ❖ My husband—I don't think I could have written this book without understanding the joy that comes from sharing your life with your best friend. Thank you for being the first reader I would trust to read the manuscript during the writing process, for the walks with Ollie (my four-footed writing partner) that cleared my head, and for finding the time in your own very busy life to make the chocolate cookies that turned out to be critical to the writing process.

- ❖ My daughter—Thank you for the daily encouragement and the joy, laughter, music, and stories you bring to my life. You always put a smile on my face when you popped into my writing room. I'm so looking forward to hearing all of the stories you will tell.

Engaged Healthy, Wealthy & Wise

Introduction

When a young inheritor announces that they have met "the one"—their chosen life partner whom they hope to marry—the wheels of the wealth advising industry whir into motion. Advisors recommend prenuptial agreements, wealth-owning families discuss how transparent to be about the family's financial situation, and white papers offer best practices about how to "onboard" the new partner to the wealth-owning family's cultural and financial ecosystem. The prevailing motivation underlying this flurry of planning is risk management, defined largely as preservation of the wealth-owning family's financial assets and cultural ethos.

But amid all of this, there is a young couple in love. What does it feel like to be this young inheritor (who might still be trying to forge a differentiated sense of self amid the backdrop of inherited wealth) and their partner, for whom all of this is new and largely irrelevant, or at least tangential to how they feel about their significant other and their vision for their lives together? How does it feel when the possibility that defines this tender time of life runs smack into the ossified frameworks inherent in most wealth management ecosystems? And how can a young couple make it through with their love, partnership, and faith in each other not only intact but stronger on the other side?

That is what this book is about. It's about the perspective of these young people who are rarely asked for their views by an industry that is employed largely by their parents' generation. And it is about how they have navigated the journey of forging a strong union and fulfilling life path with their chosen partner amid the complexities of inherited family wealth.

Our industry seldom considers this topic, and when it does, we hear mostly about the downsides—how hard it can be for young inheritors to trust a new partner's intentions, how money may be lost in marriage, and how much risk is introduced when new partners are invited to the family governance table. In short, we hear a lot about what can go wrong.

We're taking a different approach. We're focusing in this book on what can go right and how—on success stories of couples who are in love, whose lives have been meaningfully improved by the presence of the other, and who view themselves as a team working together to navigate the land of love and family wealth and construct a life of purpose and meaning.

Refocusing the lens

Our aim with this book was to refocus the lens—to hear directly from the couples on the receiving end of the wealth advising industry's many common practices that impact this stage of life. The 22 couples whose stories are captured here are all (still) in their first marriages, range in age from their early-30s to their mid-70s, and predominantly (77%) involve the pairing of a partner who views themselves as an inheritor with one who does not.

We were blown away by what we heard in these couples' stories—the struggles they have encountered attempting to reconcile love and family wealth, and the ingenuity, courage, and resilience they have demonstrated in making it through. Each of our interviews traversed the hallowed ground of love, trust, and wealth—we delved into how the couple first met, how the reality of the inheritor's family wealth was first revealed, how and in what ways family wealth has swirled around most of the important things in their joint life, from their marital planning to their child-rearing to their relationships with the rest of the family to their divining their life's purpose, and how they have kept their union strong through it all.

Many (but not all) of our discussions involved both partners, and it was a joy to hear their interactions with each other—how they chimed in, occasionally finished each other's sentences, and generally supported each other as we explored these (often difficult) topics. We found that even for the couples who have been married for decades, the memories of this stage of life—when their marriage was new and they were first confronted with the complexities of reconciling inherited family wealth with their relationship—were crystal clear and often still laden with emotion.

Beyond the couples we interviewed, we thought it was important to contextualize their perspective with other voices. We spoke with inheritors who are single and are still traveling the path of finding a partner and grappling with the ways in which inherited wealth can complicate that journey (more on this in Section One). And we spoke with several wealth-generating parents who have done their best to ensure that their own wealth transfer planning strategies do not impede their children's ability to forge strong unions with their chosen partners. Finally, to round out these first-person perspectives, we talked with industry experts ranging from attorneys to philanthropy advisors to consultants specializing in inheritor individuation, and we reviewed (and included salient points from) the literature in our field relevant to this topic.

Our firm and the advice we give our clients have forever been changed by what we learned in this process and especially in the voices of those whose lives have been impacted by the strategies our industry recommends. It is our hope that many others in our field will be too once they hear these stories. I am indebted to the interviewees for their willingness to share candidly with me and only hope they will feel I've done their stories justice and that the insights they generously shared will spread far and wide. To preserve their anonymity, I have changed names and identifying details throughout, but all quotes are verbatim.

How this book works

This book is split into three sections: On Your Own, Just the Two of Us, and Beyond Us. It is designed to mirror the arc of life that we saw our inheritor interviewees traveled—first on their own, attempting to individuate and forge a capable and authentic sense of self amid inherited wealth, then in the early and formative days of their relationship with their chosen partner, and finally expanding out into the life the couple designs beyond themselves (including as parents, as members of a broader, combined family, as agents of their own wealth advising ecosystem, and as contributors to the broader world).

Section One offers a road map for any inheritor struggling with these complexities, told in the words of our many interviewees who have successfully navigated these very challenges and eventually emerged on the other side fully engaged in their own life. If you already feel confident in your sense of self (and comfortable with the wealth you will inherit and how to be honest about it with others), you can skip to Section Two, which begins the moment you and your partner meet. And if you are already happily paired but you and your partner are just beginning to contemplate parenting or how to assert your own wishes relative to the broader family's wealth management framework, you may want to start with Section Three.

Throughout, you may find that particular sections resonate more loudly because they reflect where you are in life currently or where you've recently been. But don't be afraid to read ahead to life stages that may lie down the road (parenting, for example). There was a recurring refrain in our interviews—many of our interviewees expressed that they wish they had been able to read a book like this earlier in their lives. This is your chance to do just that and to shape your future informed by the benefit of our interviewees' hard-won wisdom and insights.

This book is for you

This book is for you wherever you are in this journey. It's for every inheritor struggling with reconciling their self with their wealth or wondering how and when to tell their partner that their family is significantly wealthy. It's for every partner who will be on the receiving end of this conversation (and everything it entails and precedes), and for every couple who has navigated this revelation but now must consider how to assert their shared values amid the infrastructure of a broader family wealth management ecosystem (trustees, wealth advisors, or family office). In short, it's for every couple navigating the land of love and inheritance as they forge a joint life path and work to integrate their hopes for the future with the expectations, complexities, and yes, opportunities that inherited family wealth offers.

It is also for the parents of these young people—often the wealth-generating generation—who deserve to understand how the strategies and structures they are contemplating will be received by the people whose opinion they often care the most about. Although I wrote this book with primarily inheritors and their partners in mind, I was frequently struck in my interviews by how differently their parents' generation would act (and feel) if they understood how their actions were perceived by their children and their children's partners. I hope that every wealth-generating parent (or generation currently in primary control of the wealth management ecosystem) will listen to these voices, try to understand and reflect on their perspectives, and allow them to inform their own.

This book is also for any advisor operating within the arena of family and wealth. As advisors, we are often hired by the wealth-generating generation to help them bring their goals to fruition. Deep down, beneath the focus on wealth maximization (or preservation), tax mitigation, and legacy creation, most wealth-generating parents first and foremost want their children to be happy—and to experience love in their lives. Armed with these stories, we can show them how to achieve this goal, or at least maximize its likelihood, and how they can create plans and structures that are conducive to their children forging a loving union with their chosen life partner and living a couple-directed, fulfilling life.

And now a note on what this book is not—it's not about divorce or relationships that are flawed from the start. Although there is much written about the rising rate of divorce, it turns out that among the demographic of our interviewees (socioeconomically advantaged and well-educated), lasting marriage is alive and well. This book is also not about later-life marriages or blended families. Our focus here is on first marriages, often begun in the 20s or 30s, between two people who are in love and whose relationship would work out if only the backdrop of inherited wealth and its attendant complexities did not get in the way.

A note on word choice and context

There is no perfect term for a young person who inherits (or will inherit) wealth. I have long chafed at the terms "next gen" and "G2" because of their implicit subordination and the way in which they link identity not only to previous generations but to the narrow fact of when significant wealth was first generated within a family. With their book *The Voice of the Rising Generation*, authors James E. "Jay" Hughes, Susan E. Massenzio, and Keith Whitaker introduced a new and improved term. Still, while there is much I like about "the rising gen," as the term has come to be known in the industry, the moniker feels like an imperfect fit for many of my interviewees who might still prefer a less generationally linked term or who may fairly perceive themselves as largely "risen."

In the end, I went with the term "inheritor," which although it suffers from the same challenge of defining an individual in relation to something outside of themselves, aptly reflects how many of my interviewees perceive (or used to perceive) their own identity. In fact, the task of needing to integrate this bequeathed identity with something that feels truly of one's own is an important part of what we will discuss in the first section of the book. I choose to interpret the word "inheritor" broadly, meaning I use it for any and all of the following: someone who has already inherited family wealth, someone who will likely inherit family wealth at some point in the future, and someone who, even if they may never inherit family wealth, was raised in an upbringing sufficiently shaped by their family's affluence and influence that they have "inherited" its impact on their identity.

I use the term "partner" throughout to refer to the inheritor's significant other, whether spouse, fiancé/e, or long-term companion in a committed relationship. And I've chosen to use the pronoun "they" throughout to imply the s/he singular—I prefer the pronoun both for its gender neutrality and its linguistic simplicity.

Finally, a note on context: this book is set largely within what is recognized in the wealth advising industry as a Western, individualist culture,[1] as this is the milieu that defined the majority of my interviewees' upbringing and orientation.

Begin today

Since the publication of my first book for our firm in 2014 (*Raised Healthy, Wealthy & Wise*—aimed at helping parents raise grounded children amid wealth), I have come to devote a large share of my time as our firm's Chief Creative Officer to trying to bring novel ideas to our clients and consulting on how to implement the lessons of our firm's books in their lives. It's been incredibly rewarding work to help people on issues that matter most deeply to them.

Still, I know that even with these efforts and our firm's increased work on projects related to these issues even with clients who have no need for our broader wealth management services, there are only so many we will be able to reach directly. My hope with this book is to get the wisdom of my interviewees into the hands of those we may never meet but whose lives might be profoundly benefitted by these stories.

If you're an inheritor or partner, I hope you'll take away from this book not only the solace that you are not alone, but also the tools you need to navigate your way through the land of love and wealth and the courage to prioritize your partnership amid the gravitational pull of inherited family wealth. If you're an advisor, I hope you'll be inspired by these stories to seek ways to shift the conversation with wealth-generating clients so that they are able to make decisions informed by our interviewees' perspective.

Wherever you are, I hope you begin today.

Section One

On Your Own

Meet Our Interviewees

....

Below are our interviewees who appear in Section One, in order of appearance:

Chapter One:

Harper: Raised in a well-known family with a nationally recognized last name, Harper grew up in Dallas, Texas, immersed in four generations of family lore of fortunes won and squandered. Drawn to helping people, she pursued a career in medicine and now, in her 40s, is a sought-after pediatric surgeon. She has been engaged once but is currently single. Ten years ago, a criminal investment manager defrauded her branch of the family out of much of its wealth.

Craig: The eldest of three children, Craig grew up in Short Hills, New Jersey, aware of his father's financial success as a high-profile Wall Street executive. Eager to strike out on his own, Craig launched a tech start-up his junior year of college. When it ultimately failed after six intense years, Craig embarked on a new career in impact investing, accepting an entry-level position at a top tier firm. His girlfriend, now wife, Laura, was an important support during this transition.

Lucy: The younger of two daughters, Lucy grew up in St. Paul, Minnesota, attending private schools but believing she was no wealthier than her other upper middle-class friends. Her life changed at 22 when the sudden loss of her father left her reeling with grief and trying to process that she was now the beneficiary of a $20 million inheritance. Now in her 40s, and with a daughter of her own, Lucy lives in Brooklyn with her husband and has found her calling running an organization that empowers affluent white women to use their purchasing power and influence to help close the racial wealth gap.

ABBY: As a 3rd generation inheritor on her mother's side, Abby grew up in Litchfield, Connecticut, hearing her mother and father talk openly about navigating financial inequality in their relationship. Abby has been friends with her partner Ben since middle school, and they now have a three-year-old daughter. Abby is a public-school history teacher in Newark, New Jersey, and has been teaching her favorite age, eighth grade, for five years.

ALICE AND TIM: Alice grew up in an "old money" family, attempting to reconcile her ancestors' names on buildings with her own family's frugal lifestyle and her feminist mother's belief that it was important she be capable of supporting herself. Alice is married to Tim, whose life changed his freshman year of college when his parents sold their multigenerational family business and became instantly wealthy. Alice and Tim met in college and have been married for 28 years. They now live in Oak Park, Illinois, where Tim runs his own artisanal furniture studio and Alice is a docent at a local conservation trust. They have three teenage children.

Chapter Two:

HELEN: Helen grew up in Portland, Maine, aware of the wealth her mother and she had inherited from her great-grandfather's textile business and the concern voiced by her father that she would be taken advantage of if people knew about it. She met her husband, Stefan, in her 20s and formed an immediate bond because they both had lost their mothers at an early age. Now in her 50s, Helen is a novelist, and she and Stefan live in the Washington, DC, area with their three teenage children.

Justin: The youngest of three siblings, Justin grew up near Seattle, Washington, hearing from his mother (also an inheritor) that he was expected to do chores around the house and earn his own spending money. Now in his late 20s, he lives in Boulder, Colorado, and works for a film company that produces environmental documentaries.

Darius: Darius grew up in Atlanta, Georgia, the eldest son of parents who immigrated from Jamaica and became successful doctors. Now in his 20s, he works for Google as a programmer and feeds his passion for financial planning by giving his friends free lessons on how they can start to save and build wealth.

CHAPTER ONE

Building the Foundation

The 20s, at least in our modern world, are about individuating—striking out on our own.[2] They are that time in life when we start to ask—and begin to fumble toward answering—critical life-defining questions like: Who am I? How am I different from my parents? How will I contribute to the world? Who will I love? And they are the time when the answers to these questions and our efforts toward discovering them begin to carve out trajectories that indelibly shape the rest of our lives.

As clinical psychologist Meg Jay writes in her book, *The Defining Decade*, "Your twenties matter. Eighty percent of life's most defining moments take place by age thirty-five."[3] Those of us older than this critical decade can probably recall seminal experiences we had when we were that age that we now credit for shaping who we are. And we can remember that thrilling moment when we first proved to ourselves that we could stand on our own two feet—that we might actually be able to make it in the world as a real live adult, no longer reliant on our parents or their support. The twenties are a critical time in life not only because we begin to find out who we are, but importantly because we begin to prove to ourselves what we're capable of.

Individuating amid wealth

In the wealth advising industry, it's long been understood that this normal process of individuation and maturation is complicated by wealth. In 2007, family wealth consultants and psychologists Dennis Jaffe and Jim Grubman published a seminal paper titled "Acquirers' and Inheritors' Dilemma" that summarized 50 years of research in the field. "This then is 'The Inheritor's Dilemma'—the daunting task of growing a strong responsible identity out of the environment of wealth," they write. "The Inheritor must still accomplish the task of any individual: to grow a productive, responsible, and well-adjusted identity within the environment of one's birth. What is under-rated is how difficult it can be to grow this identity when the land of one's birth is Wealth. The very nature of the environment makes this growth a uniquely daunting task."[4]

Why is this? Why is it harder to individuate when you've grown up amid wealth? There are multiple shelves of wonderful books that dig deeply into this topic (see my Recommended Reading for a list!) but to summarize, in our experience, individuating amid wealth is more challenging for three primary reasons:

- Shame about having been given an unearned advantage
- Shadows of parents/wealth builder looming large
- Support that undermines capacity

Shame

Those of us who spend our days working with individuals who have inherited wealth know that shame is a commonly expressed emotion. Nearly 40 years ago, John Sedgwick, an inheritor himself, published *Rich Kids*, a 300-plus page profile of the lives, emotions, and struggles of 50 of his inheritor friends. Amid the pages, which ultimately depict very few friends feeling happier or more fulfilled as a result of their inheritance, Sedgwick includes this stunning explication of shame—where it comes from and how it feels:

"For all rich kids, the act of inheritance is entirely passive. Yet this sometimes makes the guilt more severe, and more permanent. True criminals, at least, have something to confess. They can receive forgiveness, they can reform, they can put their sins behind them. But rich kids start to feel they are the sin themselves, and every crime that was ever committed out of greed now hangs on their heads. They see the inequity that lies about them, or read about it in their money mail, and they think they are responsible for it. Because they are on top, they must be squashing those on the bottom. This is the true embarrassment of riches.... To clear themselves they often feel...an unspecified and diffused need to do penance, to suffer in some way so as to square things with the almighty dollar."[5]

The inheritors I know who feel shame know exactly what Sedgwick is talking about. If anything, the intervening 40 years that have passed since Sedgwick penned these words and the societal and cultural shifts that they have brought have only made it worse. In many ways, this shame has now been taken up as a generational anthem, fueling articles with headlines like "The Rich Kids Who Want to Tear Down Capitalism"[6] and reflected in a presumption among many of a certain age group—and perhaps political persuasion—that wealth accumulation is in and of itself immoral.

It's important to note that not everyone feels shame. We've seen in our practice wealth-origin stories that seem to inoculate inheritors from shame as well as strategies that allow inheritors to overcome shame and move forward to confident, self-fueled, purpose-driven lives (what most of this chapter will be about). But for those who do feel shame, it's real and can lead to a paroxysm of paralyzing guilt that can prevent them from purposefully engaging with their wealth ("I'll be less tainted if I don't use it or acknowledge it") or even moving through developmentally beneficial stages like earning an income ("Why should I earn money if I don't need it and if my doing so will take away from someone else who might deserve it more than me?")

Shadows looming large

Most young people growing up in a family with wealth hear stories about the individual or generation that built the wealth. For some, this person is close at hand, a father or mother with tremendous career and financial success. For others, it's several generations removed—the grandfather or great-grandfather who grew up poor selling newspapers and then founded a publishing company eventually worth millions, or billions. No matter how far removed or close these wealth-building individuals are, their success looms large. It's challenging for young people just beginning to carve out their own path in life to reconcile this already demonstrated and lauded success with the primal drive to go beyond your parents, to do something that is better, or different enough, to demonstrate and validate your contributions to the world.

Eileen Rockefeller puts it this way in her lovely memoir, *Being a Rockefeller: Becoming Myself*: "I am part of a long line of venture capitalists and philanthropists. It's hard to talk about my grandfathers without them taking over. Their accomplishments overwhelm me. I feel small and insignificant in comparison."[7]

In addition to this sense that young people individuating amid wealth can have—that they are small by comparison—there are corollary effects of the wealth-builder's success that can exert influence over a young person's fledgling trajectory as they are just starting out. The wealth advising industry now aptly describes this through the metaphors of a black hole and an incoming meteor, thanks to two seminal books by authors Jay Hughes, Susan Massenzio, and Keith Whitaker. In their 2014 *The Voice of the Rising Generation*, they use the image of a black hole to describe how the wealth builder's dream can "silence the dreams of rising generations" through the power of its gravitational pull.[8] And in their 2012 *The Cycle of the Gift*, the same three authors explain how a financial gift can act as a meteor that "flies from the giver to the recipient, often appearing on the recipient's horizon with no warning."[9]

Support that undermines capacity

Young people who grow up amid abundant financial resources are faced with an unusual problem, but a problem nonetheless—too much help. There are numerous well-meaning people—parents, financial advisors, trustees, family office executives—who proactively offer help with everything from paying the rent to managing the bills to finding an apartment to rent, etc, etc. For a young person just struggling to make their way in the world, these offers of help can be tempting. How do you muster the strength to say no when you're not quite sure how you'll do it on your own without the help? And how do you politely decline when doing so might make you look ungrateful to parents making heartfelt gifts or disloyal to generations of expectations about which services the family office should provide. Yes, it can be psychologically challenging and emotionally exhausting to say no. But saying yes is ultimately worse. It deprives you of the chance to prove to yourself what you are capable of on your own. It's akin to drinking saltwater to quench your thirst when stranded out at sea—satisfying in the near-term, but ultimately self-defeating.

The Way Through

These are real problems. The aim of this section is to give you a way through. Why start here? How is this relevant to a book that's primarily about finding and building a life with your chosen life partner?

Because, as the late Zen Master Thích Nhất Hanh writes in his book *How to Love*: "You can't offer happiness until you have it for yourself. So build a home inside by accepting yourself and learning to love and heal yourself."[10]

Or, as inheritor coach Myra Salzer says in her wonderful guide, *The Inheritor's Sherpa*, you need to love yourself and figure out who you are as a precursor to a relationship "because you want someone to fall in love with *you*."[11]

So how do you overcome shame? How do you move out from under a wealth generator's looming shadow? How do you resist support that ultimately undermines? The answer to all of these questions is the same—it is to first build, brick by brick, a sense of your own individual capacity and self-efficacy. Many of the young inheritors I know have successfully traveled this journey. They've proven to themselves through years of effort that they don't *need* the money—to live, to feel whole, to enjoy life, to find love—and in doing so, they've found a freedom in their relationship to their inheritance. They can now choose, with agency, to engage with it. They can now "own" it because they are not dependent upon it. They can answer the question, "If the money went away tomorrow, would I be okay?" with a resounding *yes*, and that allows them to be okay with the fact that it's still here. For many, this was a two-stage process—going away and proving to themselves that they could be independent and then coming back and reengaging (with the wealth, the family office, the choices and opportunities wealth makes possible) from a position of authority and a grounded, foundational sense of self.

Parenting yourself

So, how do you make this happen if you're still struggling on this path? In my first book, *Raised Healthy, Wealthy & Wise*, aimed at helping parents raise grounded children amid wealth, I talked about the four success factors that I observed all of my interviewees (children raised with wealth, now grown into content, self-motivated adults) had in common:

- Demonstrated ability to earn their own money
- Motivation toward achieving personal goals
- Grounded sense of self not wrapped up in issues related to wealth
- Ability to overcome setbacks[12]

The rest of that book focused on stories my interviewees shared of how their parents helped them cultivate these success factors in their lives—the parenting behaviors and messages they believed most contributed to their strong sense of self.

But what if your parents didn't emphasize these messages in your upbringing? Or what if they tried, but you find yourself looking at this list and realizing you are still trying to master these milestones? Then this chapter's stories are for you.

Part of what we realize when we grow up and begin to individuate on our own is that our parents are fallible, they're human, that no matter how hard they tried, they couldn't possibly raise us into being ideal humans because they're not ideal humans themselves. Continued growth toward that ideal is on us. We have to pick up where our parents left off—and the fun part is that now we get to be in charge! We can set our own goals, decide what we want to be able to say is true for ourselves, and then go out and make it happen.

The stories and framework that follow will show you how to do the work to master these success factors in your own life now, and in so doing, prove to yourself what you're capable of.

Earning a strong foundation

In 1943, psychologist Abraham Maslow first proposed his theory of a hierarchy of needs—often depicted as a pyramid, ranging from physiological needs on the bottom to love and belonging in the middle to self-actualization at the top.[13] He postulated that we are all motivated ultimately to pursue self-actualization (defined as self-fulfillment and the realization of one's potential), but that failure to meet lower-level needs can disrupt this process. Individuals lacking in foundational needs will be motivated first to remedy this lack before feeling free to pursue higher needs. Conversely, if a person aims to fulfill a higher order need without first securing the basics, the effort will lack integration and ring hollow.

Maslow's theory has been much discussed, debated, and expanded upon.[14] But for our purposes, it's thought-provoking to notice that the needs at the bottom of the pyramid—the physiological needs of food, clothing, and shelter, and the safety needs of health and financial security—are highly correlated with the needs we satisfy when we support ourselves. They are the needs that largely fall under the "living expenses" line item on a financial budget, and while it's true that money can't buy all of them (health, for instance) it's also true that money is necessary for the attainment of most.

Now, for an interesting thought experiment: what if, in order for the needs at the bottom of the pyramid to truly be fulfilled, you have to pay for these things yourself? What if you need to *earn* these levels? Perhaps it's impossible to feel that you've met these needs when a little voice inside your head reminds you that this food, shelter, security, etc. could go away tomorrow if someone you have no control over changes their mind (say, a trustee fails to make a distribution or a parent decides not to renew an annual gift?)

If this is true, we do a disservice by encouraging young people to focus on self-actualization (finding your passion) without first talking about the necessity of mastering these fundamental milestones of adulthood and proving to themselves psychologically that they have the wherewithal to meet their basic needs. The inheritors I know who've done this have benefited twice over—not only did they emerge with a deep trust in their own capacity, but importantly, they took from the experience a sense of satisfaction and contentment that itself was a critical stepping-stone on their path to self-fulfillment.

Factor 1: *The critical shift in outlook that follows supporting yourself*

We can see from our Maslow thought experiment that so much of the process of successfully individuating is about what a young person thinks about themself. And how a person thinks about themself follows causally from what they've proven to themself they can do. Or as some say, confidence follows competence. This is work that, by its very nature, cannot be outsourced—someone can tell you over and over that you're capable of something, but until you do it, it's hard to truly convince yourself that they're right.

We saw in our conversations with our interviewees that the actual act of supporting yourself was both protective and freeing psychologically—its power lay in the number of beneficial ways that it shifted how our inheritors thought about themselves and trusted in their capabilities:

1. Conquering fears

Tangled up in the complex web of self-doubt that inheritors often wrestle with is a distinct thread of fear. What if the money goes away? And the corollary questions: Will I be able to make it? Will I still be me if the wealth part of me no longer exists? These fears can eat away at an inheritor's sense of self until they are faced head-on. And the best way to face them is to live at least some period of time in this reality—living only off of funds you provide for yourself, as if the money had already gone away—and proving to yourself that you'll be just fine.

There is a tremendous amount of confidence that comes from knowing you would be prepared for any eventuality. And sometimes it turns out to not be just a hypothetical. Our interviewee Harper grew up intent on supporting herself because her mother "always instilled in me the importance of me as a female having my own sense of security and stability, away from family and away from a man. There was never a question that I was going to figure out how to be self-supporting in some way." Drawn to helping people, Harper pursued medicine, eventually becoming a sought-after pediatric surgeon.

When she was in her mid-30s, Harper's family's investment advisor was arrested on charges of fraud, and she learned that much of her family's wealth was now gone. "While I was happy to be a doctor," she says, "I didn't think that I was actually going to have to do that to pay the bills. And then when I was faced with it, that more than anything, became my identity. When the financial privilege went out the window, I probably did cling to my professional career as not only a lifeline to support myself, but also an 'Okay, I am somebody on my own aside from this.'"

Now ten years on from that life-changing moment, she reflects, "I think that my identity, who I am today, has so much been crafted by the fact that I have self-supported. I do know that if something were to go wrong, I can do this. And that the things that I have right now in my life are because I've worked really hard for them. And so, I have a nice car, and I can have nice things, and it's because I've worked for it, and that feels much different than it did years ago when it was just being paid for by my parents."

2. Reclaiming financial agency

It's common for inheritors to view money (and its attendant world of wealth advisors, investment managers, lawyers, accountants, etc.) as the exclusive domain of their parents or broader family and utterly divorced from their world and what they perceive as their sphere of influence. This can be okay, even healthy, up to a point—to create enough space from the family wealth infrastructure to carve out your own path and invest in your own capabilities. But this avoidance and "othering" of all the instruments of wealth management can become problematic if it impedes the inheritor's developing financial agency or prevents them from feeling empowered in the financial world.

We've seen that the surest way for inheritors to feel agency when interacting with the financial world is to seek advice and guidance about money they feel is truly their own. Typically, this happens around the time of a first job and involves questions about how much of the earnings should be invested in a 401K or how to construct a budget now that there's a predictable paycheck and short- and long-term goals. The nature of these interactions is entirely different than when an inheritor is told, cajoled, or incentivized to receive education about money they will inherit. The difference lies within the inheritor themself and whomever they perceive being in charge of these interactions. When they know it's them (versus a parent or family office executive), there's an entirely different level of curiosity and commitment.

Our interviewee Craig shared with us how this played out in his own life. The eldest son of a high-profile Wall Street executive, he grew up feeling that money and finance were the domain of his father. He remembers a disdain for "financial services amongst my peers" many of whom were in similar positions of being raised in well-off families. It wasn't until Craig launched his start-up in college that he realized he needed to familiarize himself with the financial world. Attempting to navigate funding rounds and discussions about capital structure "made me realize that I knew practically nothing about finances besides buy low and sell high. In turn, I was compelled to educate myself."

Doing so was eye-opening and eventually prompted him to reflect on the earlier disdain that he and his friends had felt for the financial world. "I now understand that I was simply insecure about my lack of financial knowledge and felt simultaneously intimidated by and envious of those who had that knowledge."

Craig's evolution is like many that we see in our work. By seeking financial advice on his own terms about topics immediately relevant in his own life, Craig reclaimed a sense of financial agency and rewrote his earlier narrative that the financial world was a domain belonging only to others.

3. Earning self-worth

Inheritors must contend with the society in which we live, which rightly or wrongly places moral and social value on work that is paid. Our interviewee Lucy, who spent years chairing nonprofit boards, recently set up a consulting firm on the side so she can experience being paid for her expertise. As she put it, "Whether or not you disagree with our capitalist system and how it's setup in America, it is still the system we are operating in. So, if you want to reject it, there's still going to be this chaffing point about your identity and others' perception of you, and your knowledge that if you're not getting compensated, it's not as valuable."

She went on to describe how, when her daughter turned school age, she was able to focus on attaining this milestone. "I was like, you know what? I'm going to emerge. I can do this now and found my own consulting firm and I can do nonprofit consulting. I can finally get compensated and feel good about that."

This sense of something being left on the table in the self-worth department is common to inheritors who have perhaps dedicated lifetimes to family philanthropy, but have never held (or been encouraged to hold) a paid job. In Jim Grubman and Dennis Jaffe's summary article about the dilemmas inheritors face, they quote an inheritor, Abby Stranahan, who though involved in managing her family's philanthropy still felt, "I know I'm doing important work, but I still would like to have a paid job. I don't want my whole identity tied up with doing things that only someone with money can do."[15]

Our interviewee Lucy felt similarly: "For me, emotionally though, income is really important. That's something that my husband and I talk about a lot, and we talk about it for our kids. Because I think it's important for people to generate income for their sense of self-efficacy and self-confidence and self-worth." As we talked through why she felt that was, our conversation came around to how important it is to wake up every day and feel like what you do matters. "And you know it because someone is paying you for it," she inserted. "It actually has a very important psychological impact and existential spiritual impact."

4. Feeling free

We know from our inheritors like Lucy how critical earning income can be for your sense of self-confidence and self-worth. But there's something else that earning your own way can provide: freedom. When you don't feel like you need your family's money to function, you have a lot more autonomy in your actions and in your life choices. This is not only about how you feel, but importantly, also about the message you are able to send to all those in your life who might (even unwittingly or good-naturedly) attempt to influence your decisions through financial support. As reporter and author Kelly Williams Brown writes in her wonderful and funny book, *Adulting: How to Become a Grown-up in 468 Easy(ish) Steps*: "It's hard to prove you are independent if you depend on your parents for things, since that is in fact the opposite of what independent means. This happens especially with money. Accepting your parents' money makes them shareholders in your life. And they probably see themselves as the kind of shareholder that gets a vote when big decisions are made."[16]

We can hear in these voices and stories the subtle ways in which earning an income shifts the landscape of self. It is a cornerstone in the foundation of individuation and a launching pad to agency and capacity. If you haven't yet had a chance to experience how this feels in your life, it's worth trying to check the box on this milestone and to embrace the attitude Peter Buffett (musician, philanthropist, and son of billionaire Warren) shares in his wisdom-filled book, *Life Is What You Make It*: "I accept and even celebrate the necessity of earning a living. Earning a living is one of life's character-defining challenges."[17]

The messy bits

So, does it have to be forever? Must you always support yourself and never use your inheritance? And must it always be entirely? Is it okay to live partially off your own earnings and partially off inherited wealth?

The answer to the first question is no, it doesn't have to be forever. But it has to be long enough that you can experience the shift in sense of self that our interviewees' stories describe. Long enough that you can expunge fear, feel agency over your financial life, forge a foundational sense of self-worth, and experience a sense of autonomy in your life choices. For some, this is several years, for others, it's a lifetime.

And on whether it's okay for part of your life to be self-supported and part enhanced by money you are given—it's a multifaceted answer. If you've experienced the milestone of supporting yourself entirely for at least some portion of your life, you are then much more likely to feel psychologically free to access your inheritance without disrupting your sense of self. If, on the other hand, you haven't yet achieved this milestone, it becomes a much more subjective answer, an elegant dance between your fledgling sense of self and the erosion of that sense of self that tapping into your inheritance may cause.

An equation for life

These issues of when and to what degree a young person should access their inheritance so that it does not disrupt their efforts to construct a solid foundation of self are among the most complex that arise in the wealth advising industry because, as we can see, the answers lie very much at the inner heart and subjective core of how the young person feels about themself. As I puzzled over the wisdom that our interviewees shared about how they have navigated this landscape and emerged stronger on the other side, I found myself wishing for a simple rule that a young inheritor could turn to to try to help guide them in these decisions. While nothing is truly simple, of course, in the land of wealth and self-esteem, I hope that, if you are one of these young people attempting to reason this out for yourself, this equation will help:

$$\text{SENSE OF SELF ON A SCALE OF 0-100\%} \quad \text{MINUS} \quad \text{\% OF LIFESTYLE PAID FOR BY INHERITANCE} \quad \geq \quad \text{ZERO}$$

Where the first term, SENSE OF SELF, is defined and strengthened by your efforts to prove to yourself your self-efficacy, competence, and ability to stand on your own two feet.

The key is to be at least neutral—zero or above. You don't want to go into the negative zone, which is the equivalent of the inheritance or family wealth black hole that we discussed earlier. So, if you feel 100% confident in yourself and know that you could handle it if your family money disappeared tomorrow (because you've actually lived like this for a while—no fair guessing!), you can handle up to 100% of your lifestyle being covered by your inheritance and you'll still be at zero, which, although not ideal, is at least not negative. Conversely, if you're just starting out and haven't yet proved much to yourself about your capacity, agency, or self-worth, even a small amount of your lifestyle paid for by your family wealth might send you into negative territory.

Sometimes in our work, we've seen inheritors effectively navigate this dance by having "skin in the game"—by having a sufficient percentage of their lifestyle paid for by their own earnings that they feel in their heart of hearts that their efforts truly matter (a down payment covered by family wealth but a monthly mortgage paid for out of earnings, for instance). To go back to the equation, skin in the game pulls the inheritor further into the positive zone because its reinforcement of self-capacity increases the sense-of-self term.

And sometimes we see inheritors who feel well-evolved in their sense of self beneficially choosing to access inheritance to fuel the important work of their life calling. Our interviewee Abby, who has taught public school in Newark, New Jersey, for five years while devoting evenings and weekends to a nonprofit she's deeply involved in, shared with us an important conversation she had with her mother (also an inheritor) a few years back.

Abby was trying to decide whether to supplement her income with money from her trust, because she hadn't done this before. Abby's mother asked her whether her friends at work had another job. Abby realized, yes: "They all do. They babysit. They tutor. Some are bartenders on the weekend." Her mom pointed out that that was a choice Abby could make. She could have a second job, or she could choose to put that time into the nonprofit—her inheritance could make that choice possible. Abby recalled her perspective shifting as her mind wrapped around the agency in that choice. "For me, that was realizing I could sort of think about money and time and the ways that

I was giving of myself in different ways."

The time and money balance that Abby was puzzling over reflects a truth we see in our work—in essence, the hours that Abby was devoting to her nonprofit became the means by which she proved to herself that she was "earning" the money she was accessing from her inheritance. Her sense of self has not been eroded by accessing her family money, because she's converting the money into her life purpose through her own sweat equity. Again, going back to the equation, Abby's efforts have had the effect of taking money that would have increased the second term and transformed it into a stronger sense of self-efficacy, which in fact increases the first term. Because sweat equity increases sense of self, it makes it possible to pull a greater amount from inheritance to support lifestyle without going below zero.

Factor 2: Work and motivation toward a compelling and challenging goal

Apart from supporting ourselves, one of the other benefits of forcing ourselves to get out there and earn a living is that it catapults us into the world of work. The second of the four success factors that I noted in my first book, motivation toward achieving a compelling personal goal, is all about work—what you push yourself to do, what you're called to do, and ultimately what you're grateful to have done.

As father of the field of family wealth Jay Hughes so eloquently writes in his book, *Family: The Compact Among Generations*: "It is critical that each family member believe and accept as absolute and fundamental truth that each individual spirit has unique work to do in this lifetime and that each possesses unique gifts that will allow him to complete it. The most self-aware, free, and happy people I've met are those who have lived out their dreams by finding their work, the thing they were called to do, then apprenticing themselves to a master to learn it."[18]

A little-talked-about reality is that finding the "unique work" that Jay speaks of is *hard*. It's a process, and it can take years of effort—some of which is no doubt spent discovering what is definitely *not* your chosen, unique work and thereby uncovering truths about yourself and your preferences. Even more challenging is that, even when you *have* found the work that will ultimately be your life's calling, there can be days, weeks, months, even years that feel incredibly tough. As Meg Jay writes in *The Defining Decade*, "Twentysomethings who *don't* feel anxious and incompetent at work are usually overconfident or underemployed."[19]

One of the side benefits of a commitment to support yourself is that it keeps you in it at work when the going gets tough. It can take a bit of an external push—say, economic necessity—to motivate yourself to get up the next day and go back to the job with the intimidating boss or difficult customer or problem that you can't figure out how to solve. And it turns out that sticking it out through these challenges is key. It's the very crux of what ultimately gives work meaning—that it requires sustained effort and that success isn't guaranteed. Austrian neurologist and Holocaust survivor Viktor Frankl, whose contributions on what makes life worth living have so inspired the world, asserted that meaning is found in work when we are "striving and struggling for a worthwhile goal, a freely chosen task."[20]

When an inheritance is too easily accessible or a parent's financial support is too readily offered, the bolster of this economic necessity evaporates, and it becomes all too easy to walk away. Or as Myra Salzer puts it in *The Inheritor's Sherpa*, "Inheritors, especially people who received their legacy at an early age, are deprived of the usual coming-of-age process. When financial security just happens, there is no incentive to develop the survival skills that most learn when earning an income, and the interaction with the world and with people that this experience provides."[21]

And what a shame it would be to miss out on that experience. Because we saw in our conversations that work was the doorway through which our interviewees discovered themselves and learned what they were capable of. As Craig told us, "My successes [with my business] became examples of what I could do myself, and as those successes grew, they snowballed my confidence in myself and my sense of independence and resilience. This was only the case because there was a direct correlation between the work that I did and the results that I personally produced."

We also saw that work was a form of armor for the self. As Harper shared earlier, her work identity enabled her to psychologically withstand the blow that her family money was gone. And, as we'll see in later chapters, work and having an identity outside of the family wealth served as an important anchor not only to inheritors but also to their spouses and partners who, as new members of the family, were equally at risk of succumbing to the centripetal force of the black hole.

So what if you haven't yet found your calling? What if you're still muddling through, going through the motions, unsure if the journey you're on will ultimately lead anywhere fruitful? Take heart in these wise words from *New York* magazine's advice column "Ask Polly" (actually essayist and critic Heather Havrilesky) responding to a heartbreaking letter from an inheritor doubting their path:

> "Talent is a story we tell ourselves. You don't know what you'll be good at until you work very hard for a long time. You find your purpose and a path by blindly doing what you can for years, paying attention to what you enjoy, surviving, and keeping your heart open. Work creates more work, and ideally, the work becomes more satisfying as the years go by. You're bored because you don't know how to work. It's very hard to thrive when you don't understand how to work or how hard work (that you choose for yourself) can function in your life or what purpose it

serves… Work is crucial. Work gives a day some shape. When you start to do work that you value (and you learn how to savor the work itself in addition to savoring the Being Done With Work), joy becomes possible. The world lights up. You understand that survival itself is worth celebrating, and that it brings with it all kinds of incandescent gifts."[22]

Factor 3: A grounded sense of self not wrapped up in issues related to wealth

As we can see in the stories above, the real magic of success factors 1 and 2 is that they begin to transform how you feel about yourself. If you've spent time supporting yourself and if you are engaged in fulfilling work of your own choosing, you naturally develop a sense that who you are is as much about your own efforts, achievements, and choices in life as about what you inherited or the advantages you were born into. Of course, there is an acknowledgment of the opportunities you were given and the privilege you carry, but this is tempered by the reality that there is something significant and real about your day-to-day life and the contributions that you are making that could not exist without your waking up daily and putting in the effort. This confidence that what you do on any given day matters, that your life is meaningfully of your own making, is the definition of the grounded sense of self that was the third success factor I observed the interviewees in my first book had in common.

Our interviewee Harper, speaking to us in a time slot scheduled around her busy surgery practice, shared with us what this feels like: "I'm 44 years old now, so I feel much more comfortable at this point being like, I know who I am, and I know how hard I worked, and I've earned all of this. Sure, you know, maybe the last name has impressed some people, but it's not going to do the work for me. In this profession, you cannot get to the place I have without working as hard as you possibly can."

Getting to this place of confidence and the type of contentment with self that Harper is describing can feel hard-won. Our interviewee Tim, who has dedicated the past 20 years to mastering the art of fine-grain woodworking and building a bustling specialty custom furniture business, talked with us about how he feels his craft saved him and gave him an anchor of self-hood amid the tidal wave of family wealth and family office expectations that defined much of his 20s.

When Tim's parents sold their multigenerational family business his freshman year in college, it felt like his family had become wealthy overnight. While his parents, then in their 60s, genuinely looked forward to how the wealth would enhance the remainder of their lives, their message to Tim that he wouldn't need to worry about work and could just enjoy life left him unmoored. "There was really no pushing in our family to be something or to make an identity outside of the money. Certainly, you know, there was no need to provide for my own financial security, because everyone, all the messages were, you know, 'there is plenty of money coming.'"

His parents' philosophy was, "'We just want you to be happy,'" he says. "And I also think they were processing and dealing with their own awareness of what the money meant because they were coming into it at the same time."

As a result, Tim spent much of his "early 20s kind of floundering without much direction, and without much incentive" to strike out on his own. In fact, if anything, the message was the opposite. Tim's parents were generous in including him in their efforts to answer the questions that arose around their wealth (Should we have a family office? Should we form a foundation? How should we invest all of this and who can help us?), with the result that the centripetal force of the family wealth, the "expectations that you participate in this process, and isn't it a privilege to be part of this process" were hard to resist.

"We kind of defined ourselves as a greater family," Tim recalls, but this collective identity crowded out his efforts to figure how who he was on his own.

It wasn't until his 30s—when Tim began to devote time to his love of wood-working, learning the fundamentals, apprenticing to a master, and ultimately launching his own studio—that he began to feel the fledgling buds of his own sense of self start to blossom. Now twenty years on, looking around a studio full of hand-carved pieces that will be shipped to grateful clients all over the country, he realizes that this studio, his art, has been a lifeline. It has fed the sense within him that, despite the wealth, despite the shared family responsibilities of wealth stewardship that he is both grateful for and occasionally burdened by, there is one piece of his life that is entirely his own. Though hard-won, Tim now truly feels that he has a grounded sense of self—that these creations, literally carved with his own hands, and the business they've made possible—are daily evidence of his own capacity and proof that his contributions uniquely matter.

In a sense this is the crux of individuation, to emerge from the chrysalis of our upbringing and, with appreciation for and acceptance of its critical role in our development, fly away confidently into our own singular butterfly life. It is a developmental journey that is by no means unique to wealth, but, as we heard from our interviewees' stories, it can be harder to break free into that life when the expectations, perks, shadows, and even *ease* of wealth conspire to strengthen the chrysalis' bonds.

If you're still stuck within the chrysalis, trying to muster the courage to begin to knock at the shell and let in some light, take comfort in the fact that this is both a journey we must all make as individuals in a life well-lived and that it can take courage and exhortation to compel even the most independent-minded of us to truly do so. American transcendentalist philosopher Ralph Waldo Emerson wrote his canonical 1841 essay "Self-Reliance" to inspire exactly this type of initiative and reclaiming of one's individual path. He writes:

> "There is a time in every man's education when he arrives at the conviction that envy is ignorance; that imitation is suicide; that he must take himself for better, for worse, as his portion; that though the wide universe is full of good, no kernel of nourishing corn can come to him but through his toil bestowed on that plot of ground which is given to him to till. The power which resides in him is new in nature, and none but he knows what that is which he can do, nor does he know until he has tried."[23]

Factor 4: The ability to overcome setbacks

The fourth success factor that I noticed in my research for my first book is the ability to weather setbacks without relying on family wealth to come to the rescue. It turns out that the ultimate outcome of a setback—success or failure—is less important than whether we can tolerate living with the discomfort of the problem long enough to make it through to the other side. We've found in our practice that when young people are given a chance to muddle through setbacks, to sit with failure and uncertainty long enough to demonstrate to themselves that they can endure, it gives them the confidence that they can weather the other struggles that life will throw in their path. They earn a resilience that empowers them to try other new things, risk more discomfort, knowing they can handle it even if it doesn't all go according to plan. As Eleanor Roosevelt put it, "You gain strength, courage and confidence by every experience in which you really stop to look fear in the face. You are able to say to yourself, 'I have lived through this horror. I can take the next thing that comes along.'"[24]

Of course, in addition to this sense of confidence, there are the many lessons the struggle itself imparts. Our interviewee Craig talked with us about the heartbreak of ultimately needing to walk away from the start-up he founded in college after six all-consuming years and how he now credits that experience (which he describes as "my ultimate failure of realizing my dream") with fostering his sense of personal accountability: "While there are of course variables that negatively affected my business that were out of my control," he says, "I look back and place the responsibility squarely on myself. Claiming absolute ownership, in comparison to blaming those variables, helped me build agency and a sense of personal responsibility. Blaming others would have stunted that."

Craig recalls how painful this time felt, how "the lack of purpose I experienced during this transition was a very specific and demotivating feeling." But, as he realized at the time, "the only path, if I wanted to regain purpose and a feeling of competency, was through." And now, when he looks around at his life five years on from that time, as he excels in an entirely new field, he credits this experience for his success. "Any sense of entitlement I might have had was washed away by this humbling event, and the process of embarking on a career path that was not only completely new, but in a field where I was insecure about my lack of experience and knowledge, significantly matured me. It helped tremendously to have the support of friends and family during this time."

Craig's last comment brings up an important point—when we say don't rely on family wealth, we're not saying go it alone. Family, friends, partners, and counselors all can provide important *emotional* help that can be invaluable as you're struggling. The key is to try your best to cope with the problem without asking for or relying on *financial* support. This distinction is both doable and important. As our interviewee Harper put it, when talking about the struggles she faced in her 30s and 40s, "A lot of the hardest things I've gone through, I've had to go through as an adult and especially within the last 10 years. And, you know, I think that a huge part of my identity is from the resiliency that I feel from having gone through that on my own. And while I did get through it, you know, with some support from the love and support of my family, the emotional support, there hasn't been any financial support. And I think it makes me who I am as a person."

Part of struggling is struggling with yourself. This can mean everything from pushing yourself to, as Craig says, "Do the thing that is (or that you *think* is) just beyond your capacity" to forcing yourself to do the thing *you just don't want to do.*

In their wise-beyond-its-size book of essays, *Minimalism: Live a Meaningful Life*, authors Joshua Fields Millburn and Ryan Nicodemus talk about two types of positive experiences, those you enjoy (fun and effortless experiences like watching a movie or eating a sundae) and those you dislike, which "for some people, includes most of the activities that are good for them, like eating vegetables, exercising daily, manual labor, conversing with loved ones each night, taking on new challenges." They go on to say that "The second type of positive experiences—the positive experiences you dislike—are the key to living a meaningful life. That is, finding ways to transform the positive experiences you dislike into positive experiences you enjoy is the ticket to changing your life long-term. This one strategy is the ticket to long-term happiness, fulfillment, and a life with meaning."[25]

So, part of struggle is a struggle with ourselves—self-discipline, delaying gratification, and dedicating time and energy to experiences that might feel unpleasant at the time but are actually key to long-term contentment. And part of struggle is a struggle with others—the unpleasantness, conflict, and complication involved in having to say no to the well-meaning people in our lives who are happy to step in and do for us what we would otherwise be forced to do ourselves.

In our conversation with wood artisan Tim and his wife, Alice, they talked about how their lives changed when Tim's family decided to set up a family office. Alice recalled how, then in her mid-20s, she had just begun to get traction and start to feel a modicum of mastery in basic "adulting" skills like paying her bills and figuring out how to rent an apartment. And then, when the family office was created, all these things that she and Tim were trying to do "immediately were lifted from us. They'll pay your credit card bills. They'll deal with your insurance. They'll deal with, you know, all the adulting stuff that we have in our lives." She continued, "And I gave it up, because I thought, we had to. I kind of got the message that's what we were supposed to do … the message of, like, well, this is what you're paying for."

Now in her 50s, she regrets that decision. "What happens is you get so divorced from reality, and you get infantilized," she explained. "Like, I don't know how I got internet, and who do I call? Do I have an insurance person? So, it was a very negative thing for us, and for me in particular. I felt like I lost my independence." She since has taken back most of these responsibilities and, as she thinks about her own three teenage children, intends to do it differently when they are that age. She sees the irony in the assumption that "what wealth can do is take the 'burden' off of your shoulders" and believes instead that "it undermines your ability to be a competent adult, frankly."

If Alice's words strike a chord, if you realize you are currently in the middle of a life in which all details, annoyances, and basic life tasks are managed by someone else, perhaps now is the time to begin to make a change. Try adopting as a mantra that you will say no to any help that prevents you from mastering skills that most other adults walking through society know how to manage. It won't be easy, but it might feel easier if you start to recognize that the "help" (no matter how much you might want it at the time!) is actually a roadblock standing between you and a necessary sense of mastery over your life. Try this reframing as motivation: instead of thinking "*I have to*" about the tasks, responsibilities, and struggles life presents, think "*I get to*"—I get to experience these things and I'm grateful to be presented with these challenges because they are the gifts that will allow me to successfully travel this developmental path and emerge on the other side as a full-fledged adult.

And know you're not alone—if you think you're uniquely incapable, enabled, dependent, or whatever other word comes to mind, know that others out there feel the same way, and your task is no harder or worse than theirs. Earlier, we heard from advice columnist Ask Polly's response to a letter from a struggling inheritor. Here's how that letter started, in the inheritor's own words: "I am 26 years old.... Most of what I have in my life is provided for and paid for by my parents. I work for my father. I can't help but feel I have been deeply enabled, but that is because I am deeply incapable. Of everything and anything, really.... I have been given everything in life, every advantage on earth, and I still cannot make it work."[26]

And here was Polly's wise response, which charts a path out of this insecurity for anyone who hears their own fears, doubts, and hopelessness echoed in those words:

> "You need to wake up and live a real life. You're like the Velveteen Rabbit: You don't want to be coddled and imaginary and safe anymore. You want to be real. But right now, there aren't many consequences to anything you do. It sounds like no one in your family confronts you, and they'll never kick you out of the house because, as you said, they don't think you can survive on your own.... And you don't trust yourself, because you're sure that you can't survive on your own. That belief may have started with your family, but it lives inside of you now. It's time to escape that prison and live on your own terms. You need to learn to work very hard just to get by. You need to start a new life and become responsible for your own survival. Having nothing to fight for is a special kind of hell.... I think you need to cast off a lot of what you have and what you've depended on for your whole life, and you need to rediscover what you could become in a vacuum."[27]

It's about time

Yes, that is a play on words. Because the process of becoming your own person and feeling confident in your capabilities is an urgent endeavor that you should start today. And it takes time—mastering the four success factors we talked about in this chapter is typically a multiyear process.

It can help to break it down into smaller pieces. Our interviewee Craig talked with us about the early days of his start-up when he was still in college. He had confidence in his brilliant idea and knew he had the technical know-how to develop it. But he was seriously lacking in most other life skills—cooking for himself, renting an apartment on his own, doing his laundry, etc. When his business took off and dragged him into the adult world of financing meetings, appointments with commercial real estate brokers, etc., he initially felt overwhelmed and underprepared. As he put it, "I could see the 'end goal' of what having agency and independence meant, but knew I was not at all close to that. I felt that it was insurmountable to reach that level of competency, mostly financially and organizationally."

But, an interesting thing happened as he continued to focus on the needs of the business day to day. These basic skills of managing his life became table stakes, the bare minimum he needed in order to propel himself on toward his larger goal of growing his business and innovating within the market. "Attaining these skills became a necessary part of pursuing a greater goal, which allowed me to make small strides and not be intimidated by the whole picture," he says. "It would have been much more difficult to learn how to take care of myself without that ultimate purpose." And he adds, "None of this happened instantly for me. One blessing from this time in my life is the knowledge of what a person can do over a long period with daily, intentional effort."

The ultimate reward

In his 2009 book *Drive*, Daniel Pink argues that, at their core, humans are motivated by three things: autonomy, mastery, and a sense of purpose. While Pink focused largely on how these intrinsic motivators play out in the workplace, the factors hold true in life broadly and are relevant here. We've seen over the years in our practice that young inheritors who have developed the four success factors have in essence also nurtured these intrinsic motivators: they feel autonomous relative to their parents and the family wealth, they feel a mastery of the basic life and survival skills required to get through their days, and they have a sense of self-defined purpose, born out of both work and struggle.

As a result, their strong sense of identity, their grounded sense of self, can be the foundation on which they layer the wealth, versus the other way around. We spoke earlier about shame, looming shadows, and undermining support and how the first line of defense against these slinging arrows is to build your sense of individual capacity brick by brick. Think of every effort to master these four success factors as another brick, strengthening not only your confidence in what you're capable of but also your knowledge of who you truly are.

And if you need inspiration along the way, come back to these wise words from Peter Buffett, who no doubt had to travel this journey and stack bricks in his own life:

> "Why work hard if one's economic future already seems secure? Why strive, if striving only brings you more of what you already have? What's left to do if Mom or Dad or some more distant forebear has already made a mark in the world and established the family's prominence? These are understandable sentiments; but they are also dangerous and subversive. They can suck the joy and the juice right out of life. So let's try to address them here and now. Why work hard? Because it's the surest and possibly

the only route to self-respect. Why strive? Because striving brings out the best in us; it tells us who we are, what we have to offer, how much we're capable of achieving. What's left to do after the family's prosperity has been established? Everything!"[28]

Chapter Two

Starting to Emerge

If you've traveled the path laid out in chapter 1, you're likely gaining confidence in your ability to be financially independent, carve out your path in life, and handle the challenges life throws your way—in short, you may be feeling like more of an adult. But you still need to figure out how to be out in the world in an authentic way with your wealth. You need a story you can tell yourself and others that integrates the honest reality of your financial resources with who you are and who you want to be. And this story needs to be born of mature reflection—it has to be more about who you are and who you want to be than who you are *not*.

This chapter is for you if you feel the way our interviewee Abby did when she was first embarking on her teaching career and had not shared the truth about her family's financial situation or her inheritance with any of her friends in grad school. "I felt like I was sort of hiding being wealthy from myself. And generally from others. Not like I needed to put on a parade or a show about it to other people, but … realizing, I need to figure this out and I need to figure out how to fit it into who I am as a person and what's important to me. Instead of just being a source of dissonance."

Now, 10 years on, Abby feels differently. She has friends she can be honest with, a community she can rely on, and confidence that her inheritance, once seemingly at odds with her deepest held values, is now allowing her not only to live consonantly with those values but also to express them on a much grander scale. Now, reflecting back, she realizes that the work she has done over these years has "helped me to solidify my own identity and feelings about being wealthy." And, as a result, she's been able "to move from a place of feeling guilty about having inherited wealth to just being able to integrate that into my own identity and story with love, and compassion, and generosity."

This chapter is about how to bring the transformation that Abby has experienced into your life. In chapter 1, we covered forging a grounded sense of self without being subsumed by the wealth. This chapter is about how to layer awareness of the wealth back in on your own terms and then to take that you—the whole you, including your wealth—out into the world in a way that allows you to connect to others and build authentic relationships.

Being wealthy amid "wealthism"

In her 1987 doctoral thesis, family wealth consultant Joanie Bronfman coined the term "wealthism" to describe the prejudiced attitudes that "dehumanize or objectify wealthy people, simply because they are wealthy," including "envy, awe, and resentment."[29] Bronfman explains how animosity toward the wealthy in America stems from our inability to reconcile two opposing American ideals: that all people are created equal, and that the "American dream" promises that anyone can become wealthy with hard work and effort. The result is that "the rich are generally admired and glamorized as symbols of the fulfillment of a dream. But, for many, they also symbolize the impossible, and they are envied, resented, and hated."

The intervening years have only made this odd mix of enmity

and fascination more pungent. Rising wealth inequality has increased the animosity toward the wealthy to the point that, among Americans under the age of 30, 40% agree with the statement, "Rich people are good at earning money, but they are not usually decent people."[30] Yet, the fascination with wealth is alive and well in everything from the stunning popularity of the show *Succession* to the daily followings of Elon Musk to the fact that perceived-to-be "get rich quick" career paths like tech founder and Instagram influencer are lauded and desired among this very age group.

What does it feel like to be wealthy amid wealthism? For young inheritors, who find themselves on the wealthy side of the fence only by accident of birth, it can feel confusing, lonely, and (although they often feel horrible for feeling this way) a bit unfair. As our interviewee Harper put it, "I'm generally perceived to be a very kind, sweet person if you know me. But I think, I'm almost guilty until proven innocent when I meet new people, because there is a perception that I'm going to be pretentious or just not the person that I am."

It can be painful to reconcile who you are at heart with society's image of you and to realize that you are prejudged before you even have a chance to show the world who you are. Even worse, though, is when this conflict lives within. It's common for inheritors to have an inner voice of "wealthism"—to share some of the same disdain for the rich that is reflected in broader society. It can be truly wrenching to try to reconcile your sense of self with some of the unflattering ways in which you might perceive "people like you." This can lead to confusion and cognitive dissonance—in short, a whole bunch of swirling thoughts, a sort of iterative, internally incompatible script that can be hard to process and even harder to work out: "*This wealth isn't me! It isn't! I didn't even earn it. But I benefit from it, so this wealth is me, so I am rich. But I don't admire rich people, and I'm not like them. But I have wealth, so I am. But…*" (and repeat).

So, what do young people faced with these swirling thoughts do to go about their lives and manage their days? Often, they go into denial, in many forms. We'll spend this next section talking briefly about how this denial (from both self and others) and its corollary—isolation—manifests, before going on to share the stories we heard from our interviewees about how they moved past this denial in their own lives.

Denial from self

Denial often has its roots in ignorance. Our interviewee Lucy, who shared with us in chapter 1 how important earning her own income has been for her self-worth, grew up playing hide-and-seek in the nooks and crannies of her family's historic, rambling, Victorian home and looking out from her window onto the expertly landscaped backyard. Yet, when she remembers how she and her sister thought about her family's financial situation, she says, "I think I did that thing where I was like, 'There are people who are definitely richer than my family. So, we aren't the wealthiest.' And then we could fool ourselves into thinking that meant we were like middle class."

Lucy never heard anything to the contrary from her parents. She says now, "I think I'm just a really good example of no-one-ever-really-talked-about-it. I didn't have any language for it. I didn't have any preparation for it." When Lucy's father died unexpectedly the year she turned 22, she became the primary beneficiary of a trust worth $20 million. She says her grief was laced with a sense of shock. "I had a very abrupt—not even poorly handled, not even *any* introduction to what was going to happen. Like, there was no introduction. I had no training. Not to mention, what does this mean? How can we support you? It was just trial by fire." She recalls now that her general feeling toward her inheritance was, "I didn't know what to do with it emotionally or otherwise."

We also hear from inheritors who *are* offered an education about their inheritance, that they often can't really engage with the information they receive. They hear the words but can't internalize, integrate, or act on the knowledge because they haven't yet reconciled their sense of self with the wealth.

Our interviewee Helen saw this at play in her life. As a teenager growing up in Maine, she would hear about the family meetings her mother would travel to, organized by the trust company managing the wealth that had been generated from the sale of her family's textile business two generations earlier. When Helen turned 18, she was asked to accompany her mother on these trips, and she dutifully attended every biannual family meeting all the way through college.

Now in her 50s, Helen can still call up like it was yesterday the feelings she had about the wealth during this time: "I was very scared of my situation. I kind of didn't want to know about it. I kind of didn't want to think about it. I'd go to the family meetings and see my trustees and always sort of get really dressed up, and be the way that I thought everybody thought that I should be, but I never felt like myself. I always felt like it was money that somebody gave me; it wasn't really mine. I didn't really understand how it was mine. I know that I inherited it. But I always felt kind of guilty about it."

Between the trips to the family meetings, Helen remembers she would be sent quarterly investment reports from the trustees with pages of numbers and charts. "I never looked at all the information that they would send me," she says. "I just kind of put it in a folder because I just didn't want to deal with it. And I didn't really understand how to read all of the paperwork."

This idea of a folder that is put away, in a desk, under the bed, out of sight (and out of mind) was a recurring theme in our interviews and is a powerful metaphor for the distance that most young inheritors feel between their true selves and the wealth. As inheritor and author Karen Pittelman writes in *Classified* (which, yes, is a double entendre meant to evoke both secrecy and class status): "The file is rarely left out on our desks. It's rarely even in a drawer in the living room or a cabinet in the kitchen. Instead it's down past creaky stairs, into the dark and dusty basement. Back there, behind a pile of boxes, is where we keep a thick and tattered file stamped 'classified'—the place where many of us hide our experiences as young people with wealth."[31]

Denial from others

When you're hiding your wealth from yourself, it's almost impossible to share it with others. You haven't arrived at language or a narrative that sounds good in your own head, much less when shared out loud with others. And even those inheritors who are making strides toward trying to integrate the wealth with their sense of self still fear that others who learn the truth about their wealth will judge them.

In 1963, sociologist Erving Goffman described "stigma" as a phenomenon where individuals are "disqualified from full social acceptance" by virtue of having an aspect of their identity that is discredited by society.[32] While being wealthy amid "wealthism" is not one of the stigmas that Goffman called out (he focused on character traits, physical characteristics, and group identity, including race, national origin, religion, etc.), it's striking how much of Goffman's theory (and those of others who have built on it, including Kenji Yoshino in his 2007 book, *Covering*) is applicable to how young inheritors often try to hide their wealth from others in an attempt to be welcomed as "normal" members of the group. The analogy isn't perfect, because the stigmas Goffman described conveyed societal disadvantages, while being wealthy conveys advantage. Yet the experience he describes of exclusion and the excluded individual's attempt to modify behavior, appearance, and association in an attempt to correct for it are remarkably similar.

Lucy talked with us about how she tried to "cover" her wealth when she first moved to Brooklyn in her mid-20s: "I think I thought

I could go through life, and nobody would know. In those years, that was my approach. And I don't think that's a good way to go. There was a lot of dissonance because there was a lot of trying to appear 'normal' and that takes a lot of energy." And there were signs that she couldn't hide, like the brownstone she was living in in Park Slope. "People would sort of be like, 'Wow, you've got a really nice apartment and you're a grad student,' you know."

And there were times that this split screen between herself and her wealth came to a head. Lucy remembers the day that one of her graduate school classes held its annual, widely anticipated, and reverentially remembered "privilege line" exercise, in which everyone is asked a series of questions (Did you grow up in a house with two parents? Did you attend college debt-free?, etc.) and each time you answer yes, you step forward.

Lucy had watched the steadily approaching date of this class with mounting dread. Ultimately, she chose to be absent that day. "I was so relieved, because I knew I was going to end up at the front of the line. And I didn't want people to know," she says. "I had been kind of, like, passing, and I didn't want people to know. I wasn't sure how I was going to handle it. I didn't know what I was going to say, and I didn't know what they were going to think about me, and I was embarrassed." Still, for the rest of her graduate program, she wondered whether she made the right choice. "I remember being, like, in my memory, this seminal moment that everyone talks about didn't happen for me. I also didn't want it to happen, but then I felt guilty that I hadn't been there."

Ultimately, Lucy's choice to be absent prevented her from being unwittingly "outed" in front of her friends and peers. She may regret this decision, but we heard a number of stories of memories seared into the mind when, despite best efforts, an inheritor was outed anyway.

Tim, now helming his own artisanal furniture studio, spent his junior summer in high school working on the factory floor of the headquarters of the paper milling company that was his broader family's multigenerational business. He had challenged himself to apply for the job with the foreman without revealing who he was (great-grandson to the founder with an uncle on the board), so that he could be treated as any other employee and be asked to work as hard. He made it through much of the summer with the ruse intact, enjoying the camaraderie of the factory floor, the challenging manual labor, and the endurance he was developing adhering to a rotating schedule of shift work.

One night in August, though, he was unloading a huge machine on the floor when his designated partner on the task, a longtime worker at the company, showed up for his shift drunk. About an hour into their work together, Tim remembers, "All of a sudden, out of nowhere, he goes, 'I know who you are.'" Tim recalls how he felt at the time. "The wheels start clicking. I'm like, oh crap, here it comes. And I wouldn't give in, and I said, 'Well, how do you know?'" Ultimately the coworker said, "Cuz you look like one of them." Tim had been done in by his resemblance to the portraits of the founder and his other distant family members hanging in the hallway leading to the factory floor. Tim acknowledged who he was, feeling like he "lost," and remembers what the guy said next: "That's cool. Your secret's safe with me."

As a result of episodes like these—both the ones that actually happen and the ones that inheritors try strenuously to avoid, it's common for young people with wealth to start to feel isolated. As Eileen Rockefeller puts it in her memoir: "Adulation, judgment, envy, and endless curiosity flew around us like a swarm of bees. I was afraid of the sting. People saw us as different, and that set us apart. Their preconception of my family as akin to royalty contributed to my sense of isolation and loneliness."[33]

The denial, isolation, and loneliness can feel even more confusing (and unfair) in situations—typically the norm in the wealth advising industry—when young people haven't yet directly received very much—or any—of the wealth. Most young people from wealthy families inherit very little money outright by the time they are in their 20s, when most interactions like these are occurring, which puts them in a cognitively dissonant position of others perceiving them as having more wealth than they actually do.

Jim Grubman and Dennis Jaffe speak to this point in their summary article about the dilemmas inheritors face, writing, "Interestingly, an important factor for Inheritors is the disparity between their own expectation of wealth, society's view of them as wealthy, and the degree to which they actually are in control of any real wealth. In various ways, many Inheritors do not come into their inheritance until they are well into adulthood…An irony, therefore, is that many heirs live with the implication of great wealth but in reality have only limited access to it."[34]

Ultimately, though, the steps we cover in this chapter are important whether or not you have already directly inherited the wealth, because the implications of the wealth—and others' perceptions of it—are there regardless. In either case, you need to figure out a way to break through the denial, combat the isolation, and forge relationships that allow you to bridge the loneliness and create authentic connections with others.

THE WAY THROUGH

There are many more stories like the ones above about the inner turmoil that can afflict young inheritors. But there are also many stories—including among the inheritors we interviewed—about how to successfully navigate this turmoil and emerge stronger, happier, and feeling more whole on the other side. The rest of this chapter will be dedicated to those stories.

The power of peers

We spoke in chapter 1 about Maslow's hierarchy of needs and how essential it is for inheritors to prove to themselves that they can fulfill the basic security needs on their own, without being dependent upon others for financial support. Once these needs are fulfilled, though, Maslow's framework defines the next psychological need as love and belonging. This encompasses everything from connectedness to affiliation to friendship to, ultimately, love.

For many of our interviewees, a critical breakthrough in their ability to feel accepted with their wealth and truly connected to others (without a need for secrecy or covering parts of themselves) came when they joined a peer group of others like them. It turned out that a chance to be among peers who were wrestling with similar struggles not only helped our interviewees begin to fulfill the existential need for belonging, but also created a means by which they could directly counter the challenges of stigma, denial, and isolation that we spoke about earlier.

Acceptance as a balm for stigma

Our interviewee Helen, who had faithfully attended family meetings throughout college, but who could not bring herself to look at the investment statements she was sent by her trustee, talked with us about how powerful the experience was for her the first time she was among peers she could honestly talk with about the challenges of inherited wealth.

Now in her 50s, she remembers that day vividly. She had heard about a group where people with wealth met regularly to talk about similar questions they all faced (What should I look for in an advisor? What is the most responsible way to manage the money?, etc.) A family member had encouraged her to attend and she had reluctantly acquiesced, but she wasn't sure she would fit in and had no idea what she would say. In the first session of the meeting, she felt frozen as she sat quietly on the unobtrusive chair she had found toward the back of the room. "I was so scared sitting there. I kept thinking to myself, '*Okay, don't talk about how much money you have, because you might have more than everybody else, and then, you know, you're going to feel like an a–hole.*' And, I don't know—I was just terrified."

As luck would have it, after the initial introductory remarks, attendees were encouraged to move about the room, and she ended up sitting next to a woman who was a bit older and who started off talking about her own family's situation and her role as the head of her family's family office. "I could tell that they were a family of substantial means, and just being able to talk to her in a way where it wasn't scary, it wasn't this terrible secret that I wasn't supposed to tell anybody," Helen said. "I was so relieved that I started crying, and I was so embarrassed that I started crying. I mean, even thinking about it now makes me kind of emotional."

As their conversation deepened, Helen started to feel the layers of stigma and denial begin to melt away. "I can't even tell you the depth to which there was guilt, and shame, and embarrassment, and fear all around us. I can't say, per se, one thing that my parents had said to me, but I think it was the little things here and there, like, you know, 'you just don't talk about it.' It [the wealth] was just so wrapped up with so much negative energy," she recalled, "and it was almost like speaking to her just released all this pressure. And it made it feel totally okay and normal." Helen decided at the end of the day to come back every month. "That place for me in the beginning became like such a solace."

Thirty years on, she views this as the beginning of a turning point for her. And she encourages others struggling as she was to try to find a way to have a similar experience. "I think for anybody it would be good to have these possibilities to come together with peers. And to actually have conversations where you don't feel like the a–hole that's complaining about how much money you have." Helen felt accepted in these meetings—she felt that there was a place, at least one place, where her whole self (including the wealth) was welcome, and that feeling of belonging started to subtly chip away at the dual walls of isolation from others and denial of her wealth that had constrained her until this point.

Courage through community

Helen's story shows how peership can forge a strong bond among inheritors who share similar experiences of being young people with wealth. But we also heard in our interviews how the sense of belonging that these peer groups foster can imbue young inheritors with the courage to reach *outside* the group and try to build authentic connections with others who don't share their experience.

Our interviewee Justin, now in his late 20s, talked with us about how this has played out in his own life. Growing up in Seattle as the youngest of three, he remembers hearing from his mother (herself an inheritor) that it was important he carve out his own path in life. When Justin reached his late teens, his older brother started raving about a peer group he had joined of young wealth holders and encouraging Justin to join too.

Justin resisted at first ("What younger brother is going to do anything that their older brother is telling them to do?"), but after several years of hearing his brother talk animatedly at family gatherings about how meaningful the group had been for him, Justin relented. His brother's urgings were compelling, but more than that was Justin's growing awareness that he wasn't comfortable talking to others about his wealth, or even admitting it to himself. "It's, you know, my big secret or whatever. It's sort of this thing, emotionally, that's been so challenging for me for a long time that I'm like, how do I deal with this so that I can sleep better and not feel like I'm walking on eggshells around people and not be uncomfortable all the time if we're talking about money and debt and stuff like that. What do I do to get to that place?"

Now a year into his time with the group, Justin feels like a different person. "If I had just joined when I was 18 or 19, when I immediately got access to wealth, oh my God, my life would have been so much easier for the past eight years," he says. Aside from the chance to talk with others like himself, he explains that one of the most powerful things he's taken from the group is the encouragement to start being honest with some of his friends about his financial situation, backed up by support if one of those conversations doesn't go well.

"What's so important about relationships is being vulnerable," he reflects. "But you really are only allowed vulnerability when you have a sense of community, and the community acts like a safety net.... I know that there's a community there for me to be caught when inevitably one of these conversations or some aspect of my identity that I can't control is perceived as wrong, and I do end up having a difficult situation with a friend or a falling out or whatever."

He thinks about the good conversations he's had with close friends over the last year and the steps he's taken to try to deepen these relationships by being open about his whole self, and says, "So, that's part of the reason why I'm doing this. I think if I wasn't in the group, I probably wouldn't be telling any of my friends. I'd be right back where I was, you know, like last year, five years ago, or whatever. So, yeah—that's what the group has allowed me to do."

Serving their purpose

We heard from a number of our interviewees that these peer groups were absolutely critical *and* that there also came a time when it felt like the group had served its purpose in their lives and it was time to move on.

Our interviewee Tim shared with us how important it had been to him to join a peer group in his early 20s, in the heady, confusing days that followed his parents' decision to sell their multigenerational paper-milling business, making all of them wealthy overnight. "It was just a release for me, you know, to learn that other people, young people, were dealing with the same problem," Tim recalled. "I think also, I learned that there were a lot of people with a lot more money than I had. So, while I was a, you know, big fish in a little pond, when introduced to a national or international level, I was a little fish in a big pond. And that just helped set perspective in some ways."

But, after five years, Tim felt like his time attending quarterly conferences with the group and actively participating in chapter meetings had run its course and was no longer providing him value. "We just kept meeting and the topics never changed. It was continuously how to deal with [the money], you know, and when am I going to feel empowered," he recalls. He started to feel impatient. "I think, you got to just kind of do something…" Now reflecting back on that time in his life almost 30 years ago, he says, "You know, I eventually kind of grew out of it because … I didn't want to be a professional victim of circumstance. And so, it was time to move on."

What Tim is describing is a normal developmental progression—an initial need for support, followed by a moving beyond and away from it after it has served its purpose (the same could be said for how we often view parental advice). Tim's psychological progression—his ability to feel secure enough to leave the peer group behind—is actually evidence of how useful it was to him at this stage of his life.

So, if these stories speak to you, if you are seeking the sense of belonging, acceptance, and release that our interviewees described, maybe it's time to consider spending time with peers who share your experience. We provide a list of places to seek this type of peer community at the end of this chapter.

The power of story

In 1994, sociologists Paul Schervish, Platon Coutsoukis, and Ethan Lewis published *Gospels of Wealth*, a study of 130 wealthy individuals and how they portrayed their lives. One of the findings of that seminal work was that "the more psychologically healthy individuals framed their life stories as meaningful narratives. These narratives served as developmental 'myths,' organizing themes about wealth that show the individual overcoming adversity and moving toward a discovered life purpose. To develop a sense of self-worth and direction, the study subjects had found a way to explain and understand the presence of wealth in their lives. A recurring theme was that discovering how to do something worthwhile or worthy served to justify their good fortune."[35]

One of the study's authors, Paul Schervish, was asked by Charlie Collier several years later during an interview for Collier's own influential and insightful book, *Wealth in Families*, whether this narrative was, for a person beginning to contemplate their wealth, a "form of the ancient myth of the hero's journey?" Schervish answered: "Yes, it's an awakening, a vision quest. A lot of these things are happening simultaneously. It's a search for his identity. It's a search for what he's going to do with his time. It's a search for what he's going to do with his money. Not that this is a terrible fate, but on some emotional level he felt something old was passing and something new was in the offing. And he didn't quite know what it was."[36]

Schervish refers to this sense of moving from the known into the unknown, these periods of transition, as "liminality." He says these are "special periods that are identifiable as psychological turning points in our lives…when we leave one part of our life and enter another" and when "what happens in terms of financial wealth is a death of an old way of thinking, feeling, and acting around the money and a rebirth of a new way."[37] He and the other authors of *Gospels of Wealth* explain that the wealthy individuals they interviewed emphasize the importance of these periods of liminality in their life narratives and "highlight the intricate process of change by which they move from one stage of their relation to money to the next and hence from one stage of identity to another."[38]

We saw this attention to these liminal periods in our interviews, too. Our interviewee Lucy, who had chosen to be absent the day of her class's privilege line exercise so her wealth wouldn't be "outed" in front of her classmates and friends, spoke to us about a breakthrough she experienced several years later when her dedicated volunteer work with a community nonprofit over several years resulted in her being asked to assume the position of board chair for the organization.

"It was that I had leadership skills. I had history at the organization. I was a giver, but it wasn't because I was being a giver. They were like, 'This woman is the right person to take on this role right now.'" Lucy felt like she was chosen on her merits, rather than her wealth. On the other hand, "I think as a board chair, you are assumed to be philanthropic, and you are assumed to be wealthy." For the first time in her life, "The role fit the wealth profile," she says, "and that unlocked so much for me." In her life narrative, she views this transition as "getting to this moment of fit," and says, "It wasn't until I had a fit that I could really come into my own, because the lack of fit was causing stress. And I didn't know that."

Getting out of limbo

You may feel reading this that you are currently sitting square in this limbo of liminality—full of questions, searching for answers, and hoping the next stage will offer resolution in a way that feels authentic to you. This next section is about the work that you can do in this liminal space to bring about a transitional moment like Lucy's and begin to feel that you have forward momentum.

Those of us who work with inheritors know that the discovery of a narrative that integrates your wealth with your life purpose is a multistep process: first, you need a sense of the story of *you*—where you've come from and where you are going, then you need a story of the *wealth*—how it came to be in the first place and then how it came (or will come) to you—and then you need to start to pull these two together into a cohesive narrative in which the story of the money fuels, and is ultimately in service to, the story of you.

We've seen in our practice that this process—combined with mastery of the four success factors we talked about in chapter 1 so that you are imbued with sufficient agency and capacity to *write* the story of you—is truly lifesaving. It absolves inheritors from shame, drives them forward with purpose, and allows them to connect deeply and meaningfully with others. We'll focus in this chapter on stories of how our interviewees navigated the first two parts of this process—owning their own story and owning the story of the money. And we'll save the last step—integrating the two—for the last chapter of the book, because it's a journey that is ongoing and, in a sense, lifelong.

Owning the story of you

Before you can begin to write your story, you have to first decide that *you* are the author of the story, not someone else. All of us come into the world as part of someone else's story—the fulfillment of a dream, the promise of a future, a chance to correct the wrongs of the past. But part of the process of becoming an adult is deciding that we now own the story of our lives, that while we may carry those expectations, dreams, and hopes with us, ultimately it is up to each of us, and each of us alone, to be the author of our one and only life.

In chapter 1, we talked about the painful transition our interviewee Craig went through when his start-up failed, and he had to embark on an entirely new path. Craig faced two important psychological journeys at that time in his life: moving out from under the long shadow cast by his father's tremendously successful Wall Street career and moving out from under and beyond the crushing sense of failure Craig felt at seeing his own entrepreneurial dreams implode. Now, five years on, Craig credits the progress he's made in both of these journeys and the commitment he's made to continue striving and push himself forward to a decision he made at the time to view his life as a story that *he* was in charge of writing. "It has helped me tremendously to think about my life as a story with myself as the protagonist," he says. "I'm the author, versus just being in someone else's story."

Craig's sense of authorship is key. Where there is authorship, there is agency, and where there is agency, there is choice, power, and possibility. As researcher, author, and phenom Brené Brown puts it, "When we have the courage to walk into our story and own it, we get to write the ending. And when we don't own our stories of failure, setbacks, and hurt—they own us."[39]

Often, though, we see young inheritors struggling with asserting this type of authorship over their own lives. From family expectations—both stated and unstated—to trustee requirements to the sting of wealthism that they encounter in daily interactions, it's not uncommon for young inheritors to feel as though they spend their lives going through the motions in someone else's narrative.

We talked with an expert in the power of storytelling, psychologist and storytelling coach Lani Peterson, about how she helps individuals begin to claim authorship. It is a landscape she knows well. "So much of the work I do," she says, is helping individuals, "who haven't, in essence, become authors of their own story. And are still feeling like somebody else is controlling their story." She says at the heart of these feelings is a sense that "our life has been controlled by external forces," and the way to reclaim agency is to understand that, while you can't control the situation you inherit (emotionally or financially), you *can* control the way you respond, the meaning you choose to make of this reality, and how you plan to harness that meaning to serve *your* purpose.

"It's about challenging the meaning that you are making of it," she says. "Because other people are making meaning and giving that to you, but what is *your* meaning and what do you want that meaning to be…So, that's the work of story. And that's where our agency and power come in…" Through this process and the alchemy that is meaning-making, Lani explains, individuals are able to transform limiting histories of shame, failure, and uncertainty into motivating hero's myths where challenges and failures cease to be impediments and instead become the very fuel that drives them forward toward purpose.

To do, in essence, exactly what Craig has done. "Storytelling can be incredibly powerful," he says, "especially when you view yourself as the person driving the narrative. Applying this framework to my life makes me acknowledge that all of my experiences so far have served a purpose, and that even though I don't know exactly where I'm going or what I'll be doing, it will be in the direction of a greater goal."

This art of meaning-making and claiming authorship of your story may seem daunting, especially if you feel like you are at the beginning of the process. Or if you are familiar with only the successful parts of the stories of the people you know in your life (your parents or the original wealth creator) and have never heard about their own struggles with insecurity, failure, or doubt.

Take heart, though—behind nearly every story of seemingly preordained greatness is a little-known backstory of a fallible human being making a conscious decision to author their own story and rewrite the limiting narrative that people (including themselves) were telling them about their potential. One of my favorites of these stories begins with the following words written on a 2000 NFL draft evaluation by a scout about a young college quarterback: "Skinny. Lacks great physical stature and arm strength. Lacks mobility and the ability to avoid the rush. Lacks a really strong arm. Can't drive the ball down the field."

Imagine if Tom Brady had let this story of his potential define his career. Instead, thanks to life-changing advice he received from sports psychologist Greg Harden that "he was responsible for his own performance in the world," he was intent on authoring his *own* story and proving the naysayers wrong. The Tom Brady legend that is now emblazoned in sports lore began in his *mind*, in his decision to claim authorship. As he puts it in the 2021 documentary series, *Man in the Arena*: "It's really a shift in the mind. You go from being a victim to being empowered by the fact that you went through something difficult, and you learned from it."[40]

Ultimately, effective authorship of your story is critical because it shifts the temporal plane—it becomes not so much about the past that you are from but the future that you are going toward, that you are in fact designing. It turns out that this hope for, and conviction in, the future, is critical for engagement in life. It establishes that there is a path worth following, that there is a yet untold future that exists and matters.

Owning the story of the wealth

Fundamentally, the story of the wealth is a story of people—the life stories, motivations, struggles, and triumphs of the people who created the wealth, an understanding of the societal milieu in which these people lived that may have facilitated or impeded their efforts, and an understanding of the impact of their actions, both good and bad, on others.

For many young inheritors, the wealth-creating person at the center of the story is a parent and, as a result, it's a story that they think they know well. But how well do any of us really know our parents, especially when we're first striking out on our own in life? The story we tend to tell ourselves, and that we tend to measure ourselves against, is the one we see—the success, the wealth that has been built, and the life that the wealth has afforded. But how did that story start? It's a useful thought experiment to ask yourself what your parents were thinking about, planning for, and struggling with when they were your age. It's a fair bet they did not start out in life intending to amass a sizeable fortune that they would eventually pass on to their children.

Our interviewee Craig shared with us how thinking this way, trying to put himself in his parent's shoes, started to shift how he felt about both his father's successful Wall Street career and the wealth that he will inherit as a result. This shift for Craig came about as he "was starting to think about a family myself and how much I want to be able to provide and realizing that my dad was motivated in the same way. We both are ambitious, but do not cut corners or prey on people."

With this realization, Craig was able to see the *beginning* of the story—he understood that his father had been motivated to support his family—and this helped Craig view what followed (the 30-year career and the wealth that it built) in a different light. Now Craig feels primarily gratitude "that I was provided a lot in life because of the work of my parents" and acceptance "that I am not a bad person for being born into those circumstances," that "this is just a reality and that my parents wanted to provide everything that they did."

And what about when young inheritors attempting to uncover the story of the wealth have to look further back than their parents to a more distant relative who was the wealth creator? Some find stories that are heroic, with uncomplicated or laudable morality—the bootstrapping immigrant, the refugee who survived and prospered. Others find a story that compounds their sense of shame—fortunes earned through industries that sowed environmental destruction, displaced peoples, or benefited from exploited or enslaved labor.

If you are in this latter group, it's important to look at this history honestly and reconcile its reality with what you now have the freedom to do about it going forward. Our interviewee Helen shared with us what it was like for her when she decided to dig into the story surrounding her great-grandfather's textile business and look beyond the memoir that lies on the coffee table at her mother's house.

What she found was complicated. There was the inspiring, rags-to-riches picture of her great-grandfather—a spark plug of a boy who transcended his own poverty-stricken upbringing to eventually employ hundreds of workers, support most of a town and its community programs, and ship fine textiles all over the world. But there were a number of details she uncovered in the margins—the ones that tended to get left out of the family lore—that she found shameful: a Native American community had objected to the siting of the factory headquarters on the river where it still stood today, female factory workers had tried to unionize unsuccessfully over their meager pay, and much of the cotton that fed the business had been produced by indebted sharecroppers in the South.

Faced with the full reality of this history, Helen mourned the loss of the simpler, morally uncomplicated story she'd known and felt a tremendous sense of guilt about the millions that were in trust in her name. This guilt, though, spurred her on. "That started the whole quest," she said, to learn more about these people—the people who didn't benefit from her family's business—and to "find out what their history was." She researched the local Native American history, studied the union campaign, and dug deep into sharecropper history at the time the business was built. She feels that this research helped her metaphorically to "be in touch with these people." And it's informed her thinking about how she will deploy the wealth in her own life. Now several years on from this process of looking at the whole story of her family's wealth, she feels it was a necessary, even cathartic, step to move forward to thinking about what she was going to do about it.

Sometimes learning about the story of the wealth can awaken responsibilities to those left outside of the wealth creation, as it did in

Helen's case. And other times, it can stir a sense of obligation to the wealth builders themselves, to continue what they started and to pass the wealth-building bug on to others far and wide.

Our interviewee Darius grew up hearing stories of how his parents had both immigrated to this country from Jamaica and met in medical school before each embarking on their own successful careers as doctors. Darius feels indebted to them for how their efforts set him up in life. "I think my story of being the child of immigrant parents, feeling the need to, you know, make their parents' sacrifice worth it, is not uncommon at all," he says. "I think, though, I am at a particularly privileged point where both of my parents 'made it.' I'm one of the fortunate few who has no student debt, who grew up with two doctors as parents, who is working at a very well paying six-figure salary job. I think for me, the more I look back on it now, I understand how my parents definitely made some intentional choices to make a better life for me."

And he feels an obligation to build on their success, "to set up my kids' lives as best as I can, like my parents did for me when they came here. So, if my parents were, you know, if God forbid something happened to them today, and they left certain assets, like how am I going to build on top of that, you know, because there are a lot of people who in that situation would definitely not use it to build, and would use it to stay at the same level and in some cases even, you know, throw it away. So, making sure I don't want to do that."

Darius works long hours in programming at Google but is drawn to his passion for financial planning in his free time. He's been frustrated by how many in his generation "aren't really thinking long-term," and by his friends who say to him that "the stock market is for rich, white people only."

He's been writing a "guide to personal finance that I've been sharing with my friends, which is a Google Doc of, you know, all the things about finance that no one teaches you," he says. "I think I write this as a way to say, 'Hey, not just financial stability, but honestly generational wealth is a thing you can move to start achieving, but you have to be willing to take the first step.'"

Darius's hope is that he'll inspire his friends to start down the road of creating the generational wealth that his parents started down and that he intends to build on. "I just think that it's achievable for many more people than they realize," he says, "but people see finance as this thing only wealthy people can think about or only rich, white males can think about." He wants to get the message out that it's doable. And with a wide body of research[41] continuing to show (as it has for decades) that about 80% of wealth in the United States is newly created on a rolling basis, the odds are in his favor.

Like Darius, Craig also feels a responsibility regarding the wealth that his parents built, especially now that he sees his parents getting older. I've been "realizing in the past five years that my parents are aging," he says. "Understanding how much they have done for me and our family, realizing that they are humans and not infallible just like the rest of us, forced me to understand that the next generation (me and my siblings) need to be able to lead the family when the preceding generation is no longer with us. This has been quite sobering but purpose-filling as well."

We can see in Helen's, Darius's, and Craig's words that owning the story of the wealth involves the same process as owning the story of you—asserting authorship and agency, shaping meaning, and then harnessing that meaning to drive the story you will write going forward. The process of reflecting on the story of their wealth spurred all of our interviewees to action: Helen refocused her philanthropic priorities, Darius is becoming a financial planner for all of his friends so that they, too, can build generational wealth, and Craig has realized he must be prepared to step into his parents' shoes to manage the family wealth when they are no longer able to do so. In other words, each of our interviewees has begun down the road of the lifelong journey we spoke about earlier of integrating the story of their own selfhood with the story of the wealth they will inherit.

It's important to note, too, that none of what we heard from our interviewees was about the details of the money (exactly how much they would be inheriting, in which account or trust it would be located, etc.) It was about the narrative around the wealth, the myth, and the process of beginning to write the next chapter in this myth.

The wealth advising industry often assumes that details are empowering—that the more details an inheritor is armed with, the more agency they will feel. In reality, though, we heard from our interviewees that details in a vacuum—without an inheritor having first built the strong identity foundation we discussed in chapter 1 and the integrated, authored story of the wealth that we discussed in this chapter—can feel irrelevant at best and destructive at worst. They can further widen the gulf between the inheritance and the inheritor's true sense of authorship over their life and the role the wealth will play in it. With every investment report that Helen received and ignored, she felt further behind and removed from her understanding of the wealth. It was only when she learned the story of how her wealth came to be and began to see herself as having a role in righting the wrongs in that story that she began to engage.

Putting it all together

We've seen in our work that when inheritors do the work of chapters 1 and 2—when they prove to themselves that they are not dependent on the wealth but then also find a way to integrate that wealth back into their own story in a way that is consonant with their values and purpose—they begin to have a delightful new feeling: freedom. Freedom just to be themselves, to define themselves, versus to *be* defined—by either the wealth or the denial or rejection of it.

We heard this freedom expressed in our interviewees' stories in many forms. There was acceptance—of self, of the reality into which they had been born, and of the autonomy and choice that still existed within this reality. As our interviewee Abby, the eighth-grade teacher who devotes her weekends to the nonprofit that is her passion, puts it, "People don't choose to be born into affluence. I didn't pick this. It just is my life. And so, I need to just allow myself to move past that and figure out what it takes for me to be authentic and have relationships that are authentic. You don't choose to be born into wealth, but you can choose what you do about it."

And there was a sense of integration, of being able to be real with others, and the almost jubilant sense of liberation that stemmed from this authenticity. Our interviewee Lucy told us about how it felt when she assumed the role of board chair and finally felt her wealth, her interests, and her talents align. She registered the change within herself—she felt that she was "coming into a place with authority and power around this role"—but also, she felt "a lot of affirmation from my staff partners about how incredible and impactful I could be when I'm integrated in that space. *When I'm who I am to others*. When I'm at peace with that, I can lead with that." This integration of who she was on the inside and the outside was a transformative shift in mindset and spurred Lucy on to launch the organization she now runs that empowers affluent white women to use their purchasing power and influence to help close the racial wealth gap. "That was really the seed for the idea," she says. "I was like, wow, if we could dispense with all the charade of pretending we're not wealthy, what would that do? How could we unlock impact and transformation if we could dispense with that shame and hiding?"

As our interviewees started to move past shame and denial, they became braver about opening up to their friends. Justin, who shared with us how a peer group allowed him to attempt to be more open with friends *outside* the group, told us that "recently, I did have these sort of 'coming out conversations,' for lack of a better term, with two of my closest friends, and they were totally supportive. They were, like, 'You have how much money?' I was like, 'I know, it's crazy.'" Justin feels these conversations have gone well. "So, the conversations that I had were really easy, because I chose two people where I knew we had an unconditional friendship, no matter what," he says.

There's one conversation, though, that Justin's been saving for last, and that's with the woman he's been dating for about half a year. "The one person that I haven't told yet, but I'm planning on it, is my current partner. So, she doesn't know that I'm a rich person."

Justin's journey of discovery and revelation—from self to wealthy peers to friends to, finally, an important partner—mirrors what we see among many young inheritors. And the slight trepidation Justin feels about opening up to his new partner is the norm. The stakes are high—he doesn't have years of history invested in a friendship to build on as he navigates the conversation, and he's nervous that the revelation will alter the course of this new relationship that is becoming increasingly important to him. We'll explore this dynamic—of being able to bring your full self, wealth included, to a relationship with your chosen partner—in the next section.

One thing is certain, though: the day Justin does choose to open up, the work he's done to know himself, to understand what he is capable of outside of and beyond the wealth, and to tell a story about the wealth that is true to himself—will enhance the likelihood that that conversation will go well.

At the beginning of chapter 1, we talked about how inheritor coach Myra Salzer says you need to love yourself and figure out who you are as a precursor to a relationship "because you want someone to fall in love with *you*." She goes on to finish that thought: "A sense of your own identity gives you more confidence and makes you more attractive to others. It also makes you aware of what you are bringing to a relationship.... If you have a good sense of who you are, you will be better able to determine if a potential partner is right for you."⁴²

The work on yourself that we covered in this section takes time—it's an evolution, and it's hard to rush growth or force the epiphanies that occur along the way. So, just begin. And you might be surprised at the way in which simply committing to begin smooths the path. Peter Buffett dedicates the last chapter of his memoir, *Life Is What You Make It*, to how true (and inspiring) he has found the following words attributed to German poet Johann Wolfgang von Goethe as he has traveled this journey in his own life:

> "Until one is committed, there is hesitancy, the chance to draw back. Concerning all acts of initiative (and creation), there is one elementary truth that ignorance of which kills countless ideas and splendid plans: that the moment one definitely commits oneself, then Providence moves too. All sorts of things occur to help one that would never otherwise have occurred. A whole stream of events issues from the decision, raising in one's favor all manner of unforeseen incidents and meetings and material assistance, which no man could have dreamed would have come his way. Whatever you can do, or dream you can do, begin it. Boldness has genius, power, and magic in it."⁴³

Peer community resources:

- 21/64—www.2164.net/convening
- Nexus—www.nexusglobal.org
- Resource Generation—www.resourcegeneration.org
- Fidelity Family Office Services—Annual peer cohort program
  Contact Jim Coutré at James.Coutre@fmr.com
- Fidelity Charitable—Next Gen Fellows Program
  Contact Elaine Martyn at Elaine.Martyn@fmr.com
- Community foundations/geographic philanthropy networks—some offer a peer cohort program for the inheriting generation members of their donor community; this is a list of the foundations that I know offer one, but it's worth checking with your community foundation to see if they do as well (or might consider convening a group):
    - Cleveland, OH—Cleveland Foundation
      Contact Kristen Grabenstein at kgrabenstein@clevefdn.org
    - Houston, TX—Greater Houston Community Foundation
      Contact Annie Hurwitz at ahurwitz@ghcf.org
    - Jacksonville, FL—The Community Foundation for Northeast Florida
      Contact Tom Caron at tcaron@jaxcf.org
    - Portland, OR – Oregon Community Foundation
      (offices around the state also)
      Contact Jennifer Curry at jcurry@oregoncf.org

- Facilitated book clubs—we may offer small peer cohort discussion groups around this book (I would facilitate). If you are interested in learning more about these and hearing when they are offered, you can find out more here:
  www.healthywealthywisecollection.com/bookclubs

Section Two

Just the Two of Us

Meet Our Interviewees

Below are the new interviewees who appear in Section Two, in order of appearance:

Chapter Three:

Hope: Growing up as a 5th generation member of a family that made its wealth in agriculture and mining in the early 1900s, Hope has attended meetings and educational retreats hosted by her family's family office since she was a teenager. She met her husband, Luke, during college the summer they both worked on her family's Montana ranch. Now, 20 years later, the couple lives in the St. Louis area, where she is a speech language pathologist, and he is a veterinary oncologist. They have two young sons.

Margaret: The younger of two siblings, Margaret grew up in Michigan, driving past the headquarters of her family's manufacturing business on her daily commute to school. In her late 20s and early 30s, Margaret worked for the family office her parents formed when they sold the business. It was during this time that she met and married her husband, Kevin, a local sports broadcaster. Now in her 50s, Margaret is amicably divorced from Kevin—with whom she is coparenting two teenage daughters—and is back on the dating scene while finalizing plans to realize her dream of launching a food truck to sell her coveted baked goods.

CAMPBELL AND MIA: Campbell was raised in Pasadena, California, aware of both the positive impact of his grandmother's philanthropic gifts to numerous local institutions and the palpable frustration his mother felt at being perceived as the "married-in" in his father's family. Campbell met his wife, Mia, during their sophomore year at college, and they now live in the Raleigh area where Mia is an international human rights attorney and Campbell works for a community revitalization nonprofit. They have a two-year-old daughter.

NICHOLAS AND SEBASTIAN: Nicholas grew up the youngest of three in Northern California, the son of parents who unexpectedly became wealthy as part of the first dot-com boom. He met his husband, Sebastian, in his late 20s, when he was just starting out in his legal career and Sebastian was working as a stylist for a high-end fashion house. Sebastian is also the youngest of his siblings and the first child in his family to be born in the United States after his parents and siblings moved here from Latin America. Now in their 40s, the couple live in Los Angeles with their ten-year-old son.

OLIVER AND HOLLY: Oliver is Campbell's younger brother (see above). He grew up heavily involved in his family's philanthropic activities and is now a child advocate in the foster care system. He and Holly have known each other since elementary school and got married eight years after their first date in their junior year of high school. Holly taught elementary school in Santa Monica before taking time off to stay at home with their three young children.

Chapter Four:

NATHAN AND LOUISA: Nathan grew up in the Phoenix area attending annual family retreats in which his mother and her siblings discussed the management of the investment assets and family foundation their parents had left them. Nathan worked for a start-up in his early 20s and relocated to Nashville when it sold five years later, reinvesting the proceeds he'd made into launching a farm-to-table food coop supplying local restaurants. It was through this that he met Louisa, a chef who had opened her own highly acclaimed restaurant two years before after a decade of earning her stripes at several top restaurants in the nation. The couple married five years ago and are expecting their first child.

AMELIA: As the eldest of four in a close-knit family, Amelia grew up in the Philadelphia area, admiring the work ethic and drive that allowed her parents to manage their loving brood while building their own highly successful careers as an investment banker and a patent attorney. Driven by her love of biology and her desire to relieve suffering, Amelia is now an infectious disease specialist. She met her husband, Liam, in college, and the two are now in their mid-30s and have a three-year-old daughter. They live in downtown Boston, equidistant from the clinic where Amelia practices and the biotech venture fund Liam joined out of business school.

HARRY AND ZOEY: As a 3rd generation inheritor, Harry grew up in the San Francisco area attending meetings with his parents' financial advisors in his teens and managing his own trust distributions beginning in his 30s. He is now a screenwriter based in Los Angeles and is married to Zoey, whom he met a decade ago when she moved to LA from her hometown in Oklahoma after college to pursue her dream of becoming a set designer. They are the parents of two-year-old twins.

GENEVIEVE AND OWEN: Both 3rd generation inheritors, Genevieve and Owen met at a mutual friend's wedding eight years ago and are now married with a two-year-old daughter. As a result of their shared experience of watching their parents' marriages end in acrimonious divorces, they attempted to structure their own marriage to avoid the same conflicts. The two are based in the New York City area where Genevieve teaches preschool music classes and Owen runs a clean water nonprofit, but they have designed their work lives to be flexible so they can also pursue their goal of sailing to 15 countries.

Chapter Five:

CALEB: The son of immigrants from the West Indies, Caleb worked his way through law school and is now one of the most successful corporate attorneys in the Los Angeles area. He and his wife, Corinna, met in law school 30 years ago and now have four adult children actively engaged in their own careers. Caleb and Corinna are thoughtful about how their affluence shaped their children's upbringing. As they now structure their estate and gifting plans, they are consciously factoring in their children's desire to make their own way in life.

DUNCAN AND BEATRICE: Now in their late 60s, Duncan and Beatrice shared a common experience of growing up hearing stories of generational family wealth that had once existed amid the reality that most had dissipated by their own childhoods. As a result, they both feel comfortable around wealth but are also driven to earn their own living. When he was in his mid-20s, Duncan founded what has become an incredibly successful publishing company, and he and Beatrice have raised their four children to appreciate both the value of the resources they'll likely inherit and the need to have their own careers and be able to support themselves.

NORA: Nora lives in Maine and is the mother of three adult children in their 30s. She and her husband became unexpectedly wealthy through his four-decade career in finance, and they talk often about how best to have a positive impact with the wealth now that their children are grown. The couple began to transfer some of their wealth to their children 15 years ago and have been happy with how each of them have handled the gifts they've received so far.

Chapter Six:

CYNTHIA: Now in her mid-70s, Cynthia learned when she was in college that she was the beneficiary of a multimillion-dollar trust. She has struggled since with the restrictive nature of the trust and with how little control she was given over her inheritance (for instance, she is not able to decide where it goes upon her death). In her 50s, after encouragement from her husband, she embarked on a multiyear process to find a new wealth advisor, become cotrustee of her trust, and separate from her family's trustee and family office in St. Louis.

YASMIN: As a 3rd generation inheritor in a prominent Malaysian family, Yasmin grew up watching her grandmother make the important decisions regarding their family wealth (as is customary in their matrilineal culture) and absorbing her mother's lessons to build wealth by buying property. Yasmin came to the United States for college and met her fiancé, Miles, who was raised in a small town in Vermont, through online dating in her late 20s. Now, four years into their relationship, Yasmin marvels at how much they've learned as they've talked through their differences in race, ethnicity, religion, socioeconomic upbringing, and familial money messages.

SCARLETT AND ELLIOT: A 4th generation inheritor, Scarlett grew up with her siblings on a horse farm in Tennessee. She first met her husband, Elliot, when they went to the same music camp at 12. They stayed friends through college but then lost touch until they reconnected at a friend's wedding 12 years later. They were married a year later. Now the couple live in Virginia where Scarlett is a music director for a theater company and Elliot runs a tech start-up. They have a three-year-old son.

DEBORAH: Raised on different coasts and in different religions, Deborah and Alan seemed opposites on paper. Yet, when they met at a party in their 20s, they bonded almost immediately over their shared experience of growing up as wealthy inheritors and being uncomfortable in the role. When they married, though, Deborah felt that Alan's family never fully accepted her—they seemed perennially disappointed that she could not fit their expectations of who Alan's wife should have been. She resolved to do things differently with her own children's partners, and now 40 years later, has been welcoming her children and their spouses into family wealth discussions for more than a decade.

Chapter Three

Meeting the One

We left off at the end of the previous chapter with our interviewee Justin getting ready to broach the subject of his inherited wealth for the first time with his new partner, the woman he's been dating for about half a year. Justin is at the beginning of the life journey we will cover in this next section of the book—the life-defining task of finding, committing to, and ultimately forging a strong union with your chosen life partner. This chapter is about the universal human drive to love and be loved, the ways in which inherited wealth can complicate this journey, and the insights we learned from our interviewees about not only *why* it's important to persist in the effort, but more importantly, *how* to navigate this path in a beautiful, partnership-enhancing, life-enriching way.

The importance of love

Clinical psychologist Meg Jay devotes five chapters in her book *The Defining Decade* to "Love," opening the first of the five with cultural commentator David Brooks's quote, "The most important decision any of us make is who we marry," and following it up with her own explanation: "Marriage is one of our most defining moments because so much is wrapped up in it.... With one decision you choose your partner in all adult things. Money, work, lifestyle, family, health, leisure, retirement, and even death become a three-legged race. Almost every aspect of your life will be intertwined with almost every aspect of your partner's life."[44]

Jay's words are true even for couples who choose not to legally marry, if they commit emotionally to building and sharing a life together. Fundamentally, Jay is talking about all that rests on your choice of "the one"—the person you hope will be your partner in all the joys, challenges, and unexpected turns of life.

Before, and hopefully underpinning, any marriage or commitment, is love. And love turns out to be a fundamental human need, evidenced by everything from Maslow's hierarchy of needs to Sigmund Freud's famous and enduring declaration that "Love and work, work and love…that's all there is." Perhaps the best explication of the true profundity and life-giving nature of love, though, appears in Viktor Frankl's *Man's Search for Meaning*. Frankl describes how, on a forced march early one morning from the concentration camp where he was imprisoned in World War II to the prisoners' daily labor site (under threat of gunfire and blows from the patrolling camp guards), "the man marching next to me whispered suddenly: 'If our wives could see us now! I do hope they are better off in their camps and don't know what is happening to us.'"

Frankl continued:

> "That brought thoughts of my own wife to mind. And as we stumbled on for miles, slipping on icy spots, supporting each other time and again, dragging one another up and onward, nothing was said, but we both knew: each of us was thinking of his wife. Occasionally I looked at the sky, where the stars were fading and the pink light of the morning was beginning to spread behind a dark bank of clouds. But my mind clung

to my wife's image, imagining it with an uncanny acuteness. I heard her answering me, saw her smile, her frank and encouraging look. Real or not, her look was then more luminous than the sun which was beginning to rise. A thought transfixed me: for the first time in my life I saw the truth as it is set into song by so many poets, proclaimed as the final wisdom by so many thinkers. The truth—that love is the ultimate and the highest goal to which man can aspire. Then I grasped the meaning of the greatest secret that human poetry and human thought and belief have to impart: *The salvation of man is through love and in love.* I understood how a man who has nothing left in this world still may know bliss, be it only for a brief moment, in the contemplation of his beloved."[45]

The challenges young inheritors can face finding love

Experiencing this salvation that Frankl describes is a desire that is core to humanness. What a true gift it is to have that loving face to focus on, that loving presence to give life meaning, even at this darkest hour. But finding this kind of love is a journey, and like many of life's most meaningful journeys, it can be a challenging road, particularly for young inheritors who find that the presence of wealth in their lives can complicate the process of trusting and opening up to a potential partner.

We talked in chapter 2 about becoming comfortable with a narrative you can share honestly with friends and others about your wealth. But, as we saw with Justin, even inheritors who are becoming comfortable sharing honestly with friends about their wealth can have a bit of trepidation about how, and when, to tell a new romantic partner.

There are the reasons commonly expressed for wariness—as one inheritor interviewed by researcher Barbara Blouin (an inheritor herself) shared, "I don't want to be taken advantage of, and … I want people to like me for me."[46] And there's the double meaning in this last point—inheritors yearn not only to be liked for themselves (versus for the money), but also to be liked for *themselves* as they truly are, outside of the money. As our interviewee Harper, the surgeon we met in chapter 1, puts it, "It is freeing to feel like there's no preconceived notion, you have no impression one way or another of me, and I could just be whoever I want without you having this filter of whatever you perceive this, you know, identity to be. And so, yeah, I think it would be freeing to kind of hide that part of me, but it's hard when you're in a potential romantic capacity. You don't want to be deceitful."

Harper puts her finger on the dilemma—it can be tempting to hide the wealth from a new partner, but it's ultimately untenable at some point if you're seeking a close relationship. Myra Salzer, in her book *The Inheritor's Sherpa*, goes so far as to say: "The demise of a relationship may be what it takes to wake up an inheritor in denial. Denial precludes the possibility of intimate relationships. When you hide part of who you are, you are not being completely honest. You are deceiving someone who is otherwise close to you and who may feel betrayed. You are also deceiving yourself by not accepting your wealth as part of who you are."[47]

The second part of Salzer's point touches on the denial from self that we spoke about in chapter 2. Those of us who work with inheritors know that a pattern can emerge when inheritors still struggling with this type of denial attempt to embark on relationships with significant others. Often, unresolved fear, shame, or insecurity about the wealth gets played out in the choice of partner—for instance, the young, unempowered inheritor choosing a financial whiz and then turning the reins over to that partner entirely in a mirroring of the relationship with a parent or trustee, or the inheritor who is so ashamed of their wealth that they choose a partner who actively disdains money and all that it entails. Sadly, the prospects for these types of partnerships are often not promising, because they offer the inheritor a solution to a problem that ultimately needs to be resolved within their own heart.

Another challenge that we often hear expressed among inheritors is that the universe of potential partners is smaller. There is a sense that one way to guard against either being taken advantage of or being liked for your wealth is to find someone in the same financial circumstance. There are problems with this approach too, though. As wealth counselor, author, and inheritor Thayer Willis writes in her book, *Navigating the Dark Side of Wealth*: "One irony of this reasoning is that it limits one's choices terribly, for at once there are only a few people who qualify as desirable prospects.... It is practically impossible to match your wealth equally with the wealth of a potential partner. Besides this, how on earth do you bring up such a private subject before you even know if you like each other very much?... If a marriage is to be built on such a limiting quality, the odds grow exponentially that neither partner will experience the rich intimacy and personal growth that marriage can offer."[48]

But there is a way through these challenges. Many of the interviewees we spoke with had navigated this very terrain and had emerged happy, confident, trusting, and in love on the other side. In this next section, we'll share what we heard from our interviewees about what worked for them.

The Way Through

As we saw in the stories of inheritors whose choice of partner was unwittingly influenced by their own unresolved, internal struggles with wealth, the first step on any successful road to love is to know who *you* are.

This is such a critical first step that it is actually one of the core tenets of an unusual course taught at Northwestern University called "Marriage 101." The course, which was the subject of an article in

The Atlantic in 2014, is focused on "walking students through the actual practice of learning to love well." Says one of the course professors, family therapist Alexandra Solomon, "The foundation of our course is based on correcting a misconception: that to make a marriage work, you have to find the right person. The fact is, you have to *be* the right person...."

Students in the course are encouraged to keep a journal and interview friends to better understand their own "issues, hot buttons, and values." Solomon explains, "Being blind to these causes people to experience problems as due to someone else—not to themselves" and that it is far better to "be aware of them, take responsibility for them, and learn how to work with them effectively."[49]

But what if you've done all of this internal work, you've identified your hot button issues, and you are ready, as the course aims to prepare students to be, to "invite in a compatible, suitable partner?" There are likely two lingering questions still in your mind: "How can I trust that this person likes me for me, sees me for me, and is not swayed by the money, either positively or negatively?" and "How and when should I tell them about the reality of my financial situation?" We'll take these one by one.

How to trust

In *The Inheritor's Sherpa*, Myra Salzer introduces the concept of a "money neutral" partner: "A couple does not need to have similar wealth or backgrounds to succeed," she writes. "But most important for inheritors, I believe, is finding someone who is neither attracted nor repelled by money. Someone who is neutral or indifferent to money is the ideal candidate for a mate."[50]

So, how do you find a money neutral partner? If you've read chapter 1 and have mastered the four success factors yourself, you have a roadmap of sorts because this potential partner will look familiar: they will be capable of supporting themselves, they will be engaged in a career of their own choosing, their self-worth will be driven by their own pursuits, accomplishments, and contributions in life, and they will be capable of overcoming setbacks. In other words, they will have achieved the 4 success factors in their own life or will be well on their way.

Our interviewee Hope shared with us the very sweet story of how she first met her husband, Luke, the college summer they both worked on her family's Montana ranch almost 20 years ago. They were part of the annual group of college students who traveled to the remote ranch and willingly worked the long hours and waited in line for dinner and the internet, all drawn by their "values around nature, and adventure, and connection, and willing to take a risk."

When our conversation turned to trust and whether Hope had ever worried about whether Luke was drawn to her wealth, she said no and explained why: "You know we weren't backpacking Europe together; we were working. You know right there—that says something about money values being on this ranch in a remote part of Montana. We were there to work, and we were good workers, so it's kind of like actions speak louder than words. We weren't sitting around. We were working through college, and he was also in veterinary school. He had done an accelerated path and was studying to be a veterinary oncologist, which, you know, in and of itself is a really great career with high earning potential, and I think, I just, I must have been able to put it together that he has the ability to earn a very nice living regardless of what money I may or may not have. So, just like the money piece just didn't seem threatening."

Hope went on to talk about what she remembers of Luke's focus in their conversations. While he obviously knew her family owned the ranch, that connection and its implications never seemed to be that important to him. "It was, your family owns the ranch, but okay, back to life. Like what are you studying? What do you want to do?" she explained. "You know that was more of the focus about what we were doing, not about my family…yeah that's nice, that's cool, that's interesting about your family and the money, but that doesn't have to drive our story, I guess. You know, we were both set on making our own way, which we have done to-date."

Threaded through Hope's recollection of that summer were all the signs that Luke was already working his way toward the 4 success factors in his own life. We see in our work that, just like inheritors themselves, partners of inheritors who have built these capacities in their own lives are better able to integrate knowledge of the wealth (the fact that their partner will likely inherit) into their life without being swayed off course. They, like Luke, find it "interesting," but ancillary to the path they are on and the contributions they intend to make in their own life. They are money neutral in the best sense—the money means little to them. It doesn't draw them in, but it doesn't repel them either. And more importantly, it doesn't subsume them—because of the strong internal foundation they have built, they are also able to withstand the pull of the black hole we spoke about in chapter 1, and as a result, are in a position to be a true support for their inheritor spouse.

So, finding a money neutral partner is a very good start. But another important part of convincing yourself that you are not only loved for *yourself* (versus your money) but also seen as your true self—outside your money—is to make sure you are coming across as money neutral yourself. Part of this goes back to the story you're telling yourself about your wealth that we spoke about in chapter 2 and to what degree you've come to a level of acceptance about that. Our interviewee Margaret, who is amicably divorced from her first husband, Kevin, and is now back on the dating scene, reflected with us on how she used to let her own inner feelings about her inheritance get in the way when meeting new potential partners and how she's decided to change that. "I think, sometimes, people were telling me who they were, and I wasn't listening because I was too busy worrying about who they think I am," she explained. "I think I've often come into relationships apologizing…I'd like to stop doing that."

As important as whether you feel money neutral in your own mind is what you are broadcasting to others through your lifestyle. Our interviewees Campbell and Mia, now living in Raleigh with their two-year-old daughter, reminisced with us about their lives when they met during their sophomore year of college. Campbell, whose family could have chosen to use their wealth to rent him a luxury apartment close to campus, was instead bunking up with 3 other roommates in a serviceable walk-up. As a result, he said, for those college years, he and Mia's lives looked socioeconomically very similar. "I mean, my parents were paying for college. Her parents were paying for college. My parents paid my credit card bills. Her parents paid her credit card bills," he said. "We were kind of in the same boat, so in terms of wealth, I don't think it really came up. We lived in the same apartment complex, that's when we started dating, so we lived in the same type of place. You know, our lives were pretty similar for those four years, five years."

What's striking about Campbell's story is that now, almost 15 years later, his parents view the family wealth as collective, and he and his brother are actively involved in managing both the wealth and his family foundation. But, in this critical developmental period of his life when he was not only figuring out who he was but also forging bonds with his life partner, the wealth was allowed to take a backseat so he could live a lifestyle not defined by his family's resources or access to it.

Ultimately, inheritors are able to be confident they are loved for themselves rather than their wealth and seen as their true selves when they live a life that is not defined by their wealth. When they have something to offer to a partner that they feel is truly their own, they fundamentally understand that it is this true core of self that is loved. Our interviewee Harper put it well as she was musing in our interview about what she hoped a book like ours would cover. She started by saying, "I mean, I think that if I were to be given this book, I would want to know how to really find and maintain a relationship with a person who is not necessarily of the same background as me, because it's really hard to find people who have the same exact, you know, multigenerational wealth situation." But then, she answered her own question, "But I think the answer to that, generally, is by maintaining your own sense of identity outside of your family. Having the sense that you've created something for yourself is so important. And so, I think that's the healthiest thing that you bring to a relationship, if you are a next gen beneficiary in some way."

We completely agree, and it turns out that this epiphany that Harper came to, which essentially describes the importance of believing in yourself as a precursor to believing in another, is at the core of love. In his book *How to Love*, Zen Master Thích Nhất Hanh writes, "When you love someone, you have to have trust and confidence. Love without trust is not yet love. Of course, first you have to have trust, respect, and confidence in yourself…True love cannot be without trust and respect for yourself and for the other person."[51]

Of course, establishing trust is only the beginning. There is everything that follows that defines and creates a deep relationship, including shared values, hopes and dreams for life, aligned views on children and career, etc. We heard touching stories in our interviews on everything from those first conversations about whether each wanted to get married and have children to a deep bond over the fact that both partners had lost a parent when young. But the type of genuine opening up that happens in conversations like these is dependent on there first being trust—on the inheritor knowing in their heart of hearts that this partner is trust*worthy*, that it will be worth investing the time and emotional risk in deepening the relationship.

How and when to tell

If you've been lucky enough to find someone you feel you can trust to love you for you, the next question that comes to mind for most inheritors is how and when to reveal to this person the reality of your financial situation. The answer feels elusive—while everyone agrees that this isn't a topic for a first, second, or third date, the longer the wait, the more time invested in the relationship without the topic being broached, the more the inheritor feels they are lying to the very person they hope to be closest to.

We learned from our interviewees that it might be that the answer to "when" feels elusive because it's an imperfect question—it implies a specific date, a duration of time that is sufficient to merit revelation, when in reality our interviewees remembered the revelation to their partners as a process that unfolded over time. It was iterative, with more revealed as trust deepened and as the inheritor themselves learned (and could internalize) more details about their inheritance. And this iterative process of revelation itself *built* trust, as the partner had the opportunity to demonstrate empathy, support, and continued money neutrality along the way.

What seemed most important was that, at each step in the process, the inheritor felt that their life was in congruence—that they didn't feel they were lying to their partner. For instance, if, as in the example of Campbell and Mia's college days, money didn't come up because it was irrelevant at that time in Campbell's life, that was okay. But, if an inheritor received a trust distribution and was meeting with a financial advisor to discuss the implications of that new wealth in their life, it seemed important that the partner knew about the distribution and the role this advisor played.

Our interviewee Nicholas shared with us how this played out in the early days of his relationship with Sebastian, his husband of fourteen years. In the first year of their relationship, they would visit each other's apartments in West Hollywood. As the year drew to a close, Sebastian suggested they move in together to save rent. That prompted a conversation about the rental amounts and revealed that Nicholas's rent was almost double Sebastian's. Nicholas felt he should explain how he was affording the rent while he was fresh out of law school and still two months away from his first job as a lawyer. "I was like, you know, I'm not going to keep this secret from you," he remembers. "I think honesty has to be the bedrock of a relationship. For me it was about the honesty of the relationship. So, by doing that I'd already committed to saying like, 'Okay, I'm going to let you know about my wealth, it's not a secret.'"

Nicholas went on to tell us how glad he was that he opened up to Sebastian. It gave him someone to talk to as he was wrestling with the impact of the inherited wealth in his life. "I was also kind of going through my own, you know, grappling, too. Here I'm just learning that I was given a bunch of wealth and still grappling with what am I going to do with it. Do I just leave it in the account and ignore it, or do I talk about it? And I always realize you have to bring your full self to the relationship. You can't just pick and choose what pieces you want to show."

And it turns out, the discussions they had, comparing Nicholas's emotions about his unexpected inheritance with Sebastian's upbringing in a family that occasionally struggled financially, was a growth experience for them both. "I didn't know what the right thing was to do [with the inheritance]. And so, I spent a lot of time talking with Sebastian about it," Nicholas says. He talked about how these conversations would unfold: "You're spending so much time with this individual," he said, it's natural to talk about "what's really bothering you. You know like, well, what's bothering me is I've got all this money, and I don't know what to do with it, you know, that's what's bothering me. And so, we would have a lot of conversations about money and wealth and, you know, how differently we both grew up. And I think he realized quickly that, you know, money doesn't solve all the problems. Money can create problems. And, I realized that like, sometimes, you don't need to think about money all the time. You can just enjoy life and, you know, you can still have a great time. So, we were learning from each other."

All in all, this process we've been discussing, of first building trust and then opening up to a partner, mirrors what we covered in chapters 1 and 2—that once an inheritor proves to themselves their identity and self-worth are not dependent on the wealth, they are able to layer the wealth back into their story. The same is true here—once an inheritor proves to themselves that their partner's love and the depth of the relationship are not based on their wealth, they are able to layer the wealth back into the story and feel free to reveal more.

Earlier we talked about how our interviewee Justin was preparing to tell his partner for the first time. Although Justin naturally felt a bit nervous about how the conversation would go, he told us that he fundamentally was feeling ready to have the conversation at this point because he knows in his heart that her feelings for him are unrelated to his wealth. As he puts it, "I feel totally comfortable enough with her to be able to be, like, 'Hey, this is my story relating to my family's wealth. And here's who I am in relation to it,' because I already feel really confident that she likes me for who I am as a person not associated with my wealth."

If you're still somewhere in the middle of this journey, either trying to find the partner you feel you can trust or wrestling with how to reveal the truth of your wealth to the person you hope is "the one," we hope that these stories of how our interviewees have navigated this path give you not only hope that there is a way through, but confidence that you can find it.

And it's worth finding. In addition to the transcendent, life-giving purpose we can all glean from the love that Viktor Frankl so beautifully described at the beginning of this chapter, we heard from our interviewees that there were important ways they felt their significant other furthered them along the developmental journey they began in Section One. In this next section, we'll share these stories and hear how the love of a trusted, chosen partner can help an inheritor further individuate, feel confident in their own abilities, hone their sense of self, and process the role of wealth in their lives.

The gifts that love bestows

In Section One, we saw how important it is for an inheritor to feel they can move out from under the shadow of their family's wealth and success and be seen as a competent adult in their own right. And for many of our interviewees, it was in the eyes of their significant other that they first truly felt seen this way. Their partners not only naturally saw them as the adults they were (versus the "next gens" they might have been seen as by their families), but also gave them a chance to be known for themselves and to be loved for an identity that was of their own making rather than associated with their family wealth.

Our interviewee Tim from chapter 1 shared with us what this felt like when he first met his wife, Alice. "I think it helps that we met in college far away from home. Because, in some ways, you know, it allowed me to be me without any strings.... I think I was being who I was with Alice from the moment I met her, you know, without feeling constrained by this other inheritor identity or pressured by it." A thousand miles away from home, the ongoing sale of the family business, and the conversations his parents were having about forming a family office to invest the proceeds, Tim felt like he could be his true self and that it was this self that Alice first loved.

Tim went on to describe how, even though his family wealth wasn't a big part of the early days of their relationship, Alice's independence and natural curiosity empowered him to take a more authoritative role when he came back to engaging with the family wealth. "I think Alice's independence has been a big part of how I've grown up, and grown into myself, and who we are as a couple, and who we are as a family," he said. "I wouldn't have asked myself half the questions I've asked myself or dealt with or struggled with or resolved had I not had Alice to at least be a different voice and a different opinion."

We heard Tim's sentiments about this deeper level of agency conferred by a partner echoed in a number of our interviews. Not only did partners, like Alice, bring a fresh perspective that allowed inheritors for the first time to step outside of and really reflect on whether they agreed with family norms, but also, importantly, partners treated inheritors like adults, expecting them to exert agency, have opinions, and generally be in charge of their own life. In other words, more was expected of the inheritor by their partner than sometimes had been expected by their own family, and they would rise to the occasion.

In addition to imbuing and reinforcing agency, we also saw how the love of a partner conferred resilience and helped our interviewees weather the setbacks they encountered in life. Our interviewee Craig explained how important his wife, then fiancée, Laura, was to him when the start-up he founded in college fell apart six years later. "Her support when that happened, in my eyes an ultimate failure, helped me realize that I had other qualities and accomplishments besides what I prized that were valued," he said. "When I thought that I was a shadow of my former self, she helped me truly understand what I could do in life.... In my head, I had lost myself. But she was still there. We were still engaged. She was even excited for me to do something new. It wasn't because of my business [that she was there]; it was because of me. And that became abundantly clear once the business was nonexistent."

In chapter 2, we met storytelling coach Lani Peterson, who talked with us about the importance of "meaning-making" when reclaiming agency as a young inheritor. An important part of this process, Lani explains, is "restorative resilience," which involves knowing who you can turn to "when your coffer is empty or you're struggling with how to rebuild yourself back up." She encourages people to think about who in their lives "restores and sustains" them: "Who do I want to connect with? Who helps me gain perspective? Who brings me joy? Who reminds me of me? Who helps me remember who I am?" For many of our interviewees, the answers to these questions were the same—it was their chosen partner. The partner was the primary person in their life who fulfilled the role Lani summarized as the guide who "helps us remember what's important to us and why, when we fall off track."

In this way, the chosen partner acted as a mirror for our interviewees—they were both the mirror that our interviewees chose because it reflected back the version of themselves they wanted to be and the mirror that helped them remain that way. This concept of a chosen friend or partner as a mirror that helps you both stay true to self and improve that self goes all the way back to Aristotle, who believed "that friends hold a mirror up to each other; through that mirror they can see each other in ways that would not otherwise be accessible to them, and it is this (reciprocal) mirroring that helps them improve themselves as persons."[52] In that vein, Craig, whose wife helped him refind himself after the loss of his business and identity as a founder, shared with us that now, "The version of myself I see in the mirror is what my wife knows I can become and needs me to become."

We saw Craig's sentiment in a number of our interviewees' stories—that their relationship with their chosen partner not only imparted self-knowledge, but also pushed them to continue to become who they most desired to be. And, as Aristotle indicated, it was reciprocal—each partner helped the other strive toward this improved version of self. Our interviewee Oliver describes how, over the years, his wife, Holly (whom he met in elementary school and married eight years after their first date in their junior year of high school) has "pushed me in so many different ways to become more the person I want to be, the father I want to be, the partner I want to be, etc." And he's done the same for her. "So," he explains, "I think pushing each other in the areas we want to be pushed in and challenging each other, I guess, has been a real important part of our day to day."

Growing together

Fundamentally, what we see inheritors finding in their chosen partner is someone to grow with. A number of our interviewees met their partners during what we noted in chapter 1 was the critical period of individuation in their 20s or even earlier, and in essence, evolved into the adult version of themselves in concert with their partner. Our interviewee Abby, the eighth grade teacher we met in chapter 1, has been friends with her partner, Ben, since middle school and together as a couple since they first started dating in college 15 years ago. "I think we've had this experience of kind of becoming adults together in our relationship," she explained. "So for us, it really involved making sure that we had room in our relationship to both be independent, and grow independently, and encourage that in each other. And I think we've sort of been able to build our identities as adults together. And so, I think we have a lot of shared experiences, and a lot of shared values that have derived from those shared experiences."

It turns out that the shared, mutual growth that Abby is describing is not just an emotional reality, but also a physiological one. In their book, *A General Theory of Love*, psychiatry professors Thomas Lewis, Fari Amini, and Richard Lannon apply insights from neuroscience to explain how the bonds of love, attachment, and intimacy regulate our daily experiences and even alter the structure of our brains: "In a relationship, one mind revises the other; one heart changes its partner. This astounding legacy of our combined status as mammals and neural beings is *limbic revision*.... Who we are and who we become depends, in part, on whom we love."[53]

The authors go on to explain that, as a result, the "prevailing myth" that "*relationships are 50-50*" is a misunderstanding of the physiology of love and that in reality, "Love is simultaneous mutual regulation, wherein each person meets the needs of the other.... Such a relationship is *not* 50-50, it's 100-100. Each takes perpetual care of the other, and, within concurrent reciprocity, both thrive. For those who attain it, the benefits of deep attachment are powerful—regulated people feel whole, centered, alive." As a result of this mutual regulation, they conclude, "partners share a single fate: no action benefits one and harms the other.... A couple shares in *one* process, *one* dance, *one* story. Whatever improves that *one* benefits both; whatever detracts hurts and weakens both lives."[54]

A shared story

We saw in our interviews that part of the *one* story that inheritors and their partners come to share is the story of adjusting to wealth, integrating wealth into identity, and finding a way to be comfortable sharing the reality of the wealth with others. This can come as a surprise to the partner, who in the beginning of the relationship views the wealth essentially as "other," as belonging to the inheritor or their family. But as the relationship evolves and deepens into the type of attachment described above, at some point a shift happens, a realization dawns: this wealth (and all of its attending challenges) is *ours*.

Inheritor coach Myra Salzer describes this phenomenon in *The Inheritor's Sherpa*: "Many people regard non-moneyed partners as lucky. In reality, [they] become targets of the same negatives that inheritors themselves experience. Furthermore, their change in circumstances can affect former relationships. Additionally, they lack the years of preparation for wealth that inheritors often have, so these challenges may hit them by surprise."[55]

We saw this in our interviews. Remember our interviewee Nicholas, who told us earlier how relieved he was when he could share honestly with his partner, Sebastian, that what was bothering him was grappling with his newly inherited wealth? We learned later from Sebastian that, as their nearly two-decade partnership has evolved, what began as his mainly offering an empathetic ear to Nicholas eventually became his experiencing the challenges of wealth firsthand. He told us about a particularly painful episode in which the relationship with his brother nearly broke down because his brother accused him of changing as a result of the wealth, and Sebastian strongly disagreed. When the siblings finally reconciled two years later, Sebastian remembers saying, "I have changed. I'm married, I'm a father, and I grew up. I'm not that same little boy that you keep thinking about."

Fundamentally, inheritors' partners have the same need that inheritors do to build a solid sense of self outside the wealth and then to find a way to layer the story of the wealth back in a way that feels authentic to themselves and supports rather than undermines who they want to be. The good news, though, is that they don't need to travel this path alone—for both partners and inheritors, these burdens can be shared. For the inheritor, there is finally someone who truly understands the challenges of integrating wealth into identity, and for the non-inheritor partner, there is someone you love who is a bit further ahead of you on this journey who you can commiserate with and learn from.

Our interviewee Holly described what this evolution has felt like to her over the course of her relationship with Oliver from their first date in high school to now, almost 20 years later. At first, she saw the wealth as something outside of herself, and this was fine with her. "I didn't want to associate myself with the privilege," she said. "The whole pull-yourself-up-by-your-bootstraps ethic was something that I idolized, I guess, and I didn't want to let go of that idea.... So, at first it was kind of easy to think it's his money and just put it on him; it was his family thing to deal with."

But over time, as Holly began to become involved in Oliver's family foundation, as she and Oliver chose careers in teaching and social work because of the economic freedom afforded by his family's wealth, and as her decision to stop working to stay home with their three children was made possible partly through distributions from Oliver's trust, it became clear to Holly that this wealth and its benefits were as much hers as Oliver's. "Owning my role in that took some space and time," she says. "I started thinking about things that he had talked to me about when we were dating that felt like *his* issues ... [and] it dawned on me, like, wait a minute, this is now *our* money."

As she was wrestling with this evolution and processing the role of wealth in her life, at least she knew who she could turn to. "It's something that Oliver has been dealing with his whole life," she said. "I was kind of late to the processing of what it all meant. And so, I sort of learned how to think about the wealth through listening to him talk through it. And benefiting from all his years of struggle and processing guilt and thinking about, you know, how to merge his values with the wealth. Just kind of reflecting on ways that he had processed things and choices he has made helped me to think like, 'Oh okay, I'm now having the same question. Here's how Oliver processed it. Does that feel good for me?'"

We can see in Holly's story that she and Oliver were in essence writing the story of the wealth in their lives together, sharing the benefits, burdens, and challenges along the way. And this is love. In *How to Love*, Zen Master Thích Nhất Hanh writes: "In true love, there's no more separation or discrimination. His happiness is your happiness. Your suffering is his suffering. You can no longer say, 'That's your problem.' In true love, both happiness and suffering are no longer individual matters."[56]

Chapter Four

For Richer or Poorer, Part I: The Problem with Prenups

We left off at the end of the previous chapter with our partners in love, united in their shared challenges and joys, and beginning to weave the stories of their lives—and their relationship to wealth—*together*, in both senses of the word. The next step for many couples at this stage in their relationship is the commitment of marriage, which, despite the anecdotal and much-reported-on decline in marriage among millennials, is still alive and well as an institution, particularly among the demographic that largely defines our interviewees—highly educated, socioeconomically advantaged, often dual-earning couples.[57]

Within much of the wealth advising industry, the announcement that a young inheritor is contemplating marrying their partner brings to mind one primary "to do" item—a prenuptial agreement. The "prenup," as it is known, is seen by many as a standard and necessary item on the premarital planning "risk management" checklist. This is because much of the wealth advising industry orients around the center of gravity of the wealth-owning "G1" parents, and the risk that is being managed in this process is the risk that some of the wealth that these "G1" parents have built and transferred to their child will be squandered as a result of the dissolution of the child's marriage.

So, this chapter will be about prenups, but from an entirely different perspective. This chapter will be about what the *requirement* of a prenuptial agreement feels like to a young inheritor and their partner when introduced by a third party (often a wealthy parent or the parent's advisor) at the point in their relationship that we've just gotten to—when in essence the inheritor and their partner feel like one.

We wish we could share the full transcript of every story we heard. This was often the most emotional part of our conversations with our interviewees—stories poured out page after transcript page, with memories and emotions still quite raw and present, even if in some cases these experiences were now 30 years in the past.

We were transformed by what we heard, and these stories have forever changed how we will approach this area of planning in our practice. We hope to share what we learned so others can benefit from the wisdom in these memories and experiences. We will show through our interviewees' stories why prenups can be particularly fraught in a multigenerational wealth context (the predominant context in which they are recommended by our industry), how the risk that a prenup mitigates is often dwarfed by the much more significant risks the process introduces into the human relationships involved, and of course, the way through—how our interviewees, their partners, and their families weathered this challenging period, created novel approaches that avoided the pitfalls of the typical process, and emerged stronger, more unified, and wiser on the other side.

One note before we begin—if it seems from this lead-in that we are anti-prenup in all cases, we're not. Specifically, we're not talking in this chapter about blended families with children from prior marriages, later-life prenups, or even prenups that essentially function as buy-sell agreements for closely held businesses. We're talking about a prenup in a first marriage between a young inheritor and their partner, designed to protect inherited family wealth (liquid and invested assets, almost always held in trust), as this is a common situation and a very common fact pattern in a significant number of cases in which prenups are introduced. Our goal is not to rule out prenups entirely, even for this scenario, but importantly to share what we learned about the downsides and risks of the typical approach and, in the next chapter, to provide a road map for a much better way to go about the process if a prenup is actually necessary (which we've come to believe is the exception rather than the norm).

Why prenups are fraught in a multigenerational wealth context

We heard in our discussions with our interviewees that the stress they experienced in the prenuptial process rarely began with a disagreement over terms. The cause was simpler and, in fact, more devastating. It was the way in which the very suggestion or requirement of a prenup by the wealth-owning family or their advisor at this point in the story itself introduced significant risk and distortion into the relationship dynamics between the young inheritor and their partner. There were four distinct areas of distortion—we'll take them one by one and describe not only how our interviewees felt, but more importantly, how they found a way to navigate through the situation and emerge with their relationship intact.

Agency

We've seen in our first three chapters that so much of a young inheritor's journey is about agency—about individuating from their wealthy family, forging an independent sense of self, feeling capable on their own terms, and finding a partner who reinforces and supports this individuation and with whom they can grow as the two work together to author their lives and carve out their own place in the world.

A threat to authorship

Now, consider how a third party's suggestion or requirement of a prenup, coming at this very moment (one infused with all the possibility and potential inherent in the beginning of a jointly designed life), disrupts all of this. Suddenly, the inheritor is no longer an adult in charge of their own life, but a subordinate in the larger system of the family wealth. Worse yet, in the most important and intimate realm of the inheritor's fledgling adult life, the family wealth (the very wealth they've struggled for years to individuate from and attempt to perceive with authority and agency) descends with an agenda of its own.

We heard from a number of our interviewees about what it feels like when this dynamic plays out and their agency is removed from the equation. For some, the decision had already been made—the first they were told of a prenup was when they were instructed to come to a trustee's office and presented with papers to sign (sometimes a week before the wedding). For others, they were "involved" in the process—provided instructions to execute on, essentially—but the prenup was presented from the outset as a fait accompli. Our interviewee Campbell, who met his wife, Mia, when they both lived in the same apartment complex in college, explained, "I never felt strongly that I needed it. It felt more like just what I was supposed to do." He continued, "I think it was being pushed primarily through my current financial advisors at the time; it was just like, what is done. And this is how it's done. And here's your lawyer, you're going to meet with a lawyer. Mia needs to get a lawyer. We're going to hire her lawyer. And this is just the way it is, you know."

Because of the gravitational pull of the black hole of the family wealth that we mentioned in chapter 1, it was often challenging for our inheritor interviewees to wield agency even when they were given an opportunity. In some cases, this was because they felt they understood so little about the prenup topic relative to the trustees or attorneys advising them to sign one. As our interviewee Helen, who had attended family meetings with her trustee through college but felt ill-equipped to understand the quarterly investment reports they sent her, recalled, "I felt like that [the prenup process] was so out of my hands. I remember the trustees saying to me, 'We need to do this.' And I was, like, 'Okay,' because I felt like I had no knowledge about any of these things. So, I just deferred to them. So, there were decisions that were made by 'me,' but I feel like kind of weren't, because I just had no understanding of what I was doing."

In other cases, it was difficult for our inheritors to wield agency because they felt emotionally paralyzed. Our inheritor interviewee Nathan and his wife, Louisa, talked to us about how the process of finalizing their prenup unfolded in the hectic months before their wedding five years ago. The couple, who met when Louisa began sourcing produce for her restaurant from Nathan's business, were aligned on their mutual goal of trying to make the prenuptial agreement as generous as possible. Still, though, Nathan found the whole process "uncomfortable and awkward." Louisa chimes in, speaking to Nathan during our interview, "I think partly in your heart, you would have preferred to not do it. But you knew that that would not be an option and was not something you were ever going to be able to confidently say to your parents, like, 'No, we didn't get a prenup.' That wasn't going to fly."

She continued, speaking to us, "So, in this way, he was doing the prenup to appease what he knew were the family's expectations, and it created a lot of challenges, because it really wasn't his thing. I think it was like an emotional iceberg-type panic moment for him, where he was like, 'Okay, intellectually, I know I have to do this thing.' But, knowing that he had to do this contract around money that he didn't earn anyway, that was given to him. And why should he get to keep money that was given to him. It just created this vortex of emotion that was very hard to work through, like very hard." In the end, Louisa explained, "because it was so much less emotional for me, and I knew it had to get done, ultimately, I got it done. I had to take it upon myself to sort of, like, drag the project over the finish line."

We saw this dynamic in a number of our interviews. For young inheritors having just recently wrestled with feelings of shame about inherited wealth, the idea of "protecting" this wealth from their chosen and loved partner can feel, at best, mind-boggling, and at worst, downright wrong. As a result, a common response is avoidance, which often means delay, either until it becomes too late to act or until, as in several of our interviewees' stories, the partner—never the initiator of the concept—steps in out of a sense of necessity to shepherd the process and get it done so that the box can be checked and the wedding preparations can continue.

These stories show us how challenging it can be for the inheritor when they start to perceive that they lack agency—that their own desires are subordinate to those of the larger family wealth system—in an area of such critical importance as the most intimate relationship of their lives.

A mirror at risk of fogging

As challenging as it can be for the inheritors themselves, it can be even worse for the couple as a whole when the requirement of the prenup and the inheritor's trapped acquiescence alters the way in which the partner *sees* the inheritor. All of a sudden, the adult whom they love and have seen functioning independently in their own life is dragged back into the role of a child taking orders from parents or a subordinate carrying out the wishes of a larger family wealth system. It can be a rude awakening for a partner to be confronted so starkly with how little power the inheritor has (or perceives themselves to have) in these broader relationships. After all, in the previous chapter we talked about how inheritors often seek partners who act as a mirror to reinforce their sense of agency and reflect back the self they hope to become (and remain). For these mirroring partners, who have up until this point considered the inheritor free—to define themselves, their relationship with their partner, and their relationship to wealth—these shifting dynamics can be unsettling, unmooring, and potentially destructive unless the inheritor and partner find a way through that allows them to regain their joint sense of agency, freedom, and possibility.

Our interviewees Tim and Alice shared with us how this played out for them when the concept of a prenup was introduced by Tim's family office in the lead-up to their wedding almost thirty years ago. The couple had met in college, miles away from Tim's hometown and the ongoing family discussions that were occurring around setting up a family office now that the family business had been sold. When they moved in together closer to Tim's home after college, Alice, who came from an "old money" family herself and had been raised by her feminist mother to always support herself, committed herself to living frugally and splitting expenses equally. When, several years later, Tim proposed on the summit of their favorite mountain in the midst of a fall hike, the two were giddy. Alice remembers staying awake half that night in their tent while Tim slept, full of love for him and anticipation for their life ahead.

When Tim shared the news of his engagement with his family and their family office, the head of the family office suggested a prenup. Tim was familiar with the concept from the peer group of wealth holders he had joined. "Everybody talked about the need to have a prenup," he said. "It was just part of the dialogue, you know, professionally and in the industry." He remembers his family office's perspective being consistent with what he was hearing among his peers, that "the best thinking of the day was, you know, if you're an inheritor, you absolutely have to have this in place." And that "it should be able to be presented in a way that takes all the emotion out of it. It's just a fact of life. And it shouldn't really be a burden to anybody. It was like,

'Oh yeah, it won't be a problem,'" Tim recalled. "And that was not the reaction I got from Alice."

Alice continued, "My memory was that, actually, when Tim told me, I was really mad, and really sad, and really scared, because I was like, 'I'm not doing this.' And the message, of course, it sends—as I'm sure you've heard 25 times in your 25 interviews—is, you know, basically, screw you, and you're always going to be on the outside. And we know that you're just after our money. That's the message you hear." Alice explained that she also felt stung by Tim's family's seeming lack of understanding of her and her family's values—that after all her efforts over the last several years to support herself, it "still was like, 'Yep, you're going to take his money, dear,' you know, from his parents and the advisors. So, I was really hurt. I just felt like they didn't know me or my family or my values at all. So, you know, I was really disappointed."

Alice's reaction came as a shock to Tim and put him in a position he realized he hadn't been in before, both with Alice and with his family. "I mean, this was really the first major kind of disagreement, you know. I was so, you know, enmeshed with my family. And I'm not sure I was ready or capable of not doing something that, you know, they told me to do. It took some time and it was a hard for me to kind of process that."

This enmeshment, now on full display to Alice and motivating Tim's acquiescence to the idea of an agreement that Alice viewed as a nonstarter, struck a chord. "One of my biggest fears," Alice said, "was that Tim was sort of being led around by the nose by these advisors and not able to think for himself. Because, frankly, the wealth was so relatively new. He came into it with no preparation. So, you know, I was worried. I was like, 'Well, here we go, Tim is just always going to take their advice.' And I came as spouses do, with this different perspective and like, you actually don't have to do everything they say."

Alice is talking about agency—her sense of dismay at her perception that Tim was abdicating his, and the need it fueled in her to find an outlet for hers. Thankfully, because of her own family's history with wealth, she had one. Alice called her own family's trust attorney, whom she knew had decades of experience with significantly wealthy families, for a second opinion. Fortunately for her, he did not subscribe to the conventional wisdom. "He said, 'Oh no, I would not advise that. I don't advise anyone in first marriages to do prenups.'" Alice shared. "So, that was really great for me to have that perspective. And poor spouses who don't have anyone to talk to like that—a professional, frankly, who's really plugged into these issues. I was very lucky, because I had those resources to be able to go right to. So, we were able to resolve it pretty quickly, because I was able to come back to Tim and say, 'I'm not doing this, and you've really hurt my feelings, and your parents have.'"

Ultimately, Alice and Tim made it through. Somewhat ironically, and as we saw in several of our stories, when they reclaimed agency and expressed that they wouldn't be signing a prenup, the family office's response was, "Okay. It was no big deal." Alice says now, "I remember thinking, 'Are you kidding me?' All that emotion and all that terrible stress, and we nearly, we didn't break up, but I wasn't going to get married under those circumstances. And when Tim pushed back a little, they're like, 'Okay, you get to do what you want. It's your life.' And I remember thinking, those are really mixed messages. Like, this is the way it's done, you know. And then, actually, when you show you have some agency, they go, 'Oh, okay, you're allowed to make your own decisions.'"

The about-face from the family office, as whiplash-inducing as it was for Alice, is reflective of standard industry best practice, which views the prenup almost exclusively through the lens of the wealth-owning family and as an almost transactional, off-the-shelf, checklist item, devoid of emotion. Alice's reaction brought the emotion—and the partner's perspective—back into the discussion and shifted the equation. When faced with her reaction and the stakes that it raised (and the possible significant risk to the relationship), Tim's family and their family office saw the issue in a wholly different light.

Now, thirty years later, Tim reflects on what he thinks was broken about the process: "There's very little discussion about message received. It's all about, well, if you have money, here's how you just move through this one chapter in your life, and here's why it makes sense, and here's why it really should be a very easy topic. Oh, and here's a way for you to talk about values. And there isn't any discussion about, yeah, the emotional impact of the discussion and those decisions, and what that meant."

Loyalty

Woven throughout Alice and Tim's story is another dynamic: loyalty. When Alice balked at the notion of a prenup, Tim was implicitly given a choice—side with his family or with her. This dynamic was evident in a number of our interviews and made it clear that this test of loyalty and the untenable position in which it places inheritors—and the potentially devastating consequences to the relationship with their partners—is another significant distortion that a prenup introduces into the equation when suggested or required by a third party at this stage.

Psychologist and relationship expert John Gottman, known for the work he and his wife, Julie Schwartz Gottman, conducted over several decades on divorce prediction and marriage stability, writes at length about the destructive consequences of disloyalty in a relationship. "Betrayal is, fundamentally, any act or life choice that doesn't prioritize the commitment and put the partner 'before all others.'" He goes on to say that "nonsexual betrayals," including "siding with a parent against one's mate" can "devastate a relationship as thoroughly as a sexual affair," and that research conducted at their University of

Washington "Love Lab" (which has scientifically observed more than 3,000 couples and operated for more than 30 years) indicates that "*betrayal lies at the heart of every failed relationship*" (his italics).[58]

Seen in this light, it's alarming that the typical prenup process within the wealth advising industry, in which a prenup is put on the table by the wealth-owning family once a marriage is in the offing, typically initiated by the inheritor's parents or by an advisor working on their behalf, often sets in motion a chain of events that necessitates exactly this type of betrayal. Just at the moment that should represent the culmination of an inheritor and their partner's commitment to one another, the inheritor is asked to side with their family, or their family's wealth (the family by proxy), at the expense of their partner.

The grand cinematic tradition is alert to this dynamic and its fork-in-the-road implications for whether a couple will succeed or not. In countless movies—as recently as *Crazy Rich Asians*, but copious other examples exist (see our recommended movie list at the back)—a pivotal plot point occurs when the inheritor proves their love for and loyalty to their partner by showing that they are willing to walk away from everything else (the money, the role the family expects them to play, etc.) in order to be with the partner. Often, a less draconian outcome emerges as a resolution, but the proclamation of loyalty and the commitment to put the partner "before all others," as Gottman puts it, often serves as a crucial turning point and necessary breakthrough to demonstrate the depth of the couple's love and the likelihood that they will triumph over the odds and succeed in the end.

We saw this dynamic play out in a number of our interviews, but we'll share the story we heard from Amelia about the events that unfolded when her parents suggested a prenup in the months leading up to her marriage to her college sweetheart, Liam.

Growing up in the Philly area as the eldest of four siblings, Amelia had always enjoyed a close connection with her parents. "I feel like I have a very close relationship with my parents, and I really value their opinion, and I really value their advice," she said. "They've always been very supportive, so it's always been nice to be able to run things by them and trust them and feel like they're advising me on what they think will be in my best interest."

About six months before the wedding, Amelia's parents brought up that they thought it was important that she sign a prenup. Their view was that, given that she was coming into the marriage with significantly more money, it would be a prudent move to ensure that she and any future children would be protected in the event of a divorce and that she would be able to leave the marriage with the same amount of money she came in with. Amelia felt like it was overkill but was willing to sign one if they thought it was important, especially since she considered it irrelevant given that she and Liam were unlikely to ever divorce.

Liam, though, felt differently. Though up until now he had been very close with Amelia's parents, he was deeply offended by what he felt was their inappropriate incursion into his and Amelia's marriage. Worse than that, he felt the entire concept was at odds with his vision of cohesion for their marriage. His view was, "We're going into this marriage together—everything is going to be shared. We're going to have one family, one bank account, one home. That's really important to me, and I feel like if we were to enter into the marriage with something like this, it'd just put a really sour taste in my mouth, and I wouldn't feel at all comfortable signing it." Also, Liam felt the request made little sense given his earning potential at his biotech venture fund and the fact that his earnings would largely be supporting the couple due to the magnitude of his income compared to Amelia's.

She remembers his perspective was, "I am providing for our family. So, for us to be put through this stressful situation to protect one account when, hopefully, one day our net worth will be significantly higher than that and, you know, primarily because of my income, like that just seems ridiculous to me."

Amelia relayed Liam's objections to her parents, but they dug in, viewing it as a fundamental protection for her. Thus ensued three extraordinarily painful months as Amelia went back and forth, torn between the two camps of people she loved most. "Actually, that was the most stressful experience in my entire life," she recalled, which she acknowledged was saying a lot given that her work takes her to virus hot spots around the world. "I felt like the two groups of people who I care about most in the entire world were pitting me against each other. Obviously, I wanted to side with Liam, because (a) I agree with him, and (b) we were months away from getting married and starting our life together and had committed to each other and to be supportive of each other. And we also shared the same financial goals, and shared the same kind of traditional family values. Meanwhile, my parents were really upset, and I think they had really strong concerns, and I know it was coming from a place of wanting to protect me and having my best interests at heart."

Ultimately, Amelia and Liam decided that they would not be signing a prenup, and that they would rather forego Amelia's inheritance altogether than introduce that dynamic to their marriage. Amelia relayed this decision to her parents in a pivotal conversation. And she presented them with a choice—they could either agree to move on and move forward respecting the couple's decision or accept the strong likelihood that their relationship with her and Liam would be permanently impaired. She recalls saying, "Hopefully, we're going to have a wonderful relationship with you like we've had my whole life, but if you're putting us in a position where we feel like you're putting pressure on us and not listening to us, that's not going to bode well for our relationship going forward. You have to respect that Liam and I are going to make decisions together. Sometimes, you're not going to love them all the time. But, you know, this has to be a priority. Liam is going to be my priority going forward. And, obviously, we're going to be considerate of you, but that's just going to have to be the way that we do things going forward."

It was a breakthrough. Amelia's parents acknowledged that they had never wanted to create tension in their family around money—that it was something that they had actually worked very hard to try to avoid. And they recognized the fundamental truth of Amelia's argument that she and Liam would have to prioritize each other and their marriage over other family members; it was in fact exactly what they had done themselves when they were first starting out.

Amelia recalls that at one point in the conversation, she said, "You just need to let this go." Looking back now, almost five years later, she said, "And they ended up doing that. And we never talked about it again." To her parents' credit and to her immense relief, the conversation ended there, and her parents worked very hard to regain the close relationship they had enjoyed with both her and Liam.

Ultimately, Amelia believes that this episode, as painful as it was, strengthened her and Liam's marriage. "It kind of forced us to get stronger and grow this independence. It basically forced us to say, okay, what is our priority? And, like, our priority is each other and nothing can touch that. To basically say out loud together, we are each other's priority. This is the precedent we need to set for the rest of our life as a married couple. That was so powerful for us. And I think in a way was probably good for our relationship. I'm sure we grew as a couple because of that."

We can hear in Amelia's words how in weathering this trial and coming through to the other side, she and Liam proved that their loyalties were to each other first and foremost. The conflict with her parents prompted a reorientation of the decision-making locus and reprioritization of relationships in the family that was probably necessary and beneficial for all of them going forward. Amelia says that, in fact, across a host of decisions that have followed—from the significant (where they're going to live) to the mundane (vacation plans)—she and Liam have been able to smoothly broadcast their wishes to her parents with the introduction, "We have decided…" and have found that her parents have been supportive and onboard.

Unity

We heard among the objections Liam expressed a defense of unity—he felt that a prenup would destroy cohesion in his and Amelia's marriage and that it refuted his basic understanding of what a marriage was—that he and Amelia would be sharing all things and were in essence becoming one.

Liam was right to be mindful of unity. As we heard in the previous chapter, physiologically and emotionally, couples share *one* story and *one* journey through life. It turns out that couples benefit when this sharing extends to their money. In the money-related chapter of his book, *Things I Wish I'd Known Before We Got Married*, author Gary Chapman (known for his framework of the "five love languages") writes: "The first foundational stone in developing a financial plan is to agree that after marriage, it will no longer be 'my money' and 'your money' but 'our money.' At the heart of marriage is the desire for unity. 'For better or worse,' we intend to live life together. The implication is that we will share our income and work as a team in deciding what to do with our money…. If you are not ready for this kind of unity, then you are not ready for marriage."[59]

Chapman's assertion is borne out by recent research published in the *Journal of Personality and Social Psychology* showing that couples who pool their money are happier. One of the study's authors, Emily N. Garbinsky, an associate professor at Cornell University's business school, summarized the findings this way: "People who pooled everything were the most satisfied. People that pooled nothing were the least satisfied. The people who had this hybrid—where they pooled some (money) and not other—were in the middle."[60]

Critics might counter that this sounds nice but doesn't apply when there is significant wealth to be protected, because things get more complicated. Complexity is certainly a challenge, but it's worth pondering the broader implications of an assumption that this research about marital happiness and sound advice from a relationship expert can be disregarded as inapplicable; what are we really saying about the potential for intimacy and success in marriage when wealth is involved, then, if these rules can't apply? It leaves us wondering if the conclusion that the rules shouldn't apply is actually the problem.

After all, five years after deciding not to have a prenup in order to protect their sense of unity (or as Amelia put it, their sense that "we are each other's priority, and we want everything about our life to be cohesive"), Liam and Amelia now view money exactly as Chapman describes and manage their finances exactly as the pooling research recommends. As Amelia explains, "In our day-to-day lives, we share a bank account. We share everything. We share a credit card. All of our assets are pooled. Both of our salaries, both of our paychecks, are auto-deposited into our joint bank account. We never talk about, like, whose money it is. So, all of that is very easy. It just seems pretty simple and straightforward."

Equality

A final distortion that the typical prenup process—initiated by a wealthy family and designed to protect their wealth—introduces into the relationship between an inheritor and their partner is a power imbalance that disrupts the sense of equality between the couple.

While the view that the primary purpose of a prenup is to protect the wealth of the more moneyed partner is standard practice within our industry, it is actually a 180-degree departure from the historical norm. Ancient marital contracts now regarded as precursors to the prenup concept—from the *ketubah* in Judaism to the *mahr* in Islam to documents tracing as far back as a 2,500-year-old Egyptian scroll—were designed to protect wives, the *less*-moneyed and *less* powerful partner, and to assure them of financial security in the event of a divorce or their husband's death. As Laurie Israel, an attorney and prenup mediator who has written extensively on the drawbacks of the typical prenup process, writes in her book *The Generous Prenup*, the current norm turns this on its head: "They [prenups] operate almost invariably to diminish the rights that accrue upon marriage to the other, 'less-moneyed' spouse. This doesn't sound like a very good deal for the less-moneyed spouse, whose rights are diminished, does it? That's because it isn't."[61]

And the power imbalance that begins with this one-sided purpose often continues through the process, as the spouse with more resources often has greater access to information, education, and advice. Our interviewee Louisa, the chef we met earlier, talked with us about what it felt like to be the less-moneyed partner on the receiving end of the announcement that a prenup would be required and that a prenup process would be underway. Even though Louisa accepted the idea of a prenup in concept (as she put it, "It makes sense as a practical, thoughtful, correct, smart thing to do, and those are things I can get on board with"), she felt at sea in the process, especially relative to the resources Nathan had available to him. "Nathan had a literal team of people helping him. And here I am, a normal person, and they said, 'Go ahead, you need to go retain a lawyer.' Okay. I've never retained a lawyer before. And everyone just says it. Like, it's a normal thing that people do. It's not normal. It's not a thing. I had a very nice life. I got to be 30 years old before I needed to retain a lawyer. Like, where do you even start with that?"

She wished there had been a book she could turn to ("How to be the outlaw in navigating a prenup") but there wasn't, and "the internet is not helpful, because you're never going to find anything from a financial place that's really authored for people in this situation." And so, she was left trying to figure out, "Well, how do I do this in a way where I don't feel like I'm being taken advantage of, or making an uneducated decision?" She recalls feeling like "it was very hard, because it feels like all of a sudden, you're left out on an island of being the person without the money going, okay, what do I do now? And everyone sort of expects you to go figure it out. But there's no blueprint for how to do that. Or if there is, I wasn't aware of what it was."

The feeling that Louisa describes of being at-sea, with no means of navigating her way through, was common among the non-inheritor partners in our interviews. When we asked Louisa what would have helped, she said, "Definitely, if anybody wants the prenup done with any sort of expediency, the non-wealthy partner needs some support, because that's definitely a major blocker."

And beyond that, she reflected that it would have been helpful if she and Nathan had been presented with a model that would have been the "generous" option from the get-go. "Everyone hears 'prenup' and they assume, okay, this is so that if there's a divorce, the wealthy person retains all their money, and the non-wealthy person gets screwed," Louisa said. She and Nathan agreed that this is *not* what they wanted, but there was no road map presented to easily accomplish this. Louisa would have loved to see "what are options that don't look like that. Like, here are the six models that people tend to go with. Which one feels like it's right for you?" Without this, it felt like she and Nathan had to fumble through the process ("it's the world's weirdest conversation, it is") to get to an outcome that was more balanced, even though their goals had been aligned from the beginning.

We heard echoes of the inheritor-partner power imbalance in our discussion with our interviewees Harry and Zoey as well, as they shared with us a decision they made once their prenup process was in motion that they now feel helped (at least somewhat) mitigate this imbalance. Zoey met Harry soon after she relocated from her hometown in Oklahoma to Los Angeles to pursue her dream of designing sets for films. It was evident from early on in their relationship that Harry's family had money (his mother's house had an elevator and floor-to-ceiling views of the Pacific), but Harry lived a down-to-earth lifestyle, immersed in his screenwriting and in collaborations on several projects he was trying to bring to life. As their relationship deepened over the next couple of years, Harry began to open up to Zoey about the various trusts he would be inheriting from and the fact that a number of them would begin distributing to him outright over the next several years.

When the couple began discussing marriage, Zoey expected that she would need to sign a prenup. "I was like, oh, if we ever get married, I know I'll have to sign a prenup," she said. "I guess I've read enough books and seen enough movies that wealthy people have prenups. You know, so it didn't come out of left field." But when the process actually got rolling, Zoey, just like Louisa, felt isolated. "I felt like I was navigating alone, just kind of valuing my own self-worth, what I was worth on paper. You know, and I didn't really have anybody. None of my friends have been in this situation."

Through a friend of a friend, the couple found an attorney for Zoey who happened to be a divorce attorney (known for her loyal clients and her thorough approach) rather than an estate attorney (as Harry's was). Zoe recalls, "As a person who had no weapons, no knowledge, knew nothing about this circumstance, I feel like she definitely had my interests at heart. She really kind of attacked it from every angle and made me feel better about it."

Harry remembers that his own attorney felt that Zoey's attorney was being too aggressive—"He expressed a lot of consternation over that fact to me and that she was approaching her job from the perspective of a divorce attorney and not a contract attorney or an estate attorney." But, looking back on it, Harry is very glad that Zoey's attorney took that approach. "There's sort of inevitably a power imbalance ... but the fact is that Zoey felt like she had a very competent and aggressive person in her corner and that's a good thing. Because, if you're going to have that negotiation happen with, you know, not addressing that power imbalance, it's going to create distrust. I think the fact that Zoey felt supported is why it worked." Zoey agrees: "I don't regret having her because I actually felt like there was someone in my corner."

While they certainly wouldn't go so far as to call their prenup process enjoyable (it is still summed up in Zoey's memory as "the only financial friction we've ever really had; the only time we've ever kind of argued where money was involved"), they realize now it's possible they got through it because Zoey felt that her relative lack of power was being corrected for by her attorney's approach. In a way, the solution Harry and Zoey happened upon evinces how truly challenging it is for a young inheritor and their partner to come through the typical prenup process unscathed, if perhaps one of the best things the couple can do for their relationship long-term is to hire an aggressive attorney for the less-moneyed spouse.

The exception that proves the rule

We've seen through our interviewees' eyes how the typical prenup process within a multigenerational wealth context can impede a young couple's sense of agency, loyalty, unity, and equality. Given the number of interviews we heard that echoed these themes, we were struck by the exceptions—the very few examples we found of couples who would *recommend* the prenup process, who actually felt it was beneficial for their relationship and their marriage, and who would do it again if given the choice.

One of these was Genevieve and Owen. Both 3rd generation inheritors, Genevieve and Owen met eight years ago and are now married with a two-year-old daughter. Both experienced their parents going through challenging divorces, Owen in his teens (a five-year litigious battle) and Genevieve just as she and Owen were starting to date. As a result, Genevieve says, "For both Owen and myself, it was no question that we were going to do a prenup for each of our own individual protection and interest. And so, no matter who we were going to end up with, that was going to be something that was important to us going into marriage." Owen agrees: "It was just so prevalent in our lives that the need for downside protection was in our view."

They both had inherited wealth through their grandparents' estates and understood their respective grandparents' wishes for how the wealth might be used. As Genevieve puts it, "My grandfather was very clear that his hope was that the money would allow for future generations to get an education without having to think about it. And so that means protecting that money for my daughter.... So, it's just putting fail-safes in place that show him that I understood the intention of that money, and all his hard work was something that I respected and wanted to protect for him, and it had nothing to do with Owen."

And the amounts they each inherited were of the same magnitude. As Owen says, "There wasn't much of an imbalance in our relationship. We both have approximately the same amount of money, neither of which was enough to do nothing for the rest of our lives, but plenty to do anything for the rest of our lives."

What we're hearing in Genevieve and Owen's story is that none of the dynamics we've seen be so destructive were at play. They both had *agency*—having lived through their parents' divorces, they each decided, for themselves, that they wanted a prenup in place. They were *unified*—the fact that they both wanted to get a prenup strengthened their sense of partnership and cohesion rather than put it at risk. Of course, there was no problem with *loyalty*, because of this agency and unity. And finally, because they each had the equivalent amount of financial resources and access to advice, there was no power imbalance that impinged on the sense of *equality* between the two of them.

In other words, the facts and circumstances of Genevieve and Owen's situation resulted in a rare alignment of stars that enabled their prenup to actually reinforce the strength of their union. Unfortunately, the exceptional circumstances of their situation—circumstances that kept destructive dynamics at bay and allowed their prenup to be beneficial as a result—proves the rule that prenups are damaging when these dynamics are present. And, unfortunately, these dynamics are almost always present when a prenup is put on the table first by an outside party (a "shadow party" as Laurie Israel calls it in her writings) unless the process is *very* carefully designed. In our next chapter, we'll see an example of a couple who benefited from just this type of gold standard process.

The "why" of shadow parties and why it matters

So, if prenups introduced by shadow parties are almost always destructive unless they beat the odds, it's worth pondering why they're put on the table by these parties to begin with.

In many cases, they are the suggestion of a diligent wealth advisor or estate attorney attempting to mitigate risk—which, unfortunately, is defined too narrowly by the wealth advising industry as *money lost* rather than human relationships damaged. We heard a number of stories from our interviewees in which, even though neither the couple nor their parents wanted a prenup, there was a wealth advisor or attorney in the mix who advised them that it was necessary.

It's worth seriously contemplating how wealth advisors and attorneys would alter their advice if they broadened the definition of risk beyond the financial to include the human risks that a prenup introduces into the equation, including potential damage to all of the following: the young couple's marriage (including increasing the risk that the marriage ends in divorce);[62] the relationship between the inheritor and their parents; the relationship between the inheritor's partner and their in-laws; and the relationship between both sets of in-laws. In other words, what if it were widely acknowledged in the wealth advising industry that the financial protections that a prenup might secure are not *costless*? Prenups might still be considered, but advisors would not feel comfortable putting the concept on the table without, at the very least, informing their clients of these risks.

Of course, the initiator is not always an advisor. Wealthy "G1" parents often bring a prenup up of their own accord. Some see it purely as a prudent protective measure—as we heard in the case of Amelia's parents earlier. And others are driven to make the request by a complex swirl of often unnamed emotions—everything from the sadness of empty nest syndrome (and awareness of mortality) that a child's impending marriage can bring to the fore, to dislike of a child's partner, to frustration at the perceived loss of control over the wealth (that they earned).

Family wealth counselor James "Jay" Hughes spoke to the latter two when interviewed by Charlie Collier for a piece about prenuptial agreements published in the book *Wealth of Wisdom*. "At the root of the [prenup] discussion," Collier writes, "is 'the parents' fear as the driving force,' says Jay Hughes.... 'They are afraid of the money getting into the wrong hands, which often means their son-in-law who is not good enough.'"[63]

So, what should parents do in the face of these fears? The answer is counterintuitive and involves recognizing the limits of control. In their book, *The Cycle of the Gift*, written to help parents ensure their financial gifts have a positive effect on their children (rather than the opposite), authors Jay Hughes, Susan Massenzio, and Keith Whitaker provide the following sage advice: "For all our powers as individuals or as a society, what we cannot control is far greater than what we can. You cannot control what your children do with their lives. You cannot control some of their most important choices, such as those relating to careers or marriages.... The natural human reaction to these uncertainties is fear, and when we feel fear, we often seek control as an antidote. This emotional progression can become a vicious circle, causing us to take rigid stances precisely when we would do best to let go."[64]

And for parents who, though concerned about the risks we've

discussed, still feel plagued by a sense that letting go is financially irresponsible, it can be helpful to reframe the issue by stepping back and thinking about how much money would truly be at risk if their adult child did not obtain a prenup and then comparing that amount to the overall magnitude of wealth the child will likely inherit. Often, at this early stage in a young inheritor's life, they've inherited only a modest amount—and almost always in the form of a trust, unlikely to be viewed by most states as a marital asset unless routinely used as such. Of course, this adult child will probably inherit a great deal more later, and perhaps outright, but that will likely be after the quality of their marriage has long been evident, and (in the case of a good marriage) their partner has long since been accepted as an integral part of the family. And if this calculation of the degree of financial risk still leaves parents on the fence, they might find the scales tipped when they contemplate what their inheriting, grown child might *gain* by *not* having a prenup. For starters, as we have seen, a sense of agency, unity, loyalty, and equality in their marriage.

Ultimately, it's because the prenup discussion so often revolves around the center of gravity of these shadow party motivations that it has the emperor-has-no-clothes quality that inheritors and their partners so often discern. While the couple is told the prenup discussion should be emotionless, that it's just an insurance policy and par for the course, they know and feel the opposite is the case. While they're told it's a great time to discuss their financial values as a couple, they know that their own goals and values are irrelevant in the discussion because they are ancillary to the primary motive of the prenup, which is to quell someone else's fears. And they understand deep down that, while there are a number of serious issues that couples entering into a marriage with disparate wealth backgrounds should discuss to ensure they are on the same page (we'll devote chapter 6 fully to these, but examples include agreeing on a spending philosophy and how to handle requests for assistance from other family members), the problem of ensuring that the wealthier party does not become less wealthy as a result of a breakdown in the marriage is usually not one of them (yet this is often the only topic a shadow party views as relevant). Moreover, the couple knows that if they are to have any chance of these important discussions going well, they will need to start them on the same side of the table, rather than while being represented by opposing counsel.

Fundamentally, the emotional motivations and goals of shadow parties run counter to those of the marrying couple, and therein lies the problem. One is focused on risk mitigation, separation, and control; the other is focused on possibility, partnership, and freedom. Our hope is that, in sharing our interviewees' perspectives, we can help meaningfully shift the center of gravity to put the couple's perspective at the core. In the next chapter, we will cover positive examples we heard in our interviewees' stories of how different participants in the family wealth ecosystem—from parents to advisors to family office executives—were able to do just that. And we will explore a better way to think about prenups—from parents' deciding not to mandate them at all to a process that attempts to restore as much agency, unity, and equality as possible in the rare case that a prenup is truly needed.

CHAPTER FIVE

*For Richer or Poorer, Part II:
Taking a Different Approach*

We were inspired in our interviews by the examples of alternative approaches—from "G1" parents who didn't require a prenup to begin with (or who made it entirely their children's decision) to others who questioned an advisor's insistence that it was necessary to an example of a mandated, multigenerational prenup process that was so well designed by a family office that it was able to largely avoid the damaging dynamics we discussed in the previous chapter. We will share these stories here.

A different parenting philosophy

In our interviews, we heard from several "G1" parents whose perspective on the prenup issue differed from the norm. Our interviewee Caleb talked with us about his wealth-building journey, from his childhood as the son of immigrants from the West Indies to his successful legal career to the estate and gift-planning decisions he and his wife are now wrestling with as they contemplate transferring wealth to their children.

On the topic of prenups, he is clear. "I'm not going to get in the middle of my children making any kind of prenuptial agreements," he says. "I think, as my children all get to 'of age,' their making their own decisions is important to me." He continues, "Also, I think, for parents to mandate it, you create a situation whereby you're almost implying that this person is not the right person for your child. And so, I don't think that's the best way to start a relationship, or to start a relationship where you're trying to have this new person join the family. I don't think it's very supportive."

He believes his view is also aligned with how his children feel. He says about his son, "I think his perspective is that the best way to go forward as a couple is to build together—that when you build together it's a stronger relationship because you both have felt that you've brought something to the table."

And he's philosophical about the risks that might be introduced if his children forego prenups: "There's this whole concept of a hovering parent who's always watching the child, and every time they have a scrape or whatever else, the parent swoops in to help them up. And the question is when does that stop? Does it stop when the child gets to three? Does it stop when the child gets to 10? When should it stop, and just allow the child to be on their own?"

Caleb's story demonstrates how parents might view the prenup question differently if their main priority were to allow their children to make their own decisions in life.

The story of another one of our interviewee couples, Duncan and Beatrice, shows how a parent might view an advisor's recommendation of a prenup differently after reflecting on how they would have felt about the requirement in their own marriage.

Duncan and Beatrice, now in their late 60s, share a common background of each growing up amid the lore of multigenerational wealth that had largely evaporated by the time they came along, motivating each to make their own way in life. When the company Duncan founded in his mid-20s took off, the couple decided that Beatrice would stay home to raise their four children. She focused on instilling in them grounded values and trusting them to make their own decisions and weather their mistakes along the way.

Four years ago, shortly after their eldest son and his college sweetheart announced their engagement, Duncan found himself on the phone with his old college roommate, now a revered trusts and estates attorney. He remembers his friend saying, "Oh my God, you've got to have a prenup. It's the stupidest thing you could ever do to not have a prenup. Don't not have a prenup."

Duncan found himself persuaded and that night relayed the recommendation to Beatrice. She, though, felt otherwise. "I said, hey, I would have resented it if somebody had asked me to sign a prenup before we got married." She also remembered how this same friend, years earlier when they were doing their own estate planning, had recommended that "after Duncan dies, we definitely should have all of Duncan's assets go into a trust so that I couldn't remarry and take all the money, and cut the kids out. My reaction was just, you know, it made me furious—the idea that somebody would trust me with the kids, but not with the money. I thought the kids are so much more important than the money!" Beatrice remembers rejecting the friend's advice back then and feeling that the advice this time smacked of the same narrow focus on the money at the expense of the human dynamics.

In the end, Duncan and Beatrice allowed their son to decide for himself whether he wanted a prenup. They felt that the money he had already inherited outright was *his* and thought it important that he feel the same way and manage it as he saw best, including sharing it with his spouse if that was his choice. Ultimately, their son chose not to get one, and they feel fine about it. Duncan says, "This is not just about wealth. This is about how you approach your children, and do you trust them? Are you going to trust them?"

In addition to hearing from parents themselves, we heard from our inheritor interviewees about the messages they recall their parents relaying about prenups. Our interviewee Abby, the teacher we met in chapter 1, remembers what her mother (herself an inheritor) told her. "I want to give a lot of credit to my mom," she said. "My mom expressed very strong feelings against a prenup and said that she and my dad had not had one and that she was really opposed to them. I think that sort of sums up her feeling, the sort of messaging she gave to me, that you don't have to assume that someone is going to be predatory towards your money."

And our interviewee Campbell, who told us earlier in the chapter that the concept of a prenup was put on the table by his family's wealth advisor and treated as a fait accompli, shared with us how the rest of that story unfolded. Initially, he and his wife, Mia, tried to heed the advisor's advice and go through the motions to make progress toward getting the prenup drafted and signed. But Campbell says, "Once we started realizing the process was becoming contentious and not happy, I sort of looked to my parents and thought, 'Well, you know, when I was growing up, I never thought of it as my dad's money or my dad's family or my dad's wealth.' And I just felt like, at that point, you know, I want to emulate their marriage and the way they raised me. I felt it was 50-50. So, I think I came back and realized, you know what, this should be an equal partnership in all respects. So that means whatever is mine is yours." Campbell and Mia decided to walk away from the prenup discussions, and they've never looked back.

A more holistic definition of risk (and success)

Still, even with all of these stories of couples (and parents) who felt a prenup wasn't necessary, there may be a lingering question in your mind: what if the marriage doesn't work out? Did we talk with any wealthy parents who didn't mandate a prenup and then saw their child divorce down the road? Or hear from any inheritors themselves who decided to forego a prenup and then eventually saw their marriage end? The answer to both is yes, and the unexpected insights we heard in these stories meaningfully shaped our views on the topic.

When things don't work out

You might assume that, in the event of a divorce, the wealthier partner—and perhaps even more so, their parents—ends up wishing that they had had a prenup after all. But we heard something different in our interviewees' stories—that, in fact, the very thought process that leads someone to question the value of a prenup to begin with (prioritizing the human considerations over the financial) shapes their perspective on any financial loss experienced even if the marriage does end.

Our interviewee Nora, mother to three adult children and grandmother to two, shared with us that she and her husband told each of their children when they were marrying about the option of a prenup but ultimately decided to leave the decision up to them. "It was a risk," she said, *but* she continued "You take a risk by letting them live their life. It's a big risk being a parent, and it's really risky when you have grown this wealth, and you've given them pieces of it. But once you give it to them, it's theirs." She said her view on this issue is in keeping with her overall philosophy toward parenting, which she says is summarized in the Kahlil Gibran quote: "Your children are not your children. [They are the sons and daughters of Life's longing for itself]."[65] She continues the thought: "They're entities who came here through you, and you got them to a certain point, but it's their journey. And I mean, you can't—you're not going to be with them on their entire journey."

When her eldest daughter divorced after six years of marriage, Nora focused more on what the experience taught her daughter than the money she risked by not having a prenup in place. It became clear through our discussion that Nora's equanimity was driven by her definition of success. If she had defined success narrowly as every last dollar preserved, she likely would have mandated her daughter have a prenup to begin with. But instead, she defined success as her children having the ability to weather (and not be protected from) the ups and downs that they will experience in life. If she had mandated a prenup, not only would it have been less likely for her daughter to regard any lessons learned as her own, but worse yet, she might actually have felt that her parents' requirement of a prenup played a role in the dissolution of her marriage. Nora concludes, "I love them to death, but they have to live their own lives, or I've failed. Someone told me a long time ago, you're not raising children, you're raising adults."

And what about an inheritor who decided to forego a prenup and then later divorced? We heard from our interviewee Margaret about how her understanding of risk evolved over the course of her marriage and through its eventual end. Margaret shared with us how she had initially struggled when her fiancé, Kevin, indicated that he thought her family's requirement of a prenup was inconsistent with the messages she had relayed up until that point. She had met Kevin, a sports broadcaster, when her family hosted a charitable fundraiser at a local sporting event. As their relationship deepened over the next couple of years and she began to explain her financial situation, she remembers "the theme was, what's mine is yours."

"I had felt the burden of inherited wealth," she explains—the feeling that "gee, this really feels like a big responsibility. And so, in thinking about getting married," she continues, "I saw that as a way to share that responsibility. Like, why would I marry somebody if we weren't then going to share that responsibility?" She remembers she had told Kevin, "If we are going to be married, you will get to appreciate the benefits of not, you know, living paycheck to paycheck. And to balance that, I also want you to share this responsibility and burden."

So, when her family requested a prenup and he was taken aback (she remembers his reaction was, "Well, wait a minute, you said 'what's mine is yours.' But this document says, yeah, but, no, it's not"), she realized he had a point. "I was like, 'Huh, yeah, that actually makes a lot of sense. Like, what I've been saying doesn't really hold water if this document says that's not the case." She was left thinking, "Do I mean the words that I'm saying? Do I really want what's mine to be yours? Am I willing to risk half of it, you know, for those words to be true?"

And she ended up concluding, yes, for a number of reasons. First, she realized, regardless of the outcome, she'd end up with enough money to be okay. In fact, she reasoned she might be *better* than okay. Her whole life, she had struggled with the fact that she found the safety net of her wealth inherently demotivating. As hard as she tried to persevere in the various endeavors she had pursued, it had always been too easy to walk away when the going got tough.

Now, in contemplating the potential financial risk of not having a prenup, she found herself looking forward to the challenge of possibly having to contend with less. "There was a part of me," she said, "that felt like, well, if giving him half of it means that I have to get a job, well, that could be good." Finally, and most importantly, she trusted Kevin. "I decided if I love this person enough to marry them, and I trust them and think they have integrity and, you know, I've judged their character such that I am willing to take this step and marry them, then why wouldn't I also trust that they're not going to try to gouge me in the end?"

So, they ended up marrying without a prenup. And when they divorced ten years later, she had no regrets. "There was no argument. I just gave him without any fight half of what were the marital assets, which was really only what my assets had increased by during the course of our marriage." Because her state (like many) didn't consider the wealth she had inherited in trust a marital asset, the financial loss was less than she'd imagined it would be.

But, more importantly, she found she was happy to give Kevin, with whom she co-parents and shares custody of their children, the money she did. "It allowed him to stay in the neighborhood we'd been living in. And that was a value to him, and I appreciate that value," Margaret said, "because it allowed my children to stay living in the house that they had grown up in," and have their dad two blocks away. She concludes, "So, it didn't really feel like I was giving this man that I no longer wanted to be married to the money. I was really giving him the money to provide for my children. I wanted him to be comfortable in the house that he was in and be able to take the kids on vacation at spring break—and, you know, have some options that wouldn't make it be so 'have and have not.'"

This was particularly important to Margaret because when her own parents divorced when she was young, she remembers how stark the economic differences were between life at her mother's house (an inheritor herself) and at her father's. As a 10-year-old girl shuttling between the two, she remembers the gulf in circumstances feeling awkward and embarrassing. She thinks this likely influenced her view that "It's sad when couples have children and are so angry at each other that they lose sight of the fact that, you know, this is still your children's family. Like even if you're not married to this person anymore, they're still your children's family."

We can see in Margaret's story that each time she broadened the definition of risk (and reward) to include the human dimension (relationships, the definition of family, or childhood memories that will be forged), the financial risks felt less significant. Wealth advisor Charles Lowenhaupt speaks to this point in his book, *The Wise Inheritor's Guide to Freedom from Wealth* when he writes: "You might ask yourself what your wealth is for and how much you are willing to risk on a marriage. You also might consider whether finances are the most significant risk in a marriage. After all, marriage is in sickness or health and may require caring for a sick or disabled spouse. Marriage may involve having children (or raising a spouse's child) through predictable periods of disruption and unexpected difficulties as well.... There are many risks in marriage, and finances may be the least significant of them."[66]

To put it another way, even though Margaret's marriage ended in divorce, in the grand scheme, the financial protections a prenup would have helped her secure seemed largely irrelevant. In fact, beyond that, the very arrangement a prenup likely would have facilitated (Margaret giving Kevin less money) turned out to be exactly the opposite of what she ended up feeling was the right thing to do.

And when things *do* (work out)

Finally, as long as we're exploring the concepts of risk and reward when things don't work out (maritally speaking), it's important to also consider the scenario when they *do*—when a couple who initially had a prenup later decides, because of the strength of their marriage and the realities of their intertwined lives, to unwind its provisions. Remember our interviewees Holly and Oliver from chapter 3 and how Holly eventually came to see Oliver's wealth (both its benefits and burdens) as her own over the course of their 20-year relationship? The couple shared with us how this evolution impacted their views on their prenup, which they had originally signed even though, as Oliver put it, "the prenup was not something that either of us wanted per se. It was something that we felt was necessary."

Initially, they explained, they didn't focus on the provisions in the prenup. They had married young and were focused on finishing graduate school and starting out in their careers. But as time went on and both chose careers in service professions they could afford to pursue only with the assistance of the family wealth (and eventually Holly left her work to stay at home to raise their children) the prenup started to seem unfair. As Oliver puts it, "We both agreed that it's incredibly unfair to be like, oh, we've made this decision together but we're still going to have this prenup in place that places Holly at a higher risk of not having a comfortable life or not having the life she expected if we somehow get divorced in the next five or 10 years. It felt sort of sexist and wrong, I guess, to exclude her for no other reason than we'd signed a prenup 10 years prior."

Holly adds, "Especially as we had kids, and, you know, it definitely impacted my career, that led me to thinking how do we place a value on the fact that I'm the one that is staying home with this child?" And it made her wonder if she would regret her decision not to invest more in her career if she ever had to support herself in the event of a divorce.

Eventually, their actions started to speak louder than the words in the document. "What happened," Holly explains, "is we just started making decisions together. And eventually, it was pointed out to us that these decisions were undoing our prenup."

"And we said, well, if that's the case, we want to undo it," Oliver chimes in. "You know, I think we both decided that at this point it is just as much Holly's money as my money." Convincing their advisors that they did in fact want to make this change was an "uphill battle" (as Oliver said, "it strikes me that sort of the default is to protect the person with money at all costs," and Holly added, "there were lots of questions to make sure that we had thought through what we're doing"), but they did eventually prevail. Twelve years after they had signed their twenty-five-page prenuptial agreement, they signed a simple, two-page document revoking it in its entirety.

A better process

And in the few cases when a prenup is actually required, there is a better process. Through my research for this project, I discovered attorney Laurie Israel, her book, *The Generous Prenup* (worth a read cover to cover), and her copious articles on the prenup topic with titles like "Ten Things I Hate About Prenuptial Agreements,"[67] and "Why Prenups are Bad for Your Marital Health."[68] After reading her writings (which are full of ideas that recognized the truths we heard in these interviews), I emerged both thrilled to have found an attorney who was vociferously advocating this more nuanced, human view and also disheartened that, despite her prolific thought leadership, this perspective is still not widely shared.

I set up an interview and felt like I had found a kindred spirit. Full of warmth and compassion, Laurie deeply understands the dynamics at play with these young couples, particularly when the prenup is desired or suggested by a wealthy parent or their advisor (a *shadow party*, as we learned Laurie terms them). She now serves primarily as a prenup mediator, dedicated to helping couples who are in a position in which they must have a prenup to find a kinder and gentler way.

"You know, some people think I'm an anti-prenup lawyer," Laurie said when we spoke. "I'm not." What she *is* is anti-the-typical-prenup-process. She elucidates a long list of reasons in her writings, but fundamentally it's because the process begins with the couple having to hire separate counsel, the discussions are largely managed through these intermediaries, and all takes place amid the elephant-in-the-room of the shadow party's desire to protect the family wealth at the expense of the less-moneyed partner's marital rights.

She prefers a mediation process in which the couple first meet together and/or individually with a mediator for a number of sessions to discover and discuss what *they* want and then seek collaborative attorneys motivated primarily to codify these wishes in writing. "Mediators are trained to 'level the playing field,'" she writes. "In the prenup context, this especially means eliciting the views and concerns of the less-moneyed spouse in a safe environment where these concerns can be addressed. An experienced prenuptial agreement mediator will be able to lead the parties towards solutions they (and their attorneys) may not have thought about. In this way, the result can be something other than a "zero-sum" game, and consideration can be provided to the less-moneyed spouse, in all senses of that word."[69]

Fundamentally, she believes in prenups that are creative, generous (for instance, paying off the less-moneyed spouse's student loans), and that create opportunities for shared financial entrepreneurship in the marriage (for instance, that the family home is equally owned and that there are other meaningful financial efforts at the center of the marriage that the couple own jointly and can look forward to building together). Put another way, Laurie prefers a process and an eventual prenup agreement that preserves agency, unity, and equality as much as possible rather than does the opposite.

Our interviewee Hope shared with us how her prenup process with her fiancé, Luke, did just that when it unfolded eight years after she and Luke first met during the college summer they both worked long hours at the Montana ranch owned by her family.

Before Hope could describe their mediated prenup process, she had to first take us back to her memories of her dad telling her when she was a teenager, "When you get married, you will sign a prenup," and the session she attended when she was 19 that her family office organized on prenuptial agreements for all 5th generation members of her family. The message was that, because the 100-member family jointly benefited from a legacy trust worth more than $1 billion, it was required that all members of the family sign prenups when they got married to ensure that the assets in this trust were protected.

Hope understood and decided about a month into her relationship with Luke to throw it out there. She said she thought to herself, "I'm not doing long distance, so this isn't going anywhere. And he already knows who my family is, so I'm just going to tell him. So, I just said, you know, 'Someday when I get married I'll be signing a prenuptial agreement.' I just said it. And I thought if that freaks him out, then that's fine, because this is just a spring fling and this is a good experiment to see what will happen. And he just said, 'okay.'"

Reflecting on it now, Hope thinks that the early timing of this revelation, although admittedly soon in the relationship, was invaluable—that "as we got engaged, we knew the prenup was already on the table. He knew. It wasn't like a big, like, 'Oh gosh, when am I going to tell him this' kind of thing. Or how do I tell him this. He just already knew. So I think it took a lot of, maybe, the sting out of it."

Hope is speaking to agency. While the decision to have a prenup was out of Hope's hands, the fact that she had been prepared with that knowledge allowed her to reveal it to her partner so early in the relationship that it couldn't have been taken personally. And, more importantly, her candor gave Luke agency. He got to decide whether to proceed in the relationship understanding that that was the requirement. And everything that came after, their seven years of pre-married life, was able to evolve in the context of this reality rather than outside of it.

And there was a final element of agency that was injected into the process by the head of Hope's family office. "She is just so good with people and relationships," Hope said. "And she really had a nice take on prenuptial agreements and still does, but I just remember it being so helpful, because she said: 'Everyone who gets married has a prenuptial agreement, and it is set by the state that they're married in. The rules are all spelled out.'"

Hope's family office head was speaking to the point that coauthors Emily Bouchard and Emily Chase Smith elucidate in their book, *Beginners Guide to Purposeful Prenups*: "Many people fail to realize that the moment you get married, you already have a prenup. How your finances will be divvied up has already been established by the lawmakers in your state through the codes that cover family law and estate planning. If you never have a prenup conversation, they'll step in and make all the decisions."[70]

Hope remembers her family office head saying, "And, so, you guys have the opportunity to decide what you want, and to put that into an agreement. And you don't have to abide by the rules of your state or maybe you'd want that, but why not just be conscious and intentional about what you want?" And she meant it—the family office mandated only that the central family trust was protected but, beyond that, their view was couples are allowed and encouraged to devise whatever financial arrangement they want.

So, Hope and Luke felt that the terms of their agreement were largely up to them to decide, but they weren't sure what they wanted or what would be possible. They decided to engage a mediator. As Hope put it, "Before we got sucked into the lawyer world of 'you must do this, and you must think about this, and you must protect this,' we went to the mediator." She continues, "We were able to sort out what we wanted with the counselor individually, and then come together and just have a clear picture. And then, you know, we had a game plan, and we kind of took control, and took that back to our lawyers and said, this is what we want."

She remembers, "The lawyers said have you thought about this, and have you thought about that? And it's like, but we have, and we agree. It was very empowering … because I think it could be extremely intimidating to walk into a big law firm and have to do a prenuptial agreement. You know, lawyers are paid to manage risk and be very critical and think about like, what is in your best interest. And I think we were able to get ahead of that by meeting with the counselor and saying what do we want."

So, not only did Hope and Luke have a sense of agency, but they were also able to feel unified in their process. As she put it, "You know, I really think we were, for the most part, on the same side of the table." Beyond that, there were specific provisions they devised in their discussions with the mediator that were designed to strengthen the sense of financial unity they had in their marriage. "I had more money and I had to say, 'This trust that is in my name will stay in my name,'" she says. "But at the same time, the trust was not so large that Luke and I as a couple couldn't overcome that. Once we were married, we started our own joint trust and since then, really, any income, anything of meaning just goes into that." Now, she says, "Our joint trust is so much larger. After we got married, that's just the trust we started defaulting to. And I think, you know, it's kind of like you're investing in your marriage." The creation of this joint trust, along with other decisions, such as that their family home would be considered jointly owned even though the down payment was made with a distribution from Hope's trust, helped boost the sense of financial equality the two felt in their marriage.

All in all, Hope says, "It was a really good process. I just think being proactive and thoughtful and owning the process was really helpful for us. And just, you know, it set us off on the right track and helped us think through, I guess, reaffirmed our values around how we spend, or save, or plan for the future with regards to money."

The way Hope describes her prenup process is the way much of the wealth advising industry says all couples embarking on a prenup process should feel. But as we have seen, the process and the context matter; in fact, they are fundamental to whether a prenup feels maritally enhancing or destructive. We concluded from our discussions and the wisdom so generously shared by all of our interviewees that in most cases, first marriage prenups are not necessary. If one is truly required, as it was in Hope's case, we recommend that couples embark on a process as Laurie and Hope described to ensure that they emerge on the back end with their sense of mutual agency, unity, and equality as intact as possible.

CHAPTER SIX

Melding of the Minds

We spoke in chapter 4 about how the prenup discussion can dominate the financial conversation leading up to marriage and, as a result, crowd out other money discussions couples really should be having at this stage to ensure they are seeing eye to eye on important issues. This chapter is about *these* discussions.

Setting the stage

When we embarked on the research for this book, we were curious about whether our interviewee couples, who were quite successfully navigating disparate financial backgrounds and discussions about wealth, had used any premarital curriculum or exercises to help them align their thinking.

The question was on our minds because one of the major surprises of the research we conducted for our first book, *Raised Healthy, Wealthy & Wise*, was that very few of the grounded and successful inheritors we interviewed had received anything resembling traditional financial literacy lessons. Instead, they had parents who had modeled grounded financial *values*, and as a result, they absorbed these values and sought out specific financial knowledge (like "How much should I responsibly spend on rent?") when it was relevant and necessary in their lives.

We found a parallel observation in our interviews this time. Although the internet is awash in all manner of premarital financial curriculum (quizzes, questions, and checklists on everything from financial details to money philosophy), very few—fewer than 10%—of the couples we interviewed had used tools like these to structure their conversations or to alert them proactively to areas of disagreement. Instead, most of our interviewees credited their relationship success and financial alignment to two things: 1) shared values and dreams for the arc of their lives, and 2) a commitment to openly communicate and discuss tricky issues, whatever they may be, as soon as they arose.

Shared values

The discovery of shared values was, in a sense, the first test of communication that our couples experienced. And for many, it happened on the first date. Our interviewee Sebastian recalled his first date with his husband of 14 years, Nicholas. He says he and Nicholas each answered three questions honestly for each other. "Do you have strong family support?—which I think is important," Sebastian says. "And second, hypothetically, do you ever see yourself getting married, having some type of union?—and again this is before marriage equality. And lastly, do you see yourself having a family?"

Sebastian continued, "And the reason we asked each other those questions is because we mutually dated other people in the past where one wants to get married, the other one doesn't, one wants to have a child, the other one doesn't. Going on dates is fun, but, you know, time is too short to just waste on someone that is going to fizzle out in a month or two. So, we both answered those questions honestly, and I really think we mutually saw something in each other, and that set the tone, I think, in the relationship, for just being honest and forthcoming."

Our interviewee Beatrice, now in her late 60s, recalled a similar connection on her first date with Duncan more than 40 years ago: "I left that date thinking, I can't believe how connected we are, in the way we were brought up, in our values. We were very on the same level." She added that it became even clearer how important this was once they were married and "were confronted with situations where shared values made a difference," like whether to let the initial buyer for their first house out of the contract when he unexpectedly got a dream job offer in a different state. They easily agreed to because, as Beatrice says, "We just thought it was the right thing to do."

And our interviewee Caleb, whom we met in the previous chapter when he shared his philosophy that it was important to him to let his children decide for themselves whether to have a prenup, talked with us about how important his sharing values with his wife has been over their almost 30-year marriage. In the beginning, he says, when they met in law school, their shared values were the spark: "We both had hopes and dreams for the future that matched and, you know, it continued from there. We meshed in terms of what our values were." But more importantly, these aligned goals and values have kept their marriage strong over the years: "Everyone continues to change as they're married, but if you have similar values or have a common goal, I think it keeps you together."

We found in our interviewees' stories that their beginning conversations about values and dreams were crucial not only because they established a connection, but also importantly because they set a precedent for how conversations about hopes and dreams would happen in the future. Jennifer Petriglieri, an associate professor at INSEAD and author of the book *Couples That Work*, writes: "Couples that work don't wait, I found, to discuss openly and deliberately what they want their life together, their couple, to be like. They do it early and often.

Otherwise, a couple's contract is set implicitly, and they end up with a sense that life keeps throwing surprises at them, their love strains to adjust, and they are not sure why." She describes the original agreements she and her husband jotted down on a beach in Sicily four weeks into their relationship. There were detailed commitments (i.e. "Our relationship would come before everything. We committed to pushing each other to live up to our potential, etc.") but more important than the details, she says, was the practice: "I realize now that what we wrote then did not matter much. What mattered was that we set the habit, early on, to talk about who we were, and what we hoped our life would be."[71]

Committing to communicate

Petriglieri speaks to the importance of setting the habit of open communication early and practicing it often. Our interviewees were proponents too. Along with shared values, our couples agreed that the key to their success—and their ability to navigate the various issues that have come up throughout their relationship around wealth—has been honest and frequent communication. Nicholas, Sebastian's husband, puts it this way, "I mean, communicating is everything, right? What you write. What you say. And what you don't say. You know, your nonverbal communication. So, embedded in there is honesty and trust, and you need all of that together to make the relationship work. When there's a breakdown, you know, that's when you have to address it, and then fix it, and be there for the person, and then it gets you back up and running."

In addition to committing to communicate openly and frequently (and not sweeping issues under the rug), we heard from our interviewees that they also felt it was important to be alert to the issues that might lie beneath the issues being discussed. Oliver, who shared with us in chapter 5 how he and his wife, Holly, eventually decided to revoke their prenup, said, "I think it's important to communicate about what our intentions are, as opposed to, you know, just sort of getting stuck in the minutia of it all. It could be an argument about schools or a budget, but it's not really about that. It's about different styles and not understanding where the person is coming from." He continues, "I feel like a large part of what has helped us is open communication. And when we have had a hard time with communication, we've sought help. We were able, through therapy and financial advisors and our own conversations, to sort of get to the other side of that."

Oliver and Holly were fortunate that they were able to find help when they needed it. The challenge for some couples can be where to go to seek this help. While there is a plethora of books and other advice counseling couples on how to communicate more effectively about financial differences, we've found that by and large the literature does not address in depth the issues we heard our interviewee couples wrestling with—the issues that tend to surface when at least one member of the couple will inherit wealth. Our goal with the remainder of this chapter is to try to close that gap.

The Way Through

We'll share in the rest of this chapter the topics our interviewee couples felt were important to address and how they navigated those discussions in a way that strengthened their partnership.

Navigating disparate financial backgrounds

We spoke in chapter 3 about how it's unnecessary and limiting for inheritors to seek out only significant others who come from similar wealth backgrounds. And indeed, our interviewee partners' own financial upbringings straddled the socioeconomic spectrum. Yet, it is true that forging a successful partnership with someone from a different financial background requires knowing how to effectively communicate about and bridge these differences.

We were inspired in our interviews by the story both Nicholas and Sebastian independently told us of how they were able to do just that in the first few years of their relationship. As Nicholas says, "When we first started dating, you know, we definitely came from two different financial backgrounds." (Nicholas' parents had become unexpectedly wealthy in the first dot-com boom and Sebastian's family had at times struggled financially.) Nicholas continues, "The beginning of any relationship is very exciting, but as you start to kind of peel the layers apart, it was very clear to both of us that financially, we were on two completely polar opposite spectrums. At the time, my spouse did not have a lot of financial knowledge or financial resources, whereas I felt like I had a lot of that."

At first, Nicholas recalled, he found this disparity challenging to navigate. "How do you kind of reconcile that in the relationship early on to help the relationship grow? You're never really taught that in school. Your parents never really teach you that," he said. "So, I kind of felt that early on it was an uncomfortable conversation. It was very hard to talk about it because I just didn't know—I didn't have the right words or the right experience. It kind of caught me off guard." Nicholas wanted to help share his knowledge with Sebastian to help Sebastian establish a stronger financial footing, but "How do you start to teach someone about finances that you learned when you were a kid, without sounding like you know everything?"

For his part, Sebastian was willing to learn. He recalls now, "I'll be honest, I had no knowledge whatsoever, of like, how to balance a checkbook. I'll be completely honest, I was horrible. Anything like, you know, being creative, artistic, I'm all over that. But, with finances, I just had no clue. And I think it was partially because of my upbringing. My parents basically lived paycheck to paycheck."

One of the first topics the couple decided to tackle was Sebastian's debt. Nicholas recalls, "I remember one of the things that we started talking about once we moved in together was kind of like, do you have any debt? That was a big transition kind of question, and he was like, yeah, I have debt. You know, he had recently switched jobs, and he didn't have a huge safety net of money when that happened. And so it was definitely a struggle where he lived off credit cards for a while. And I said, you know, it probably would be great if, you know, we just combine our money and, you know, we can work with paying off that debt. And then, you know, we'll be in a better situation, and he was very open to it."

Next, they got to work on Sebastian's credit score. As Sebastian remembers, "When you're with your partner, you should be honest, and I told Nicholas, my credit is not that great. And, sure enough, he started to help me. He's like, 'We're going to work on your credit,' and in two or three years we turned that credit around, and now my credit is, like, in the 800s/900s. And he taught me how to save, how to budget, and I think just being transparent helped." More lessons followed, including investing and opening a retirement account for Sebastian, which has now grown to a sizeable amount.

What struck us as most remarkable about this story, beyond Nicholas's textbook approach to sharing financial literacy lessons, was both his and Sebastian's frequent use of the word "we" throughout. Nicholas saw Sebastian's debt, low credit score, and lack of retirement savings as equally his challenge to address. As Nicholas put it, "I saw ourselves as a unit. We're a family. Our finances are together. I was like, you know, we're both working so let's get our finances in order. And I'm glad we did because that was something that really helped us from day one."

Through his actions and approach, Nicholas was living out the sense of unity that we spoke about in chapter 4. In turn, his commitment to unity ensured that Sebastian didn't feel talked down to, as Nicholas had originally feared might be the case. In addition, the couple's joint commitment to honest communication allowed Sebastian to feel comfortable revealing his financial challenges. As he puts it now, "My idea of what a union should be is that you have to be forthcoming in a relationship in every angle. And I didn't believe in keeping secrets from Nicholas because I didn't feel like he was keeping any secrets from me. And, I think in a relationship, you evolve together as a union. You have to kind of pick each other up at your lowest moments and cheer each other on as much as you can, because we all have our good days and bad days."

Now, almost two decades into their partnership, these early days of financial revelations have faded into distant memories as Nicholas's and Sebastian's lives have evolved, their net worth has grown, and their day-to-day is absorbed in the happy chaos of managing their careers and raising their 10-year-old son. But we hope other couples struggling to navigate disparate financial backgrounds might be inspired and buoyed by their story and their generosity in sharing it with us.

Deciding whether, how much, and in what way to use inherited family wealth

The psychological journey from viewing an inheritance as outside oneself to possessing sufficient agency, authority, and capacity to view it as truly your own is a journey that for some inheritors can take a lifetime. Regardless of where an inheritor sits on that journey, it's important that their partner sit beside them and that the couple sees eye to eye on whether to tap into inherited family wealth. In our first book, *Raised Healthy, Wealthy & Wise*, we shared the story of William who viewed "the demise of his first marriage as a failure inextricably linked to this question of *whose money is it anyway* [his or his parents']?" William explained, "My ex-wife saw all this money out there that I never really felt was mine. She felt she had to play this role, going to charity events and being on boards—and I had to pay for it all with money I didn't feel was my own."[72]

Thinking together about how much to tap inherited wealth

As we talked about in Chapter 3, partners can help each other along this journey—they can cowrite their story of wealth and wrestle together with the philosophical and emotional quandaries of whether, how much, and in what way to use the family wealth. Our interviewees Nathan and Louisa shared with us how this comes up for them. As Louisa puts it, "If you're used to being very financially responsible, you know, what does financial responsibility look like when you have access to these funds? Is it *not* spending it and letting it be there and using your life to sustain it? Or is it spending it to, you know—I don't know? It's hard to know." She continues, "I think we've for the most part done a good job sussing out what makes sense."

But it's an issue that they continue to discuss and puzzle over. Nathan agrees and adds, "You know, how do you look at the money you have from your family? What is it for? It's like, what's the purpose here? Are we supposed to just be hoarding it away in like, a safe full of gold bars someplace? Or the flip side?" Nathan and Louisa haven't yet resolved these questions, but they are working them out *together* and as a result, ensuring they are aligned along the way.

Beyond coming to agreement on how the two of you view the issue, it's also important to consider what others might think and be aligned on how much you care about their reactions. Our interviewee Abby, the eighth grade teacher we met in chapter 1, shared with us the discussions she and her partner, Ben, recently had when they were contemplating moving from their functional 3rd floor walkup to a newly built, three-story, single family home in a coveted part of town with a shaded backyard in which their daughter could play. They realized a move like this would broadcast the realities of their financial situation to a wider group of friends and acquaintances and discussed, as Abby recalled, "How do we feel about that? And sort of getting on the same page with, you know, [the fact that] a number of our friends would be like, 'Whoa, you guys really have more money than I thought.'"

The couple spent several long conversations talking about, as Abby put it, "would people in our lives think of us differently if they knew that we weren't working for everything we have? But, you know, our conclusion was like, well, no, because we are who we are." She continued, "I feel at this point in my life more secure in my identity, I guess, as a person. I've established who I am, and what's important to me, and how I relate to other people, and so these other material signifiers feel less impactful."

Investing in your marriage

For those of you who might now be having similar discussions about whether to tap into inherited wealth and for what purpose, we also wanted to share what we learned from our interviewees about which uses of inherited wealth they found to be fulfilling and beneficial for their partnership. In chapter 5, we heard from attorney and prenup mediator Laurie Israel that the best prenups are creative, generous, and facilitate opportunities for shared financial entrepreneurship, or as our interviewee Hope put it, "investing in" the marriage. It turns out we saw in our interviewees' stories that the same holds true for uses of family wealth. When couples tap into one partner's inherited family wealth to strengthen the sense of agency, unity, equality, and joy they experience in their partnership, it tends to be relationship-enhancing, rather than the opposite.

Our interviewee Cynthia told us how she found a way to do this even though her influence over the disposition of her inheritance is limited. Cynthia learned when she was in college nearly five decades ago that she was the beneficiary of a multimillion-dollar trust. Although the trust's provisions don't allow her to provide for her husband at her death, she has found other creative ways to enhance the financial equality in their marriage. As she explains, she wanted to "try to start to equalize the property ownership."

She began with their home. "I owned a house, the house where we lived. And we renegotiated the mortgage and put the deed in both of our names." Then she moved on to shore up the financial security her husband would have outside of her inherited wealth. "Because of the way the trust was written," she explains, "I was withdrawing quarterly amounts. I did not have to account for what I was spending money on. So, out of the quarterly amounts, we took some of that and invested it into his being able to self-finance his retirement, because he was not going to be provided for if I died first. And he didn't want to be in the position of asking our kids to provide for him." While Cynthia hasn't equalized the property ownership entirely, she says that these and other efforts she's made have been "symbolically positive" in their marriage.

We heard a host of examples like Cynthia's in our conversations with our interviewees—everything from a couple accessing an inheritance for a down payment on a home they would jointly own and pay for going forward, to an inheritor using part of an inheritance to provide a means of financial security for their partner who (like Cynthia's) was otherwise cut out of family wealth, to couples' using inherited wealth to help them grow their family (by paying for fertility treatments or surrogacy). Each of these instances increased the sense of unity and equality between the couple by converting assets that had belonged to one partner into a jointly shared endeavor that was meaningful for them both.

Deciding how to handle financial requests from family and friends

In chapter 3 we touched on the fact that one of the things that can come as a surprise to the non-inheritor partner is that, at some point along the way, their friends and family begin to view them as wealthy—and more specifically, as being capable of providing financial support if needed. The issue of whether, to what extent, and in what way to help a friend or family member in need of financial support is one of the most emotionally vexing that we see in our work. It can also be a source of conflict between partners if they don't strategize together about how to handle these requests, from the subtle to the overt, when they occur.

Our interviewees Campbell and Mia, who met in college and were inspired by Campbell's parents' equal marriage to forego a prenup, discussed with us how this issue has come up for them. In the past few years, they've begun to give money to both Mia's mother and brother. The decision to help Mia's mother was easy—she is active in their lives, beloved by their two-year-old daughter, and extremely appreciative of their annual gift, which eases the financial stress she experienced after the divorce from Mia's dad. But the gifts to Mia's brother are another story—he rarely visits and the gifts seem to strain their relationship; still, he continues to ask for support and it's clear he needs the financial help.

Mia wrestles with what to do. "I think that's actually the most stressful part of our finances," she says. "How to deal with my brother, because it's hard to not attach strings when giving someone money, and then be disappointed with actions or relationships and how that plays out with how you feel about giving them money." She continued, "It's a very hard and nuanced thing, and I struggle with what is the right thing to do, my emotions around that, and the expectations that I put on people when giving them money. It's been easy with my mom because we're very close and she's a very active part of our family and just a generally amazing person and would be there regardless, but with my brother it's been much more challenging."

For his part, Campbell empathizes with and shares Mia's frustration. Yet, he has also tried to be supportive of whatever decision Mia makes. As he puts it, "As I've told Mia all along, it's her money as well. So, it's like, however much you want to give your family, you know, remove me and my opinions from it."

Stories like Mia's and Campbell's were woven throughout our interviews. There are rarely easy answers in these situations—only difficult trade-offs to balance. On the one hand, compassion and a sense of equity can tug at the heart and weigh on the conscience (as Mia put it, "I feel very lucky and like I can share my luck with my family members who aren't so lucky"). On the other hand, a relationship involving financial dependence between two adults is typically emotionally fraught—resentment is far more common than gratitude, the dependency often becomes perpetual, and ultimately, neither party (giver nor receiver) is left satisfied.

What is important amid this stew of complex emotions and wrenching decisions, though, is that the couple remain on the same page, work together to weigh the options, and share jointly in the emotional costs of whatever decisions are made. It can sometimes feel embarrassing or awkward for the partner who is on the receiving end of these requests to bring them up—especially if they occur frequently; yet open communication is critical and allows the couple to not only remain a unified team but also help each other navigate this complex emotional terrain. Puzzling out the ethical quandary of whether and when to help and discovering where the inner boundary lies between extending a kindness and feeling taken advantage of is nuanced emotional work. It is far easier to do this in partnership with the person who not only knows you best, but also understands, as you do, the complexity that comes along with wealth.

Beyond the emotional support, open communication also allows couples to work out strategies and establish rules and boundaries that help make it easier to field or redirect incoming requests. Among the strategies we heard working well for our interviewees were: 1) agreeing to never respond to a request immediately without discussing it first as a couple and then having a joint response (sometimes this step alone deflected a request); 2) paying for bills (like utilities or rent) directly rather than sending cash; 3) being honest with family members about whether you are willing to cover the bill for dinners or experiences out or would prefer to choose a venue that all can afford and share in the cost equally; 4) being realistic about the likelihood that any money loaned will be returned (and treating it perhaps as a one-time gift instead); and 5) agreeing on a script that you can share with family that helps set expectations about your ability and willingness to help. Ultimately, we saw in our interviewees' stories a recognition that it's important to decide as a couple what you feel comfortable with and what you think is right, and then use this thinking to guide your behavior—in other words, to focus more on what you can control (aligning your actions with your conscience) than what you can't (whether the recipient's reaction is what you would hope for or expect).

Aligning spending philosophies

Our interviewee couples also found that it's important to align spending philosophies even when there is potentially the cushion of an inheritance in the mix. In fact, particularly if the inheritor member of the couple might have established their spending habits when there was additional family financial support available, the couple might find that a recalibration is necessary now that they are on their own and trying jointly to build their financial life.

Amelia, who shared with us in chapter 4 how she and her

husband, Liam, ultimately told her parents they would not be signing a prenup, talked with us about the spending discussions she and Liam had in the early days of their marriage. Amelia had established her spending habits in grad school, when her parents had deposited a monthly stipend into her account to cover her living expenses. "I just felt like, oh, this is my allowance to spend in my bank account," she said. "I never really tried to save that money or anything. I was like, this is my money to spend, right?" "So," she continued, when they first got married and she was working at her infectious disease post-doctoral position and Liam was starting out at a biotech venture fund out of business school, "I continued to do that. Like, oh, I'm walking by the store. I'm going to buy this dress because it's cute. No, I don't really need it for anything."

This continued for a while until one day Liam said, "You know, if you buy a $100 dress every week, that's a lot of money." She remembers he went on to share his view, which was that "We have a chance to start building wealth; this is our money that we're working really hard to make and we want to kind of think about our financial goals, and our goals are to buy a house." He was encouraging her to think about "how much you're spending and whether you need to spend this money" given the alternative, that "if we invest it, it will grow a lot." Amelia recalls now, "Quite frankly, I just hadn't really thought about money that way before. I was just sort of used to buying what I wanted to buy, spending what I wanted to spend, and not really thinking about it because I knew it was within my budget, I guess, of what I have." Amelia thought about spending differently after the conversation, she says. She realized "that this isn't just my money. This is our money. And if I'm spending it now, I'm basically taking money out of our pool of savings."

We found that a number of our interviewee couples had similar discussions around calibrating spending and that it helped to devise simple rules to ensure coordination and alignment. In fact, doing so was part of how Nicholas and Sebastian worked together to improve Sebastian's credit score. They reasoned it was important for each of them to keep their own credit cards so that Sebastian would be able to improve his score, but they needed a way to coordinate spending.

As Nicholas remembers, "We made a deal early on in the relationship—like you can charge whatever you want to your credit card, you know, it's our shared resources. It's our money. But if you're making a big purchase, and I think at the time early on in our relationship I think we had set it at around $200 or $300, like, let's just talk about it." He continues, "I think we just kind of came up with it one day when we were talking. And it, it really, really helped a lot in the relationship. And I don't think we even had a lot of arguments regarding credit card bills and what we were spending, because we knew we kind of had that flexibility for the lower things we could pay for, but once we got to a certain level or certain threshold, it was considered a couple's purchase."

Empathizing with each other's spending hang-ups

We heard from our interviewee couples that sometimes, more complicated than discussions around the *amount* to spend are conversations about *which* purchases are worth spending on and why. The definition of what is valuable—i.e., worth spending money on—is essentially an emotional decision reflective of how much worth a person places on a whole host of underlying intangibles—everything from the discipline of frugality to the power of independence to the convenience of time saved to the freedom of choice. We learned from our interviewee couples that it's important in spending discussions to peel back the onion to get to these underlying motivations, as they are often a source of conflict if left unnamed. This can be particularly important when the presence of an inheritance can shift the optics and make expressions of frugality seem fueled less by economic necessity (requiring no further discussion) than by personal preference (by nature, subjective, and therefore up for debate).

Our interviewees Nathan and Louisa, whom we met in chapter 4 when they described their uphill battle to craft a generous prenup, shared with us how they learned to empathize with and offset each other's spending idiosyncrasies. As Louisa puts it, "Every person has sensitivities about money. And the most important thing you can do is figure out where your sensitive zones are and where your partner's are, so that then you can support them through it." She continues that they've learned it's important to "figure out what the triggers are for each person—what are your 'triggery' things that you get squirrely or weird about spending money on? What are the attributes of those types of purchases? And are you and your partner squirrely about the same things? Or are you squirrely about different things?"

For Nathan and Louisa, it was different things. Although he grew up attending family retreats to discuss the management of his family's multigenerational wealth, he "gets worried about the little stuff, because there is very much a culture in the family about, you know, not paying more than you should for a thing." And she, who prides herself on the moxie and financial resourcefulness that allowed her to succeed as a chef, has no trouble with small purchases but gets sticker shock when she has to make a purchase with multiple zeroes involved.

She told us of the paralysis that had descended just the night before our interview when she was ordering a new washer, dryer, and fridge on sale. "It's like $5,000 worth of appliances, which we can totally afford. But for me, I've been financially independent for a long time. You know, you've got to make sure you can pay that bill. I am very proud of the fact that I have never gone into debt. Like, all the stuff, the emotional shit of putting $5,000 down, and actually putting the credit card number in. I know we can afford it, but it's emotionally more expensive for me to actually type the credit card number in than it is for him."

She says that Nathan could sense her anxiety and knows her well enough that he came over and said, "So, I've got my laptop and I'm going to do it right now."

"And ten minutes later, we'd bought the appliances. He knows me well enough that I don't have to say all of this, because we've been doing this for seven years now," she says.

Meanwhile, when he starts to comparison shop on strawberries, she tries to help him keep things in perspective. It wasn't easy for them to get to this mutually beneficial equilibrium. Louisa says, "There was a ton of conflict that led to this level of understanding, because he would be absolutely insane about something that I'm like, 'Come on, man, you're loaded. How are you giving me a hard time about this $150?' And then I'd be going nutso about something, and he'd be like, 'It's not like we don't have the money, what is the problem?'"

She continues, "We had to go through the ringer on that, but of course, the benefit of hindsight, I would say, is that it's such a great exercise to have gone through. If you can figure out what the triggers are for each partner, and then, once you know that, be on the lookout for those landmines in your relationship, then it is easier because the other person knows how to talk you through it or can help step up to the plate on some of those. And we both have become way, way more comfortable about the things that used to make us uncomfortable. Now that we're in tune, we have a very nice, financially complementary approach to things, because we can work each other through the other person's hard stuff and sort of take that baton back for the things that will be more difficult for the other person."

Authors, marriage experts, and husband and wife team John Gottman and Julie Schwartz Gottman write, "The truth is we're all savers and spenders at different times."[73] The trick in a relationship is to be able to understand and empathize with when and why your partner chooses to practice each behavior, especially if their rationale differs from your own. Oftentimes, this thinking relates to messages each partner heard growing up in their origin family, as it did for Nathan.

We all have money messages we absorb growing up that we carry around in our heads and unwittingly repeat or rebel against. It's worth going through the exercise that Nathan and Louisa did of trying to reflect on and articulate the messages they were living out unconsciously. With reflection, you have choice—you can think about which messages you value, which others you might want to discard, and most importantly, how you and your partner can either align your messages or work together to balance each other's out. At the end of this chapter, we've recommended resources to help you in this exercise.

Navigating and learning from each other's wealth cultures

Our interviewee Yasmin shared with us what it has been like for her and her fiancé, Miles, to learn from each other's distinct wealth cultures. Yasmin grew up in a prominent Malaysian family, spending time on the weekends with her cousins rotating among the family's several compounds, and watching her grandmother, "the queen of the family," make all the "big and final" family wealth decisions as is customary in their matrilineal culture. Miles, on the other hand, grew up in a three-bedroom farmhouse in the small town in Vermont that his mother (an inheritor herself) and father relocated to in their late 20s to live a simpler life.

Yasmin came to the United States for college but spent the first few years dating mostly men from back home. As she recalls, "Something that was really important when I was looking for someone in the past, one of the criteria that I looked for, was someone who understood me financially and understood where our families came from—you know, where his mom knew my mom and our families ran in similar circles and all that. I thought that was what I wanted." But, as she moved to New York for work and invested several years in building her career, she began to realize that "I didn't have the same notions of what 'home' meant as my former partners did. I think that I was a little too westernized for them, or I wanted to stay in America a little longer."

She decided to broaden her search and filled out an online dating profile. In several months, she matched with Miles. Now engaged, they've been together for four years and spent much of the pandemic living with his parents in Vermont. She marvels sometimes at this turn of events. "But," she says, "I think I've gained an added perspective being with someone who didn't come from a similar background." She goes on to explain all she's learned: "He's actually taught me a lot about what it means to gain wealth in this country that is so different from how to gain wealth in my culture. He's taught me a lot about the market and a lot about investing in America. He taught me how to build credit, which I had no credit, because I had zero debt. We don't believe in credit cards back home. We pay for everything in cash. So, it was such a different conversation that I was having every day about money, and about how to build your wealth."

As their relationship deepened, she discovered that it wasn't just the financial details that were different—it was also the messages she and Miles had each heard growing up. "My mom's money message is 'God will always provide.' I grew up always thinking there's a safety net under me, that I don't have to worry." Miles, though, was encouraged by his family to earn his own way and be entrepreneurial. As a result, she says, "he pushes me to think about things differently, because I am now living alone, and I'm independent, and I want to be more independent. He's like, 'You've got to start thinking about your future.' And I'm, like, 'Yeah, you're right.'"

But as much as she's learned, Yasmin also feels that she's taught Miles. She was schooled by her family to always be on the lookout for property to buy, to "mark your territory," "put a stake in the ground," and understand the nuances of real estate market fluctuations. As she puts it, "His family, they talk about stocks. Our family talks about real estate. So, as much as I'm learning from him about stocks and investing and bitcoin, I'm also teaching him about buying land and looking at property values and what the real estate market is like. So, that's been very interesting to do with him and fun. It's been a really good way to spend time together, but also to learn about how to make each other better in a sense and learn about each other's cultures."

What we heard in Yasmin's story is that, more important than the differences between her and Miles's inherited money messages and expertise are the curiosity and openness they've each brought to learning from these differences. That and the running conversation they've had since they met that has allowed them to continue to uncover, explore, and ponder them. "I'm just in awe of all the things that are so different about the way that we see so many things," she says. "So every choice that we make, every decision that we make that is different from what the other person is used to, it turns into a talk. We point them out. It turns into a 'Why would you do that?' You know, 'Why is this so different from my life? Can you tell me more about it?' We don't like, brush them under the rug or ignore them or think that they're silly. We talk about them."

Calibrating the role of work against the backdrop of inherited wealth

A final topic we heard our interviewees describe as important to be aligned on was the role of work in their lives. This is a deep and complex topic, spanning a broad landscape from the psychological (each partner's sense of contribution, meaning, and purpose) to the logistical (geographies, work schedules, allocation of household duties, and implications for childcare). While this is a topic all couples designing a life together must navigate, the presence of an inheritance introduces dynamics that can be destructive if not forthrightly recognized and addressed.

Our interviewees Scarlett and her husband, Elliot, described how these dynamics have come up for them. The couple met at music camp when they were 12, stayed friends through college, and then married a year after they reconnected at a friend's wedding 12 years later. Over the course of their six-year marriage, Scarlett has worked as a music director for a theater company (a job she loves *and* is able to afford only by tapping into her inheritance), and Elliot's earnings have fluctuated from sizeable (when he worked for a tech company) to unpredictable (now that he runs his own start-up).

An issue they explained they've tried to pay attention to over the last several years is Elliot's sense of his economic contribution to their marriage and his emotions around that, especially during the unpredictable earnings periods when his monthly contributions to their joint checking account dipped. As Scarlett says to Elliot during our interview, "We had one conversation where you admitted to me, the phrase you used was you have like, a little bit of a 'caveman feeling' about being able to provide for your woman." She continues, speaking to us, "He put it in such great language—he was like, 'I know this is basic, and I know this is stupid or not stupid, but it's basic.'" Elliot adds, "I think Scarlett knows that work and accomplishment and self-sufficiency are important to me. And I think, from my end certainly, I never want Scarlett to feel like, you know, taken advantage of or that I'm not doing my part. And yeah, I do think the gender aspect plays into it also."

Naming the "gender stuff"

The couple share with us how they've dealt with this issue. Elliot says, "I think it's that constant checking in and just being sensitive to it, while, you know, just trusting intentions and motives all around and having that self-security to know that, you know, the other person respects and loves you." Scarlett jumps back in and adds, "I would say that *naming* the gender stuff is helpful too." Elliot agrees. "I think both of us are trying to be enlightened and sensitive to things and aware of it," he says. "But that doesn't mean that it never has any type of pull on you."

It turns out that these gender-role dynamics that Scarlett and Elliot have found their way through pretty adroitly are a known phenomenon in the wealth advising arena. In 2001, coauthors Jay Hughes, Jacqueline Merrill, and Joanie Bronfman published a seminal paper on the topic titled, "Reflections on Fiscal Unequals," the term they coined to refer to "the financial situation in which the woman in a relationship with a man has more money than the man." [74] Their goal was to articulate the nuanced ways in which deeply rooted historical gender norms, often internalized by the couple, can pose challenges in these relationships unless honestly recognized and candidly and compassionately addressed. The paper talks openly about male self-esteem and how it can be difficult for a male who has internalized the idea of being a provider (what Elliot referred to as his "caveman feeling") to square that with the strong likelihood that their economic contribution may be eclipsed (sometimes significantly) by their wife's inherited wealth. These are issues that can run deep—as author Jay Hughes (they each wrote 1/3 of the paper individually) writes, "In nearly every case I have studied or participated in, the couple in the relationship is struggling to assure that the man has true 'face,' integrity, dignity, and respect for himself."[75]

Of course, both this article and the research that has followed and expanded on it[76] enthusiastically welcome changing gender norms and the ways in which these changes are allowing the rules to be rewritten. Yet amid this enthusiasm is also the recognition that rewriting these rules and redefining roles is, in reality, an ongoing conversation a couple must have, and that it is one that typically goes better if the couple can be honest and open with each other, as Scarlett and Elliot have been, about how these internalized dynamics may be weighing on them.

The research also recommends strategies for navigating this landscape. As author Joanie Bronfman writes in the original "Fiscal Unequals" paper: "Couples need to respect what each other does. I don't believe men need to match the financial capital of their female partners, whether it be through earning or investment, but they do need to have a commitment to a calling or profession. This kind of commitment provides individuals with an identity and a frame of reference that is not based on the relationship or the money." She continues that both "Women and men function best around money in their relationships with each other if they are both self-confident and competent.... A healthy self-esteem comes from being aware of one's skills and competencies, undertaking self-development and achieving autonomy."[77]

Put another way, each partner (however they define their gender) needs to cultivate the four success factors that we discussed in chapter 1. They need to forge a sense of self that is strong enough to withstand the gravitational pull of the black hole of the family wealth and be able to point to something in their life that feels truly their own, makes them feel as if their contribution is unique and valuable, and imbues their life with meaning. Couples who ground their conversations in these issues—meaning, contribution, and purpose—rather than dollars and cents, find that they are able to transcend the constraints of internalized scripts and align around the issues that truly matter. Or as the third author of the "Fiscal Unequals" article, Jacqueline Merrill, puts it when sharing what has worked in her own "fiscally unequal" marriage, "The focus on our callings and priorities has removed fiscal inequality, and the inherent power issues therein, from the central arenas of our lives."[78]

Charting a joint path, and figuring out the role inherited wealth will play on the journey

Couples who regularly discuss meaning, purpose, and contribution are a step ahead in jointly charting the course of their life. Earlier in this chapter, we heard from author and professor Jennifer Petriglieri on how important it is for couples to talk openly and frequently about the life they would like to design. She expands on this point with the following observation: "Unlike what many people think, couples don't fail because they don't support each other. They fail because they are not sure what it is that they are supporting, and why. What a good life means for them, what they need and want, and therefore what they can let go of, and what they must keep pursuing, even at a cost."[79]

When there is an inheritance involved, part of this ongoing conversation about what a good life means is about what role the inheritance might play, if any, in manifesting this life. What dreams might an inheritance allow to come to fruition? Or, as Jacqueline Merrill writes, "What exactly are financial resources meant for in my life, and in our life as a couple?"[80]

Entertaining these questions, puzzling through answering them, and figuring out the role an inheritance might play are not easy tasks. As our interviewee Sebastian told us, "It's confusing at times. Confusing because, you have the trust, but you don't want to use it as a crutch either, and just trying to find a balance." He continues, "You can take more risks. You know, let me venture off and try this new career or this new business platform. You're given more chances. But again, you don't want to take too many chances. It's trying to find the right medium."

As with the other topics we've covered in this chapter, though, the very fact that this is a challenging landscape means that it's not only beneficial but necessary for partners to discuss so their thinking is aligned. The process of shaping a joint life can be as simple as cowriting a list of five-year goals and as comprehensive and elucidating as the "discovery" process Jacqueline Merrill describes in the "Fiscal Unequals" article[81] in which the couple ponders deep questions, articulates their own mission statements, and then crafts a joint statement for the two of them together. Regardless of how you get the conversation going, it's important to keep it alive and continue to jointly dream together and write the story of how you want your lives to unfold.

Making the time to talk

We've talked a lot in this chapter about communication and about the deep topics worth not only covering once but also revisiting as life, you, and your partner evolve. So, how do you make time for these conversations? And how do you ensure that you continue to prioritize them as life, work, family responsibilities, and a whole host of other worthy distractions get in the way?

For some of our interviewee couples, the daily commitment to not sweep issues under the rug was enough to keep things on track. But we also want to share with you here the novel ideas we heard for how couples intentionally made time for these conversations, in case these strategies might be helpful to you.

Our interviewee Deborah, who bonded with her husband Alan more than 40 years ago when they met at a party and realized within minutes that they were both inheritors and uncomfortable in the role, was eager to share with us something that she felt has made a difference in their marriage. A couple years after their wedding, the financial advisor they were working with at the time "told Alan and I to go away together for a weekend. We made up our own agenda, and all we talked about was money and what money means to us and how money is affecting our lives." Deborah continues, "And we were serious. We went and we stayed in this nice hotel, and we didn't have to go anywhere because all the meals were there, and we talked about money all weekend. I don't remember what we even talked about, but I remember for years afterward that it was really helpful. It really helped."

Deborah and Alan were able to kickstart a deeper understanding of wealth and its impact in their lives by intentionally making the time to talk. If you feel that you and your partner might benefit from a similar reflection and greater alignment on the issues we've discussed in this chapter, this idea of a dedicated weekend away might be worth a try. You can come up with the agenda on your own, as Deborah and Alan did, or start with the section headings of this chapter as a guide.

And what if you've already had these initial deep conversations and are now looking primarily for a means to remain aligned as life evolves? We loved the idea that our interviewees Scarlett and Elliot shared. "We do a thing called the State of the Union every year," Scarlett says, "where we go out to dinner at a restaurant that is not in our neighborhood, like not a regular restaurant, and the idea is that we talk about the things that have come up throughout the year." Elliot chimes in, "It's forced time to reflect," and Scarlett adds, "I look forward to it because it feels like maintenance that is important and helpful."

Whatever the method, the point is that the conversations happen. And that they evolve as you do. In the end, what we took away from our interviewees' stories is that, whether they were talking about wealth or spending, gifts or goals, there was a consistent through-line, which was the more fundamental question of who each wanted to be, who they wanted to be as a couple, and how their answers to these questions could evolve and change while still allowing them to see eye-to-eye, support each other, and ultimately continue to author their joint story.

We liked how our interviewees Oliver and Holly summed up this issue. "We are very open and honest with each other and communicate," Oliver says, "and I think that that has allowed us to sort of move through these different periods of our life, whether it's wealth or family or children or other things that are vexing for us." Holly adds, "Also, let each other change over time, because, you know, we're definitely different versions of ourselves now than when we got together. And, you know, we help each other process when we're struggling with what we want to do with life or what's happening. So, we're kind of partnering on that journey of figuring things out and changing along the way."

> *Resources for reflecting on money messages:*
>
> ❖ 21/64—Go to https://2164.net/product/money-messages/
>
> ❖ My Family History of Money Exercise—pages 129–130 of *Eight Dates: Essential Conversations for a Lifetime of Love* by John Gottman, Julie Schwartz Gottman, Doug Abrams, and Rachel Carlton Abrams

Section Three

Beyond Us

Meet Our Interviewees

Below are the new interviewees who appear in Section Three, in order of appearance:

Chapter Seven:

Valerie and Donald: Now in their mid-60s, Valerie and Donald met and married in their early 20s, the week after they graduated college. They still remember the premarital program they attended and the united vision of their marriage they crafted during their conversations that weekend. Now, 40 years, four children, three countries, and two founded companies later, they are enjoying a new chapter in their lives, redefining their role from engaged parents to welcoming in-laws and loving grandparents.

Jonah and Isabelle: Now in their late 30s, Jonah and Isabelle met in business school 10 years ago and now have busy careers in the tech sector and two daughters under four. Jonah remembers growing up aware of his father's increasing corporate success but also his parents' tempering messages that they would rather spend their money on his and his siblings' education and family vacations than material things. Isabelle's family struggled financially when she was a child, leaving her with difficult memories of boom-and-bust years and a deep appreciation that Jonah didn't care about her lack of financial resources when they met.

Chapter Eight:

CARTER: The eldest son of Haitian immigrants, Carter spent his childhood in France before coming to the United States in his teens. He met his wife in medical school and the two have both built successful medical careers, he as a neurosurgeon and she as a cardiologist. They live in Westport, Connecticut, with their two teenage sons and talk regularly about how to imbue in their children the work ethic and sound values they absorbed in their own less-affluent childhoods.

STEPHANIE AND NOAH: Stephanie credits her drive to be self-sufficient to the stories she heard growing up about how her very wealthy grandparents lost everything in the Holocaust and had to start over from scratch when they escaped to America. She met her husband, Noah, through friends when they were both early in their careers in New York City after college. Now in their early 40s, Stephanie is an editor at a top publishing house, and Noah runs an investment fund focused on renewable energy. They have two young sons.

DOMINIQUE: Dominique is the Chief Marketing Officer of a global advertising company. She and her husband, a successful entrepreneur, are children of immigrants from Central America and the Caribbean. Dominique spent her teen years straddling her working-class upbringing and the affluent milieu of the boarding school she attended and chose a school that would expose her three children to socioeconomic diversity to counterbalance the affluence of their home environment.

Chapter Nine:

STEFAN: Stefan is married to Helen. He grew up in Belgium and came to the United States for graduate school in his early 20s. He met Helen shortly after, and the two formed an immediate bond because they had both lost their mothers at a young age. Now, the couple have been married for more than thirty years and live in the Washington, DC, area where Helen is a novelist and Stefan manages a European investment fund. Together, they have worked for decades to separate from Helen's family's trustees so that they could manage their wealth and parent in a manner aligned with their values.

PENELOPE: Penelope was raised in North Carolina, the eldest of three children of a successful furniture manufacturer. She and her siblings have a close relationship with their father but don't know how to begin a conversation with him about how to effect a successful transition of leadership of the business. Penelope also wishes her father would share more details about the family's financial situation, and she hopes to be more transparent with her children about the realities of the wealth they will inherit.

Chapter Seven

Meeting the Parents:
Staying "We" Amid the Rest of the Family

So far we have heard from our interviewee couples primarily about how they have ensured that the relationship between the two of them is strong, grounded, and resilient to the challenges that come their way. But, as every couple in a long-term committed relationship knows, it's not just the two of you. As *Love Languages* author Gary Chapman writes, "If you think that after the wedding that it will just be the two of you, your thinking is wrong. You are marrying into a family, for better or worse."[82]

To complicate matters, within the wealth advising industry, the whole topic of marrying into a family is too often seen primarily from the perspective of the wealth-owning family that a new spouse is joining. The jargon reveals the emphasis—new partners are "onboarded" into the wealthy family's culture, discussions center around which meetings these new partners can and cannot attend, and partners are sometimes even referred to as "out-laws" rather than "in-laws" (or partners use the term "out-law" to describe themselves, because it aptly reflects how they are made to feel).

We're taking a different approach. We spent time in our interviews hearing from the partners who have been on the receiving end of these planning efforts about what it feels like to be in their shoes.

There is not a lot of literature in our industry that gives voice to this perspective, and we aim to close that gap. We will also share the best practices that emerged from the stories we heard—the conversations, invitations, and approaches that actually help a new partner feel included, heard, and valued.

Our goal is to provide a road map for young inheritors struggling with the issue of how to better involve their partners. It often falls to the inheritor to mediate the relationship between their family and their spouse, or as wealth advisor and author Charles Lowenhaupt puts it, "It is up to the wealth inheritor to protect a spouse from the exclusion that comes with the label 'in-law.'"[83]

Inheritors in this position often feel at sea, not having context for what degree of inclusion is optimal or how other families are successfully navigating this issue. We know from numerous conversations with colleagues in the philanthropy field that a hot topic at "next gen" donor forums (when the wealth-generating parents aren't in the room) is this issue of spousal involvement—what is normal, what is best, and how to resolve a mismatch of expectations on the issue between parent and child. If this is the situation you find yourself in, we hope the stories in this chapter will highlight best practices and give you the tools you need to advocate in your family for an approach that will work best for you and your partner.

While we're centering this chapter on the partner's experience and on what we heard works to help them feel truly welcome in the inheritor's family, we also want to make another point that came across loud and clear in our interviews—that it's important to treat each partner's family equally. In a marriage, partners are working together to understand each other's broader families and blend traditions, cultures, and values to hopefully create a whole that is greater than the sum of its parts. Too often, our industry focuses only on the wealth-owning family, its traditions, values, and requirements, and the best way for the new partner to feel a part of these. Beyond the practices we'll cover here that help a partner feel included, perhaps the loudest signal is that the traditions, values, and rituals of their own family have an equal voice.

The partner's experience

We were struck in our interviews by the wide variability in partners' experiences. Some were fortunate to have joined wealth-owning families who welcomed them with open arms. They felt not only included, but also seen as their authentic selves and appreciated for what they could bring to the table as a new member of the family. We'll share their stories—and the best practices we gleaned from them—later in this chapter.

For others, though, it was different. We heard about how complicated it can be when the center of gravity orients around the wealth-owning family and the partner is expected to occupy a role that conforms to this orbit. Our interviewee Deborah, who bonded quickly with her husband, Alan, over their shared discomfort as inheritors, described to us how it felt when she joined Alan's family. "I never really felt that they were happy about Alan marrying me," she said. "I always felt like I was an interloper, like I was there but I wasn't." She remembers feeling that "I needed to adapt totally to their culture. I could bring nothing of my culture to their family. It was all their family. And if I wanted to be close, if I wanted to be involved, I had to be like them. And that was how I was welcomed."

Deborah's situation evinces the subtleties of this issue of spousal inclusion. On paper, and to all external appearances, Deborah looked "included"—she attended family business meetings and was assigned a role on the foundation. In reality, though, she had no voice. As she put it, "I was included but needed to be quiet." The one time she attempted to break the mold, offering to interview family members to build consensus around the mission of the foundation and to compile a report, there was little reaction to her findings. "Nobody was particularly interested in anything I had to say. And I think that sums it up. Nobody was interested in anything I had to say. So, I stopped saying anything." Years later, Deborah still feels stung by Alan's family's rejection and by their lack of interest in who she really was or what she had to offer. A silver lining is that she has vowed to do things differently with her own children's partners and has been welcoming them to family wealth discussions (where they have a seat at the table *and* a voice) for more than a decade.

We see embedded in Deborah's story a dynamic we heard in several of our interviews, that partners trying to forge a role for themselves within the orbit of the wealth-owning family often feel stuck between two suboptimal poles—being excluded on the one hand and being wholly subsumed on the other. Our interviewee Alice, who had a close relationship with her husband Tim's family and who was asked to join the family foundation shortly after their marriage, spoke to the latter and told us how critical it is when "coming into a family, to try to hold on to your values and your perspective."

She remembers her early days on the foundation, trying to strike the right balance between demonstrating sufficient appreciation for being included and breaking from the norm enough to offer her own perspective. "I was caught up in trying to impress my in-laws, trying to dig in, but trying not to take over or be inappropriate in some way. Trying to be part of the family, but also trying to forge my own path. And trying to fit in, but also trying to maintain my own family identity," she remembers. Tim's family was loving and welcoming, but still, the messages felt a little mixed. "I mean, it was like, 'We love you and we trust you. And we want you to be fully a part of this, but at the end of the day, you have to listen to the foundation director who Tim's parents hired. And, you know, don't say too much because you are still a spouse.'"

Now, 30 years later and reflecting on the complex emotions she was wrestling with at the time as she tried to carve out an appropriate and authentic role for herself, Alice sums up the lesson she took away as "Just advocate for yourself. Or, if you can't, you need to have some support outside of this family. You know it's not like you're right 100%—it's just that you deserve to be heard."

In both Deborah's and Alice's stories are lessons about how challenging it can be for partners to enter the orbit of the wealth-owning family and not feel either rejected or completely subsumed by its gravitational pull. Advisors can help partners in this role by being sensitive to this dynamic and by facilitating opportunities not just for a new partner to be acculturated into the wealth-owning family but also for the family to seek out and welcome a new partner's fresh perspective.

A final challenge we heard partners wrestling with as they joined a wealth-owning family was the tsunami of industry jargon they encountered in everything from investment reports to family governance best practices, and how this incomprehensible language and the equally foreign industry norms it describes can make a new partner feel like they have lost the race before they've even begun.

Our interviewee Louisa described how this felt for her in the early years of her marriage to Nathan. She remains grateful to Nathan's family for including her in family meetings as soon as she and Nathan were engaged. "I've been really fortunate because Nathan's family is very transparent," she says. "Once you're in, you're in…. But," she continues, "there is so much, like, jargon and lingo and structure and inherent understanding of what it means to be a family that comes from wealth that if you are not from that background, it's almost hard for anyone to even explain it or to realize that they may be talking about these things that you would never know about, because it's so normal."

She says this is particularly true in Nathan's family where he and his siblings have been attending family wealth retreats since childhood.

"So, all of a sudden," she says, "they'll get going on a conversation and you're like, 'I feel like an idiot.' And that is a feeling that's very uncomfortable. Because it felt like I was out of my depth, and not because I wasn't, you know, an enthusiastic person who's excited to meet new people and be a gracious guest or any of those other things, but because there's an actual knowledge base that I didn't have." And she notes that there was no equivalent for Nathan as he tried to navigate her family. "I don't think there were any times in understanding the players and the routines and the habits and the traditions and dynamics of my family, where Nathan was sitting there going, 'I feel dumb.'"

We'll hear later in the chapter that there were a number of things Nathan's family did to help bridge this gap and ensure that Louisa felt included and valued despite this imbalance in preparation. But her words are a reminder of how distancing jargon is and how subtly it increases the barriers to entry when a new partner is joining a wealth-owning family and hoping to play a meaningful role.

The Way Through

We'll devote this next section to the best practices our interviewee couples shared with us about how partners were made to feel welcomed into the wealth-owning family and valued for the perspective they brought. We wondered when we spoke with our interviewees whether it was possible for a partner to be made to feel both fully included and yet free enough to preserve a sense of their own identity outside the orbit of the wealth-owning family and its needs and wants—in other words, is it possible to successfully navigate the two poles we heard Deborah and Alice struggle with above? We heard from our interviewees that it is not only possible but doable, and we hope these stories inspire you as you are trying to navigate this balance within your family and relationship.

Inclusion

Often, we hear wealth-generating parents genuinely wondering whether it's appropriate to involve their children's partners in discussions of family wealth. In short, the answer is yes. Family wealth counselor and author Jay Hughes speaks eloquently on this point in his seminal work, *Family: The Compact Among Generations*. "Families think of themselves as being related through blood," Hughes writes. "The paradox is that no family ever begins with blood relations. All families begin by an affinity of two people who seek to begin a common journey. As soon as a family begins to think of itself as related by blood, it has actually abandoned its dual heritage and based its idea of family on a fallacy."[84]

In a later chapter, Hughes expands on this point and what it means for the role partners should be given in family decision-making. "Holding tight to the principle that only shared 'blood' entitles a member to participate in family governance requires that many persons be excluded from it and thus from family decision making," he writes. "Ironically, this out-group consists of people who consider themselves family members and whom the family considers in all other respects to be family members. In a world in which we seek individual freedom and in which that freedom is largely defined by our direct participation in the decisions that affect us, such exclusion guarantees that many family members will feel that they're at best 'nonfamily members' and at worst slaves to the governance system. No one chooses either role voluntarily."[85]

We couldn't agree more. In fact, we find that family members find a way to be heard one way or the other—it's usually far more constructive for official processes to give partners a voice than to force them to try to advocate for their perspective from the sidelines. And family members who are officially included tend to feel far more affinity for the wealth-owning family than they would otherwise. Wealth counselor Ellen Miley Perry speaks to this point in her book, *Wealth of Possibilities*, writing, "Simply stated, small tents with hard rules of inclusion encourage out-cast family members to look for new tents."[86]

A final argument for inclusion is temporal—this generation's "outlaw" is often next generation's matriarch (or patriarch). Those of us who have worked with wealthy families long enough know that this evolution is common—time marches on, young "next gens" and their partners become parents, and eventually these parents set the wealth management (and distribution) strategy for their own family. Given this reality, it's best to operate under the assumption that this will be the outcome from the get-go. Doing so not only better prepares partners for their eventual likely role but also provides them with an inclusive model they can emulate when it's their turn to welcome newcomers.

So, what actually works to help a partner feel included? We heard in our interviewees' stories about several key efforts that truly mattered and made the difference between inclusion in name only (as we heard about from Deborah) and inclusion that felt real. We'll take them one at a time.

Being trusted with transparency

Our interviewees Campbell and Oliver remember being aware when they were growing up how frustrated and hurt their mother felt that she was treated as an outsider by their father's wealth-owning family. Now both married, the brothers feel grateful that their partners have had a wholly different experience, largely because of their mother's commitment to ensure that their wives never felt as she did. From early days in each of their relationships, their partners were welcomed to family meetings and included in transparent discussions about family wealth.

These efforts have made a difference. Oliver's wife, Holly, says,

"Oliver's mom actually voiced her discontent with being excluded from conversations and her intentions for me and my sister-in-law to always be included. So, I think Oliver's parents kind of went above and beyond to just be generally welcoming. And, I think having been able to have open conversations with Oliver's parents about wealth and values makes it all feel easy, or easier. It makes me feel a part of the family." Campbell's wife, Mia, agrees, "I think Campbell's parents were very different from what I perceived as the stereotype of family wealth. They were very open to talking about it. And I've always appreciated that particularly about Campbell's mom. She's always looped us into all the conversations."

Transparency can be conveyed in lots of little conversations or one big one. Louisa remembers that soon after she and Nathan were engaged, they were at his house and his parents took her aside for an hour and explained the history of the family's wealth, the structure of the family office, and the broad outlines of the role she would be invited to play. "It was clearly a tacit approval and acceptance and comfort level that you're here," Louisa recalls. It felt to her that they were saying, "We are very excited that you're here. And now, we're going to sit down and talk about this thing." Years later, she remembers how meaningful it was to her. "I don't know if it would work for every family, I suppose. But everyone's always looking for the approval of the family and the in-laws. When you're joining a family, you want to feel like you're welcome there, like people are excited that you are part of it. And I think having that conversation was very helpful." It also quelled any lingering questions in her mind. "It makes it much harder to go, 'Do I know everything? Am I still being kept in the dark? Do they really want me here?' Because there's so much old context and history and politics that is part of the family dynamic that it sometimes gives you whiplash when you're the new person. And so, having that comfort to sort of talk to his mom or dad or have a group conversation is something we've leaned into numerous times since then."

We can see in this story the power of transparency. The underlying message that is conveyed when someone is given access to information is that they are *trusted*—they are on the inside, and there is no question that they belong there. It sends a powerful signal not only, as Holly said, that they are now "part of the family," but also that the family is confident they will remain in this role. Considering these deeper messages—trust and faith in the longevity of the relationship—that are conveyed through the sharing of information, it's no wonder that partners read the opposite into decisions to withhold information and feel deeply hurt as a result.

Being valued for your talents

When our interviewee Hope met her husband, Luke, 20 years ago, they were both working on her family's Montana ranch. Even in those early days, she saw his work ethic up close and observed how he tapped his mathematical mind to dream up ways to improve the processes on the ranch. Hope described to us how, in the years since, her family and family office have also noticed and appreciated Luke's talents. He was invited to join family office meetings shortly after they were engaged, and now, almost 15 years later, he is the Chair of the family's investment committee, a role he enjoys and balances deftly with his full load as a veterinary oncologist.

Hope's family offered Luke something better than a seat at the table—they recognized his unique strengths and invited him to apply those strengths in a meaningful role. "So he feels very much heard and very much a part of the process," Hope explains. But she adds that her family has benefited, too, by being able to leverage Luke's expertise. "It would be such a disservice to the family to leave Luke out," Hope says, "because he's super mathematical. And how easily that translates into a financial mindset and thinking about investments, and asset allocation, and risk management." She continues, "Luke is so smart and has so much to give to this family, if you were to cut him out and just say 'Only Hope gets to come to the table,' they would be missing out on so much."

She summarizes her view as, "How can you not include spouses? When I hear about families who say spouses are not invited to meetings, I'm like, but they hear about the meeting probably that night, you know, lying in bed, like the whole download. So why not just go ahead and include them?" She credits her family's approach with not only helping Luke to feel included but also mitigating the power imbalance that can arise when only one spouse is viewed as being on the inside. She says, "My family has done a great job thinking about human capital and thinking about Luke and me as a couple. I just feel like it's neutralized this whole idea of who is the family member, who isn't, who has money, who doesn't. It's just a nonissue in our relationship."

Being given the lay of the land

Joining a family can at times feel like being dropped onto a new planet—where the language is inscrutable, the customs are opaque, and the inhabitants laugh at inside jokes you don't understand (and may not find funny even when you do!) This culture shock is normal and can mean that, even when families make an overt and intentional effort to be welcoming, new partners may struggle to adapt to what feels like foreign terrain. We were inspired by stories we heard about families who recognized this dynamic and provided the newcomer with a guide—a mentor or trusted person they could feel comfortable talking with, venting to, and asking for guidance.

Earlier we heard how Louisa felt a bit out of her depth when conversations in Nathan's family devolved into family office and investment jargon. But this discomfort was tempered by the fact that at least Louisa felt like she knew the players. Shortly after she and Nathan were engaged, the couple attended a family wedding. "Every single one of his aunts and uncles made a point of coming over, chatting with me, and talking a little bit about the family dynamics," Louisa remembers. "Not even the money stuff. But you know, every person has their flaws, here's the deal with this person and that person. And here's who you should talk to if you're feeling confused about something. They were sort of just letting me know that I was super welcome, but that, yeah, of course, it's a family. There were dynamics at play, and here is a little baby road map for how to handle them."

She was in awe. She felt not only welcomed but that she had been handed a treasure map with the decoder key. All of a sudden the uncharted sea of personalities—with all of the unknown hazards she hoped she didn't unwittingly trip—became navigable. And these relatives gave her a guide. They all, to a person, pointed her to one aunt who "plays the peacekeeper role" and is "everybody's pal, team Switzerland, all the way. They were like, if you're struggling, call her."

And she did. Later that summer, when Louisa was finding it challenging to navigate her new role in the family, she reached out to this aunt. "It was like a two-hour conversation. I vented all this stuff that I was not understanding. Why is it like this or why did they say that or that made me feel so crappy," Louisa recalls. "And you know, she had a good perspective. And also, I just needed to say it to somebody who understood." Louisa emerged from the call renewed. Not only did she have a better understanding of family dynamics and how to move forward, but perhaps even more importantly, she felt that her uncertainties, fears, and concerns had a place with*in* the family, rather than only outside of it.

When families are thinking of who might serve as this guide, it can be helpful to think about who has traveled the same journey as the new partner. Our interviewee Sebastian described to us the close friendship he and his mother-in-law have developed over the last two decades. The two bonded over their shared middle-class upbringings and the tensions each had experienced with their siblings as their own financial resources grew. Especially in the early years of his relationship with his husband, Nicholas, as Sebastian was wrestling with setting boundaries with his family members and managing their expectations about financial assistance, "I was fortunate I had my mother-in-law who went through similar dynamics with her family who I could lean on for support and a shoulder to cry on." He continues, "She has been a big support system because she kind of was in the same shoes that I am in. I think having someone like that is helpful. It can kind of guide you and give you that support, because the problem is you can't have these conversations with your regular friends, because they're not going to understand your struggle."

Having your family treated equally

There are a number of substantive issues to be worked out when couples attempt to bridge two origin families—from holiday plans to traditions to expectations of togetherness to time with grandchildren, the list is long and potentially fraught. The key, though, is to approach these discussions with equal weight on both partners' families. This is not a given. In fact, the norm in the wealth advising industry is to do the opposite—to orient around the wealth-owning family and to plan family retreats, meetings, and vacations with only that family (wealth-generating parents, their adult children, and perhaps also their partners) in mind. While this planning is not intended to be exclusionary, it often operates in a vacuum with little consideration for how these plans interact with the traditions, schedules, and vacations that might be the norm for the partner's family. A fairly common example is an annual family retreat or multigenerational vacation that occurs every year over the same holiday, making it impossible for a couple to alternate that holiday between both sets of families.

Charles Lowenhaupt raises this issue in the chapter he devotes to marriage in his book, *The Wise Inheritor's Guide to Freedom from Wealth*, encouraging couples to discuss the following questions: "How will you define and think of your family? Are the families of both partners to be considered equal? Or will the family of wealth have preference or some higher standing or decision-making power? And why? If the answer is yes because they control the purse strings, you need to discuss whether that will be satisfactory to both of you."[87] And we would add, even if the answer is yes only because the wealth-owning family has more meetings, vacations, or retreats, it's worth considering the impact of this dynamic and the message it sends to children or any other family members who might be taking note and drawing the conclusion that the wealth-owning family seems to always take precedence.

So, how to avoid this dynamic? We heard in our interviews that efforts at inclusion were noted and mattered. Our interviewee Isabelle told us how much it means to her that her husband Jonah's parents go out of their way to include her family members when planning activities, buying tickets for her brothers to join them for sports games when they are in town and inviting her parents for Rosh Hashanah. "One of the nice things about his family," she says, "is they make everybody feel super comfortable. They've been very inclusive of my family from the beginning, like my whole family."

And just as important as inclusion was curiosity—having a genuine interest in learning about the partner's family, their traditions, and customs, and respecting these as equally important. Doing so leads to more equitable allocations of time (such as alternating holidays between families and vacationing with both sides) and reinforces to the partner that they, and their family, have a voice that matters.

Our interviewee Yasmin recounted to us what a positive impression it made on her that her fiancé Miles's parents were curious about her culture. While Yasmin and Miles might both be described as inheritors (their mothers were each born into wealthy families), they grew up amid money messages, religions, and cultures that were quite distinct. "Miles's parents are very open to learning about my culture and learning what I value," Yasmin says. It started with food, as the four ate meals together for months during the pandemic. "We all love food, and I love to cook. So, I would come and introduce Malaysian food to their family, and we would cook together." And it moved on to religion. "His parents have so many questions about what being a Muslim is and especially what being a moderate, nonobservant Muslim is and the different traditions that we do. I mean, especially, fasting is something that's so interesting to talk about with them. Yeah, they've been incredibly welcoming."

Autonomy

Hopefully, with the above best practices in play—providing partners with information, giving them not only a seat at the table but a voice, valuing them for their contributions and talents, equipping them with a guide to help them decode the foreign land of the family, and treating their own family and its traditions as equals—new partners will feel authentically included and welcomed.

But we discovered in our interviews that this authentic inclusion, while necessary, is not sufficient. Partners also have to be granted autonomy—the right to turn down the invitation to be included with no feelings hurt or bridges burned. In other words, the decision about whether or not to accept an invitation (to join the board, serve on the foundation, attend family retreats, etc.) has to be the *partner's* to make. And they must have the ability to say no without being judged for attempting to live life on their own terms.

So how is autonomy conveyed? Here is what our interviewees told us mattered most.

Being given the space to live a couple-defined life

For many of our interviewees, autonomy began with space—being given the space to prioritize their own life and to strengthen their foundation as a couple, free from the distractions, burdens, and countervailing priorities of the broader family. Charles Lowenhaupt speaks to the need for this space, writing "The family of an 18-year-old may center on his parents and his siblings. The family of a 38-year-old should center on his wife and children. Your extended family should stay extended, and your immediate family must be nuclear.... You must analyze every element of family bundling—what the family does together—and pick and choose only what makes your spouse comfortable."[88]

Inheritor Eileen Rockefeller speaks to this dynamic in her memoir and describes how it influenced her decision to move across the country from her family early in her marriage to her husband, Paul. "I had watched other family members move in and out of marriages," she writes. "I did not want our marriage to be corrupted by the pull of the Rockefeller name, or the pressure to join family events. Saying no would have been much harder had we lived within easy commute from New York. I knew I was making the right choice, even though it was hard to be three thousand miles away from my family."[89]

We heard about the benefits of geographic distance from our interviewees Valerie and Donald as well, although in their case it was unexpected. Shortly after they married 40 years ago, Donald's employer asked him to head up their São Paolo office. Valerie remembers the first several months of life in Brazil as "very, very difficult," but says now, "Our moving to Brazil and being there for over two and a half years was probably the single most important decision we made that strengthened our marriage, and in a way that could never have happened if we had stayed close to home." She continues, "Primarily, I think it was that my parents weren't there to interfere. They weren't there to give their opinions, which they never held back on. They weren't there for me to run to if we had an argument. I mean that was a big one. And we did it together. We had each other. We really only had each other." Donald agrees and muses, "The idea that us moving to Brazil turned out to be important is a retrospective one. We didn't know it at the time." He's not surprised, though, as he believes that "all significant growth happens outside of your comfort zone."

Space away from family allows a couple to move through a developmental stage that is not only necessary on its own but also may be an important prerequisite to the couple effectively managing broader family involvement down the road. Family business consultants Stephanie Brun de Pontet, Craig E. Aronoff, Drew S. Mendoza, and John L. Ward write, "A young couple needs some time alone, not because the spouses want to avoid the family or valued traditions, but because they are working to establish their own traditions and boundaries on which they want to build their family. They must be encouraged to truly harmonize as a couple and a nuclear family unit before they can comfortably be a part of the larger family system."[90]

And just as important as the work the couple does together during this time is the message that is conveyed when they are granted it. When couples are given space away from family obligations, the message they hear from their families is "We accept that your life as a couple takes priority." In the world of family wealth, that message is powerful and realigns the center of gravity from the wealth-owning family and its needs to the young couple and the new life they are building together.

Being able to decline invitations to serve in family wealth management roles

As much as our interviewee partners appreciated being invited to join (family meetings, boards, foundations, etc.), it was equally important to be free to decline. Abby shared that her family has invited her partner, Ben, to sit on the family foundation board, but that he prefers to spend his time elsewhere. "My family has been very welcoming," she says. "But Ben is not interested, which I can totally understand. There are certain things that he is just like, 'I don't want to spend my time on that.'" Abby knows that Ben weighs the time he would need to devote to this effort against time he could otherwise invest in his company or spend with the couple's three-year-old daughter. And she also knows that her family is okay with this because other family members have done the same in the past and modeled that it's okay to prioritize nuclear family obligations over broader family ones. The offer stands if Ben ever changes his mind, but in the meantime, he can rest assured that his saying no hasn't ruffled feathers.

Sometimes it's a more subtle offer that a partner wants to decline. Many new partners find after joining a wealth-owning family that, on a purely economic basis, their career is optional. Not only may there no longer be an economic necessity for them to work, but there may also be a subtle, gravitational pull on their time toward the myriad responsibilities involved in managing family wealth (for instance, an implicit assumption that their calendar be kept open so that they are free to attend family meetings, interview wealth advisors, sit on the foundation board, participate in site visits to charities, etc.).

Alice felt this when she joined Tim's family 30 years ago just as the family was going through the process of setting up a family office. Up until this point, Alice had been focused on her career. "But the message to us when the founding happened was that 'You don't have to work. We just want you to be happy,'" she says. As generous a message as that was intended to be, Alice found over time that its implicit assessment that her work was unnecessary combined with the family's recurring invitations to be involved in the collective wealth management efforts crowded out her own working life.

It can take some courage (and a recognition that this is even happening) for a partner to resist these invitations and preserve a part of their life that is focused on something other than the family wealth management ecosystem. But it can be critical for their sense of identity. Earlier we heard how much our interviewee Mia appreciates that her husband Campbell's parents are open about the details of their family wealth and loop her into planning conversations. She is also grateful, though, that their expectations of her involvement are minimal, allowing her the time to be devoted to her career as an international human rights attorney. "I get a lot of sense of identity and self-worth through what I do," she says, "and I like the fact that I still do it despite having the ability not to do it and having my same lifestyle. It just makes me realize how much I love, love it. I think I would have a very low self-esteem and very low self-worth if I just quit. My work gives me an outlet for everything—for critical thinking, for friendships, self-worth, for feeling like I'm giving back.… And I think having that as a separate part of me from my relationship with my husband, my child, or with this money gives me a sense of independence and happiness that, you know, I could do this, regardless of whether we lost all our money."

Being encouraged to voice new perspectives

And what about when a partner does want to serve in a family wealth management role? As we saw in Deborah's story earlier, a seat at the table doesn't necessarily guarantee a voice or convey a sense of autonomy. This occurs only when a partner is encouraged to voice an outside perspective and believes that others might actually be open to hearing this perspective. Louisa and Nathan described to us how she and several other newcomer partners to Nathan's family have formed an "in-law focus group" of sorts, to advocate for changes like alternating holidays between both spouses' sets of families and preserving vacation time for nuclear family and friends, etc. "We haven't backed down on certain things, which has caused some conflict," Louisa said.

But she credits Nathan's family with ultimately making room for their perspective and adopting the changes they suggested.

Consistent with what we heard from Mia, Louisa credits her career with giving her the confidence to advocate for her outsider perspective. Nathan agrees that Louisa's sense of independent identity has helped her in this role. "In my mind," he says, "money is definitely an amplifier of family culture, and in many cases, family conformity. So, if you don't come in with a strong sense of independent identity, then I think one of two things happen. Either you end up just going with the flow, which can be okay if you're somebody who's comfortable and okay with that and able to achieve your own goals, happiness, satisfaction within that framework. Or you end up in a situation where the family member spouse has to essentially play defense on your behalf—because it's really easy for the family to come together and close ranks." He is glad that Louisa can hold her own and that his family sees the benefits of the changes she and the other in-laws have recommended.

We were inspired by Nathan's family's evolution and how closely the place they ended up—with a peer group of in-laws advocating for fresh perspectives that eventually effected change—matches what an expert we spoke with described as best practice. As the Executive Director and President of the nonprofit organization 21/64, Danielle Oristian York spends her days helping wealthy families communicate more effectively across generations and training other industry professionals to do the same. She thinks the wealth advising industry "should spend more time on the in-laws." She says, "I think there's a real opportunity to look to in-laws, successful in-laws, who have maintained the balance of their individuality. They have gifts that the born-in don't have, which is that they really did live a life outside of this family before they joined it. Family members can look to them as a source of learning and growth."

Danielle encourages wealthy families to ask themselves, "How might this person contribute?" "How do we make more room for this person?" and importantly, "What might we have to change about ourselves individually and collectively?" to do so. And she believes wealthy families need to recognize that it is unrealistic "to think that grown people entering into a marital relationship with their spouse, their chosen person, should somehow succumb to another family's entire culture and leave their culture behind."

She applauds in-laws who do exactly what Louisa has done. She says, "I have several client groups where the in-laws call themselves the outlaws because they are non-the-whatever-family," she says. "And you know what they do? They embrace their identity. They create their own peer cohort. They find their ways of navigating" and figuring out how to balance the benefits they value that come with being a part of the family "with the strings attached that they don't like." She concludes, "They do in many ways what we encourage inheritors to do, which is to figure out your role—make choices about what you want to do or what you don't want to do, and establish boundaries in your relationships with your parents and other family members."

As Danielle points out, underlying the seeming "born-in" vs. in-law divide is the emotional reality that, in many ways, inheritors and their partners are in the same boat. They both would prefer to be included rather than excluded but need an offer of inclusion that allows them to preserve their own identity and sense that they are leading a self-driven life. Recognizing that they share this commonality can help inheritors and their partners ease the insider/outsider divide.

Growing together

Bridging two families and acculturating to each other's family isn't easy. As our interviewee Amelia puts it, "It's a huge task to assimilate into a new family. You've spent your entire life—25, 30 years—knowing only one certain way. And now, you're expected to integrate into a new family with different traditions and navigate these hurdles together with your partner who might have different strategies for handling certain things." She continues, "So, I think my biggest takeaway from this whole experience is, it's okay that it takes time. It's not going to be perfect, and there are going to be things that don't go smoothly, and I think that's fine." Echoing what we heard earlier about the marrying couple needing to take priority, she says, "I think the key, at least for us, is that we've made a decision together as a couple that we're going to put each other first. And then we'll go from there, and everything else will sort of fall into place as long as we stick with that model."

As Amelia says, marrying into a family is an adjustment, and there are bumps along the road. But if a couple can stick together, they find they are not only able to successfully travel the path but that the journey is worthwhile. We heard from a number of our interviewees about how their relationship with their in-laws has enriched their lives.

Earlier, Valerie and Donald shared how formative those first two and half years of their marriage were in Brazil, away from family and forced to rely on only each another. But Valerie also told us how important the example set by Donald's parents has been in her life and in her efforts to be the mother-in-law she wants to be for her own children and their partners. "Donald's parents were amazing," she says. "They were the most unconditionally loving parents I think I've ever met. So, having experienced that unconditional love and that freedom to be our own couple without this extreme pressure to also be making their life happy at the same time has been a really good example for me. And of how to be a better mother-in-law."

Now, as in-laws themselves, Valerie and Donald say, "Basically, we've thrown open the doors to our home. And we've thrown open the doors to our heart." They try to treat their children's partners "like they're an integral part of this family, realizing there's another family that they're part of too.... And realizing that they need space to create their own family."

We heard in these stories a truth that we see in other aspects of our work with wealthy families. When couples are given freedom to choose their level of involvement with each other's family, they are often more likely to seek out a relationship and to appreciate what it can offer. Our interviewee Sebastian shared with us how his husband Nicholas's parents are always careful not to overstay when they come to visit. But he so loves talking with his mother-in-law that he calls her every couple of weeks. "We end up talking for an hour or two," he says, "and the conversation goes from one thing to the next and we'll go full circle." Reflecting on the two decades that Nicholas's parents have been in his life, he says, "I'm really blessed to have incredible in-laws. I can honestly say they're almost like my second parents. I really look up to them for their guidance and advice. And I know my spouse definitely appreciates the unity that I have with his parents." When his own son is an adult and "has his own family," he hopes to follow their example.

Chapter Eight

Becoming the Parents

In 2008, wealth counselor John L. Levy published *Inherited Wealth: Opportunities and Dilemmas*, informed by his 25 years of counseling on issues related to inherited wealth, interviews conducted with inheritors, and his own personal experience with inherited wealth. In it he writes:

> "It has been interesting and encouraging for me to see how often young people free themselves from the problems that tend to accompany inheritance when they become involved with the challenge and the excitement of raising their own children. Wealthy young parents who feel wounded or diminished by their experience of inheritance can approach the nurturance of their children as a challenging opportunity to break the negative pattern of past generations. Such parents often find great meaning in helping their own children to avoid some of the pitfalls and problems that they experienced. They can also find great satisfaction in seeing their children grow up less troubled by these problems and with sound values. They will also be aware that whatever they are able to accomplish with their children will probably be passed on to subsequent generations."[91]

We agree. We have seen that, for many young inheritors, the act of becoming a parent is a chance to start anew. There is an exhilarating freedom in being able to write the rules and design a family culture of your own choosing. And we find that inheritor parents are often primed to be uniquely self-aware and effective parents to their own inheritor children—they have spent a lifetime thinking deeply about issues of inheritance and identity, they have matured into an assessment of which aspects of their childhood benefited or impeded them, and they have an urgent motivation to improve upon suboptimal parenting patterns of the past.

Laying the groundwork for intentional parenting amid wealth

In our experience, though, it's not enough to know what you *don't* want to do, or which parenting behaviors you don't want to repeat. It's critically important to know what you *do* want to do (what your goals are for your children, the experience you'd like them to have with inherited wealth, and the impact that that wealth will have in their lives), *and* to have the intention, discipline, and consistency in your daily parenting to manifest these goals.

I've seen this in practice. My first book, *Raised Healthy, Wealthy & Wise* (2014), focused on the parenting messages and behaviors that are effective when trying to raise children to be grounded and motivated amid wealth. I interviewed dozens of grown, grounded, self-motivated, and content inheritors and asked them which lessons from their parents they credited with helping them to become this way. I hoped that the inspiring stories they shared—of parents' holding them to limits, requiring them to work, allowing them to earn their own success (and recover from failure), and modelling and communicating sound financial and life values—would serve as a handbook of sorts for any parent attempting to set their child on the right course amid abundance.

In the years since its publication, I've spoken widely on the book and its lessons and have been gratified to hear at some of these talks from parents who have read the book (or read it together with their spouse) and used it to guide their parenting. I've also worked with couples one-on-one to help them incorporate these lessons into their parenting. This is rewarding work—it's heartening to see the relief on a parent's face when they have a plan that is aligned with their goals and understand how the plan translates into their day-to-day parenting reality.

This work has shown me that successfully incorporating the book's lessons into day-to-day parenting requires two important prerequisites: first, parents need to be on the same page about their parenting goals; and second, parents need to be committed to a proactive, intentional, and disciplined approach to parenting (as one of the challenges of wealth is that it falls to parents to recreate lessons that necessity would teach by default). This chapter is about these prerequisites.

The reality is that questions of wealth and parenting manifest in nearly all aspects of parenting life, including where you choose to live, the values and lifestyle you model with your own behavior, the expectations you set for your children, the work you choose to do, and how you choose to communicate with your children about your wealth. We won't cover in depth the best practice strategies in all of these areas as I cover these topics in my first book; instead, we will focus here on the topics our interviewees felt were important to discuss so they could align their thinking in these areas and ensure they were sufficiently on the same page to co-parent effectively.

Our interviewees' stories also demonstrate the importance of a proactive commitment to parenting intentionally. This step of committing is one many couples skip over during the hectic pace and busy jumble of modern parenting life. There is often a sense that good intentions will carry the day, but in our experience, good intentions rarely motivate the optimal parenting action when confronted with a crying toddler (or obstinate teenager or struggling 22-year-old). It takes an extraordinary amount of discipline to parent well, especially amid wealth. Each day presents trade-offs between outcomes you might personally prefer (or certainly would prefer in the moment) and that will be better for your child in the long-term. When these choices present themselves, it's easier to remain disciplined and choose the latter option when you have thought about the fact that you will be presented with these dilemmas in advance and have committed to acting with resolve when they arise. And it's easier to choose the latter option when both partners are in lockstep. You can support each other and lend each other moral support if ever either of your fortitude waivers.

Agreeing on the life you'd like to design for your child

Our interviewees all expressed a hope that their children wouldn't be isolated by their wealth or entitled by their privilege. And they understood that there were levers they could pull to increase their child's socioeconomic fluency, enrich them with a deeper understanding of the realities of life, and imbue them with skills that not only built their confidence but helped them relate to others who have learned these skills out of necessity. Here were the levers our interviewees felt were most important to be aligned on and intentional about.

Where you'll choose to live

From the size of your home to the wealth of your zip code, the decision about where to plant roots is one of the most significant you and your partner will make in your efforts to design your children's childhood. Your choice will define your children's concept of home and inform their innate sense of what is normal for the rest of their lives. Given the import of this decision, it's worth thinking about this choice with intention and considering whether the place you would want to live is aligned with the character traits you hope your child will absorb. And if there are aspects that are out of alignment, it's worth talking about how you feel about these and what your narrative to your children will be to either flag or reconcile these inconsistencies.

Several of our interviewees were raised by inheritor parents who had themselves asked this question and moved as a result. Miles's mother was raised by a wealthy family in Greenwich, Connecticut, but as his fiancée, Yasmin, explained, when Miles's mother reached her mid-20s, "She wanted a really simple life and left it all to move to Vermont." Yasmin reflects, "And so I think Miles, my partner, grew up in a really wholesome and simple life with parents who had a lot of wealth but wanted to impart simpler values to their children." Our interviewees Louisa and Nathan shared that his parents did the same and moved from an exclusive California enclave to Phoenix when he was 10. As Louisa puts it, "Nathan says over and over that one of the best things they did for him was leave that environment."

But it can be challenging to know what is truly best for your child. Our interviewee Carter and his wife chose Westport, Connecticut, for the schools, but now wonder if they made the right decision. "I think being Black folks in this country who are, you know, probably in the top 0.5% of wealth or net worth, or what have you," he says, "presents some additional incremental issues raising Black sons, because elements of identity arise, or maybe even lack of identity, that is essentially brought about by being in overwhelmingly white schools, neighborhoods, and social structures. It can be alienating and very, very challenging. And this is something that my wife and I talk about all the time. And we talk about this with other Black families who are wealthy, that there's a sense of isolation because there aren't very many Black families that are doing well in America, particularly in the northeast." He concludes that he and his wife wonder "If we really have done a good thing, or maybe a disservice to our sons, in terms of giving them everything and moving to an area where they are two out of the ten Black kids in the school."

Our interviewee Caleb expressed a similar sentiment and said that he and his wife "have had these debates for a while in terms of what's the right thing to do for your children." They moved from a more diverse neighborhood to a predominantly white suburb when their eldest child was in middle school. Whereas their eldest son experienced and remembers both communities, their younger children were only in grade school when the family moved and "so they haven't had that chance of seeing anything different than the environment where they are very much one of a few folks of African-American background." He continues, "And so then the question is, how do you make sure that your children feel comfortable being around a wider array of people, including people who look like themselves?" Caleb and his wife eventually made strides toward this goal by finding a peer group of other Black families who were feeling similarly.

What we heard our interviewees wrestling with was the way in which location can be a double-edged sword. The very places you might choose for the amenities they offer may also double down on the isolation that can come with wealth and, by reducing socioeconomic and racial (given the existing racial wealth gap in the United States) diversity, draw a tighter circle around the world in which your child feels comfortable and understands how to operate. It's worth having a meaningful conversation with your partner about the circle you would ideally like to draw for your child and about how you will manifest this in your child's life if the location you choose ends up being too constraining.

What you'll sacrifice to broaden your child's concept of "normal"

A frequent question I hear from parents is "How much can I enjoy the lifestyle I'm able to afford versus hold back so that my children don't absorb a vision of life that is too narrow?" I tend to think of lifestyle choices as a language you are teaching your children to speak. If they learn to speak only a "five-star" language, the percentage of the world they will be able to converse with and relate to will be exceedingly small.

But the process of building your children's fluency in these other languages—from one- to four-star and everything in between—requires some sacrifice on your part. It requires you to spend time purchasing products and living experiences that are below the level that you can afford. This is certainly a "first-world problem," but it's worth seriously strategizing with your partner about how you will provide your children with exposure to these other languages because, in my experience, this is not a parenting behavior that comes naturally.

Our interviewees shared with us how they have done this in their families. Stephanie and Noah live in New York City and love taking their two young sons to basketball games. But they think carefully about which seats they buy. Noah says, "I wanted our kids to enjoy the sporting events because they enjoy the game, not because they sat in the first row. We would never sit courtside. It's not the experience and the appreciation we want them to have." Stephanie chimes in, "And there have been times when we've bought nosebleed seats on purpose, so that they would go and learn not to complain about it. And if they were like, 'Oh, these seats are terrible,' we were, like, 'You know what, isn't this better than not coming at all?'" Stephanie and Noah were in alignment on the message they wanted to convey to their children and through commitment and intentionality were able to see it through.

Our interviewee Dominique talked with us about how her family plans vacations. She and her husband have prioritized travel (because as she says, "to poorly paraphrase Mark Twain, travel is the antidote to ignorance") and their family traveled to 15 countries by the time her eldest son was 10. But Dominique and her husband noticed that all this travel was having an unintended effect. Their son "would have these wild ideas about vacation, and we realized, why wouldn't he because he doesn't see any restraint. He just knows we go on a trip."

Dominique and her husband talked about it and decided to make some changes. They put their son in charge of planning their next annual family trip for the five of them and her parents. He had to pick a destination, research excursions, and bookmark possibilities, so he would be exposed to "all the layers of planning a vacation and not have this idea that 'All I have to do is show up.'"

And he had to fit all of his plans into the moderate budget they provided. "We would say, you have X thousands of dollars, and that has to include airfare, it has to include lodging, and you've got to think about how much we're going to spend daily on things like food, excursions, and all that." She continues, "It was messy in the beginning. Obviously, we didn't give him a credit card and say have at it. He couldn't hit spend on anything. And every time, I kid you not, he would come back and say, 'you know, if I had a little more budget.' And we would say, 'This is the budget.'"

Holding this line was the hard part. As Dominique puts it, "It made us be disciplined because we had to model for him. I mean, if he says, 'I just need $5,000 more,' that's not a big deal amongst ourselves, but because we want to model this for him, we maintain that hardline. Like, 'no, son, this really is the budget.' We're trying to both hold ourselves accountable as well as teach the children."

Now, four years later, Dominique says her son is so expert at vacation planning that "he'll do a family presentation with a PowerPoint and everything. He gives us seating assignments so that the chatterers aren't sitting next to each other." And he's become so adept at budgeting that he now routinely comes in under budget.

We loved this story not only for how masterfully Dominique's son learned to vacation-plan, but more importantly because of the level of commitment and alignment Dominique and her husband demonstrated in executing on this idea. It took discipline—and yes, even a bit of sacrifice—to forego the trip they might have gone on if they had allowed their son to increase the budget. But this sacrifice has been worth it to give their son an innate understanding of an experience (how to plan and enjoy a vacation when budget is a constraint) that for most people is the norm. They have made him more socioeconomically fluent, meaning they have given him an ability to relate authentically to the many people who have this experience in common.

If these stories have inspired you to make some changes in order to improve your child's socioeconomic fluency, you can begin by taking an inventory of everything your child experiences (the size of their house, the vacations they go on, the restaurants they eat out in, the clothes they buy, etc.) and ask yourself how your child would answer the question, "What level of this experience is affordable by most people?" Would they know? Would they have any exposure to what the median (or "normal" for lack of a better word) experience feels like?

Being unable to answer this question—or to understand what that experience feels like—leaves a child isolated from most people and reduces their appreciation for luxuries that take most people years (and good fortune) to attain. What's more, this narrowness can become a real handicap when your child eventually embarks on their own journey of self-sufficiency. If they've experienced, lived in, and have felt comfortable in a range of socioeconomic experiences, they'll be far better equipped to embrace whatever level of lifestyle they will be able to afford on their own.

What you'll require of your children even if it's not economically necessary

Parents need to be in alignment on what they'll require of their children. Much of parenting well with wealth involves insisting that your child do things that either are 1) not economically necessary for them to do (like getting a summer job), or 2) easier for you to do yourself (because completing the task is always simpler than motivating the child) or hire someone else to do (like keeping their room clean or doing their laundry). Insisting on things that are not necessary (in the short-term) is hard. It can feel artificial. Parents feel that they'll be found out or that a perceptive child will question their logic, and they will have to explain themselves (a conversation with your child I wholeheartedly encourage, by the way).

Pushing through these countervailing forces requires fortitude and a dogged focus on the future and the capacities and resilience you are attempting to imbue in the adult you will be raising. It requires a steely moral conviction that your insistence is necessary and the willingness and patience to explain your position to your child. Beyond all of this, though, it requires parents to absolutely be on the same page. Children are incredibly adept at discerning which parent is more lenient or easier to persuade. Parents can save themselves hours of conflict (with each other and with their children) by agreeing ahead of time on what their fundamental expectations will be and committing to back each other up in holding the line.

The good news is that it's never too early to have these conversations and to get on the same page about your expectations. Nathan and Louisa are expecting their first child but have already talked for several years about how they want to parent. One of the expectations they've agreed to is that their child will have a summer job. Louisa remembers that growing up as one of three in a family without a lot of extra money, she and her siblings were all expected to have summer jobs. "I was babysitting by the time I was 12," she says. "Worked every summer in high school. Getting into the work world was no big deal. It was part of the expectations. That's the way I was raised."

In Nathan's household, though, it was different. "He didn't have a job in high school," Louisa said. Looking back on it, the couple reason that that was probably because Nathan's family traveled during the summers and that made his having a job logistically challenging.

They've agreed that they would prefer Louisa's experience for their child, and they recognize that following this approach may take some sacrifice on their part. It may mean not traveling as much as they would like or staying put for the summer so their child can clock in at a five-day-per-week job during normal business hours. They're clear-eyed that they may have to give up some of their own lifestyle perks in order to help their child become an "independent, well-functioning adult." As Louisa puts it, "That is something we've spent a lot of time talking about. I think the guidepost for our parenting decisions will not be what's best for us, but what's best for our child—and not in the moment, but in terms of creating a person who's ready to go out and be an independent person, regardless of how much money they have access to at some future point in life."

Sometimes you and your partner can have these discussions years in advance. And sometimes they need to happen in the moment. This is particularly true in the arena of teaching children how to handle their own day-to-day personal responsibilities. Our interviewee Dominique told us that she and her husband "have a list of pedestrian things that the kids can't leave home without knowing how to do, and their own laundry is one of them." When they first started in with the laundry expectation, though, things didn't go well. "We literally had a week or two where it was tie-dyed," Dominique says. "They ruined so many clothes, and my husband was like, beside himself." Dominique remembers the discussion in which she and her husband regrouped and recommitted to the plan. Dominique remembers saying, "They're kids. No one cares. Tie-dye is a thing. The bigger point is they need to learn how to do their laundry, and now is the time. They can't wait until they're adults." The two agreed, and eventually the laundry began to come out the same color it went in.

After this success, Dominique and her husband moved on to the cooking. Now she says, their eldest "probably does 50-60% of the evening cooking, and that's by design." But it wasn't always perfect with this effort either. "There were days and weeks where the food wasn't good," she said, "but we just kept eating it until it became good."

We can see in Dominique's story that the process of teaching your children how to handle their own personal responsibilities requires significant commitment. It's critical that you and your spouse are able to remain disciplined and aligned through the tie-dyed clothes, inedible food, and many other hurdles that will arise along the way. The incentive is that in doing so you will have raised a child who not only feels competent that they can take care of themselves (and eventually others), but also is able to relate to everyone else for whom doing these things for themselves is an economic necessity and basic reality of life.

How you'll create opportunities to allow your children to earn their own rewards

Another aspect of parenting well amid wealth that requires creative thinking and, as a result, benefits from you and your partner thinking about it ahead of time, is how you will create opportunities for your children to earn their own rewards. Wealth counselor, author, and inheritor Thayer Willis speaks to the need to do this in her book *Navigating the Dark Side of Wealth: A Life Guide for Inheritors*. She writes: "Keep this firmly in mind in regard to discipline and self-indulgence: *Children need to earn their rewards.* It gives them something to look forward to, which is highly important in preparing for adulthood. Providing them with occasional carefully chosen treats is fine, but indulging their every whim is not only ill-advised but also not very smart. Indulging your every whim where your children are involved is even less smart."[92]

We couldn't agree more. In fact, our interviewees shared with us powerful memories of how thrilling it was when their parents allowed them to experience the feeling that they had earned something on their own. Helen, who grew up in Portland, Maine, aware that her mother had inherited wealth through her great-grandfather's textile business, recounted to us the summer in her childhood when she and her brother were allowed to earn the money to buy a moped.

She opened the story by telling us, "There's one moment when I was younger that is imprinted in my mind, and my heart, and my soul, and it's so funny. And it was that, at one point, my brother and I said we wanted a moped. And my parents said, 'Yeah, well, if you guys want to get a moped, you have to buy the moped.'" She continues, "So, that suddenly made my brother and I spring into action, and I got a bunch of babysitting jobs. And my brother started a newspaper route. And eventually, we were able to earn enough money to get like the lowest level of moped. And I remember we had to share it. So, one day I would ride it. One day he would ride it. Our moped was so much slower than everybody else's. I would ride like crazy to try to catch up with everybody—like going down hills, I would never put on the brakes, and have it just go so fast, because I just wanted to catch up with everyone else."

She continues, "I just love the fact that they did that. And it was like we worked so hard, and we were so proud of that. I remember that I felt kind of proud that not a lot of other kids had to buy their own mopeds. Most kids, their parents gave them the newest, fanciest one, and each kid in the family got their own, and my brother and I had to share it. So, I think that was something my parents did that was really, really good."

Imagine how Helen's parents would feel if they knew that now, almost 40 years later, Helen can still recount this story in such detail—she can still remember the joy of flying down the hill and feel the pride that she felt in herself in that moment. A childhood of stringing together many moments like these is fundamentally what most parents want for their children.

But it takes work, and restraint. It's often easier to buy something than to think up ways for your children to feel like they earned it. And it takes a willingness to inconvenience (and perhaps create conflict with) your child by turning the task over to them. After all, when parents in a wealth-owning household try to insist that a child earn their own rewards, the child often picks up on what they perceive as illogic and points it out, occasionally with indignation. Parents faced with this reaction need to be prepared not only to remain aligned and stick to their plan, but also to explain to their child why they are doing this. I've seen in my work that a transparent message works best: "Of course I could buy this for you; but I want you to experience the satisfaction of being able to buy it for yourself."

There is another gift that parents impart when they allow their children to earn their own rewards—the ability not only to delay gratification but, importantly, to taste the sweetness of a reward that has long been anticipated. Our interviewee Justin, who grew up near Seattle, told us how his inheritor mother helped him experience this feeling. He started the story saying, "And this is one of my favorite memories, and I do carry this with me. I never had an allowance. But every month, as long as I did all my chores, which was like taking out the trash and emptying the dishwasher, my mom would take me to this music store in our town to pick out one CD that was like, 10 bucks." He remembers, "I could only get one. And it was, like, the most important day of the month when we would go there, because I was like, okay, I can only get one and I had been, like, wanting all these. You know, I love music, and I was, like, so entrenched in finding music from a really young age. So, I would spend hours in the store just trying to find the perfect album."

Justin told us that sometimes his mom would become annoyed by how long he was taking. But she kept bringing him every month for several years. "It wasn't just like, 'Oh, here's your allowance for the month. Here's 20 bucks.' It was like, 'Your allowance is that you can go and pick out a CD.'"

Think of the time Justin's mom invested in creating this experience of delayed gratification for her son. But it was worth it. Fifteen years later, this experience is still palpable for him. We were struck by the words both Helen and Justin chose when telling us these stories—Helen was "imprinted," and Justin still "carries" this memory with him. These words demonstrate how profound these experiences of earning rewards and delaying gratification can be to a young person, and how important they are developmentally to the young person's burgeoning sense of self. If you and your partner ever feel your resolve flagging when attempting to insist that your child earn their own rewards, remember how their future adult self will likely remember and recount the experience.

What it means to provide for your child

Ultimately, you and your partner need to ensure that you see eye-to-eye on what it means to provide for your child. Most parents subconsciously have a vision of the life they want to make possible for their children. This vision is often informed by each parent's own upbringing and represents an effort to either repeat the past or correct for it. It's important to ensure that you and your partner's visions are aligned, because it is often this subconscious vision that is in the driver's seat in in-the-moment parenting decisions.

Our interviewee Sebastian described to us how his vision has evolved over the years of marriage (and conversations) with his husband, Nicholas. "When I grew up, we were a middle-class family," Sebastian said. "We didn't have much, but I know when I wanted to have a child, I said to myself, 'Oh, I'm going to give my child everything. Give her things I couldn't have.'" But now he feels differently, informed by the discussions he and Nicholas have had over the years and the many experiences they have shared that have shown him the challenges that can come with excess wealth. As Sebastian put it, "It's about trying to find a balance, because you don't want to give them too much or spoil them too much."

Sebastian and Nicholas have brought their visions into alignment, and that makes it easier to agree on the many day-to-day choices parenting presents about how much to indulge your child. It's worth exploring this topic in depth with your partner so that you can get to the same degree of alignment. It can be difficult to change parenting behavior without understanding its underlying motivation, and it's often a misalignment in this underlying vision that is the source of parenting conflict.

Remember too when you're talking with your spouse to discuss not only the *money* you'll provide for your child, but also the *help* you'll provide, through your own efforts or influence, and where you will draw the line. Those of us who work in the wealth advising field know that the help parents provide their children (with everything from doing their homework to finding them a job) can be as damaging to the child's psychology as any money the child is given. Most parents understand this intellectually, but find it almost impossible to restrain themselves from helping when the opportunity presents itself. Refusing to help not only goes against most parents' natural instinct but also runs counter to another truth in our field—that one of the uses of wealth (or influence) parents typically say most appeals to them is using it to make a difference in the life of their child.

Because holding the line is so difficult, I've found it helpful for parents to have a simple aphorism or concept they can rely on to remind them of why it's important to minimize their role in their child's efforts. One I think works particularly well because it is so visual is a phrase coined by family wealth consultant Kristin Keffeler: "Put your hands in your pockets." As Keffeler writes in her book *The Myth of the Silver Spoon*: "It's a very effective but often underused parenting technique where, if you want your kids to learn something, don't do it for them; put your hands in your pockets and allow them to do it for themselves."[93]

I also find it useful for my clients, when their children ask for help, to keep in mind the following Sufi poem that author Lynne Twist references in her book *The Soul of Money* when writing about parenting effectively amid wealth:[94]

> "I asked for strength
> and God gave me difficulties to make me strong.
> I asked for wisdom
> and God gave me problems to learn to solve.
> I asked for prosperity
> and God gave me a brain and brawn to work.
> I asked for courage
> and God gave me dangers to overcome.
> I asked for love
> and God gave me people to help.
> I asked for favours
> and God gave me opportunities.
> I received nothing I wanted.
> I received everything I needed."
> —Hazrat Inayat Khan

What work ethic you will model

A final topic that we heard from our interviewees was important to discuss with your partner and get into alignment on was the type of work ethic that you want to model for your children. A chapter in my first book is dedicated to how parents can effectively inculcate a solid work ethic in their children. Chief among the findings of my research is that it is critical for parents to model a strong work ethic themselves. But this can be a challenge if you feel like your wealth has complicated your own work path or allowed you to design a life in which your own work is not particularly demanding. You might find that there are changes you want to make before your children begin to draw conclusions from the example they observe.

Our interviewees Harry and Zoey told us that they talk frequently about this issue. Harry is a screenwriter and Zoey is a set designer, but for a number of years, Harry's inherited wealth has made it possible for the couple to take work only when it fits in around other priorities in their family.

Now that their twins are getting older, though, they are working on changing this. "Both of us want to be more dedicated to our work so that when they start to come of age, they can experience that rather than be told," Harry says. "You know, you've got to work hard, right? I think that sort of leading by example is something that's important to us. And so, both of us have kind of redoubled our efforts to achieve. And put ourselves out there in a way that maybe we wouldn't have if we weren't concerned about the example that we are setting for them."

Zoey adds that they feel setting this example is particularly important given the other examples their children will see in the family—"Harry's cousins and how the wealth has affected them and seeing that, you know, nobody holds a job." She continued, "I think that's just something we want to make sure we don't instill in our kids."

Harry and Zoey are right to recognize that their own behavior will matter. And they're right to be thinking about it now, when they can begin to put in motion the changes they will need to make.

Two is better than one

As we can see from this section, the topics couples need to discuss and agree on in order to parent effectively amid wealth are deep and complex. But the good news is that you have each other. You have the benefit of two childhood experiences you can draw from. You can think about each of your experiences, lessons learned, compare and contrast pros and cons, and ultimately choose the approach you prefer (or a combined or wholly new approach that works best for you). The benefit of thinking deeply about the differences in your experiences is that you can use these differences as an advantage rather than a source of conflict.

And don't be afraid to get into the nitty-gritty when contrasting experiences. In parenting, the devil is in the details, and the more granular you can get in your vision, the better. As we saw earlier, Nathan and Louisa discussed summer jobs. Our interviewees Scarlett and Elliot talked about college funding (they preferred his experience of being involved in investing his 529 plan as a teenager to hers of not understanding what college cost) and spending in high school (again, they preferred his experience of receiving an allowance he could supplement with his earnings from summer jobs versus her experience of having her parents' credit card, which she says, "I would never give to my son").

Whatever the details, we hope these stories model how you and your partner can begin these discussions and the planning they inspire today so that you can look forward to co-parenting effectively and manifesting the goals you have for your children.

Putting it together: Creating a parenting plan

Some of my most fulfilling work is leading couples through the process of introspection, self-reflection, and goals articulation required to create (and stick to) a parenting plan that aligns with their hopes for their children. It's rewarding and cathartic for couples when this process reveals insights, flags areas where parenting behavior may be misaligned with goals, and identifies changes parents can make in their day-to-day behavior to more effectively bring about the outcomes they envision for their children.

A process to get started

While it can be helpful to have a coach or guide to facilitate you and your partner going through this process, you can also begin on your own by setting aside time together to contemplate and discuss the questions below. The goal of this process is to think deeply about your hopes for your children and the impact that you would like wealth to have in their lives and then use this thinking to assess whether your own behavior is consistent with these goals. The introspective thinking required is similar to the identity journey we covered in the first section of this book; the difference here is that you now are imbued with the agency of a parent. You are now in the powerful—yet paradoxically humbling—role of being the one whose decisions and actions might affect generations to come.

Questions for discussion with your partner (whether you already have children or they are contemplated down the road):

1. How do we each define success as a parent? What would constitute a job well done? What are our goals for our children, for the values we hope they will absorb, and the skills, capacities, and character traits they will develop?

2. What is the role we hope wealth will play in our children's lives? How would we want our children to describe the impact that wealth has had in their lives when they're grown?

3. For each of the first two questions, are our visions aligned? Why or why not? If not, are there aspects of each other's vision we can agree with? The goal is to build toward a consensus vision and to take note of areas where your visions are misaligned or inconsistent (as these are likely to cause friction down the road).

And some additional questions for couples who already have children:

4. How would we assess our success relative to our goals so far? Be honest with each other about where you think you're meeting your parenting goals and where you are falling short.

5. Where would we most like to close the gaps between our vision and the reality?

6. How might we change our day-to-day parenting behavior to begin closing these gaps? Which of our parenting behaviors, although well-intentioned, may be eliciting outcomes that are in conflict with our goals?

This last question is one where it can be particularly useful to have outside help. But if you're doing this on your own, try walking through a typical day in your parenting life and think about each of your parenting behaviors. Then look at each from the perspective of your child and ask whether the message your child would receive from the behavior is consistent with your parenting goals. For instance, if a stated parenting goal is that your child should be capable of managing their personal responsibilities on their own, but a parent is still cleaning the child's room or making the bed (or allowing it to remain unmade), this is an area where a change in parenting behavior could be effective.

Looking within

In addition to taking a hard look at parenting behaviors and the messages they send, successfully closing the gap between the goals you envision for your children and the reality that currently exists often involves looking within. Sometimes, our best parenting intentions are stymied or derailed by unspoken fears or uncomfortable personal histories that hijack our intentions. As we learned about earlier, both the inheritor and their partner go through their own journey adjusting to wealth, and parenting has a way of revealing any aspect of that journey that is still incomplete. The two of you can help each other to reflect honestly about your unspoken fears: What still makes you uncomfortable about wealth? What do you worry about when you think of how wealth might affect your children? Are there areas in your life you still feel like you struggle with as a result of wealth?

While the process of calling up your deep-seated fears or anxieties about wealth can be unsettling, ultimately, it's necessary not only so that you can parent with a clear-eyed approach (versus one that is influenced or blown off course by subconscious insecurities or concerns), but also so that you can model a healthy integration of identity and wealth. In their article summarizing the dilemmas inheritors face, family wealth consultants and psychologists Dennis Jaffe and Jim Grubman write, "The thoughtfulness by which parents teach their children seems to be connected to the parents' own stage of development and self-understanding. If parents have grown to a more mature view of money and wealth, they are then able to convey it to their children...."[95]

Wealth counselor and inheritor John Levy expands on this point, writing in his book:

> "It is important for wealthy parents to teach their children constructive ways of living with their wealth. This starts with the parents themselves being relatively comfortable, clear, and balanced about their own wealth, free of both pride and shame about it. Parents need to start with a good look at themselves, searching out their own attitudes toward affluence and what comes with it, and then working through whatever they find that is

unresolved, as best they can, in order to avoid contaminating their children. Parents need to demonstrate healthy and appropriate ways of using money wisely, avoiding the extremes of profligacy and penury. The manner in which parents manage their own money inevitably serves to teach their children about ethical and psychological values far more than what the parents tell them."[96]

We couldn't agree more. It's worth reflecting on what your children would currently be taught by the way in which you manage and think about your money. Or said differently, if wealth is a tool, what kind of tool would your children conclude it is, based on your own behavior?

We'll devote more time in the last chapter to thinking about the uses of your wealth, but for now it's enough to think about the story your children would write from your actions and whether it's the narrative you would choose to be written. In fact, it's often the parenting role itself that acts as a catalyst for couples to begin to think more proactively about this issue. As our interviewee Oliver put it, "I think having kids sort of crystallized for us that we are going to be dealing with this wealth in one way or another, and it's better to start being more intentional about it and figuring out how to use it for better things or to serve others or to sort of do things differently, as opposed to just ignoring it and not dealing with it."

We also saw that when our interviewees had a clear sense of the purpose of wealth in their lives, it was easier for them to weave these values into their day-to-day parenting messages around money. Our interviewee Dominique talked with us about the process she had just gone through with her teenage son to set him up with a debit card linked to an online account funded with his own money and the intense negotiations the two of them had to determine which expenses he would be responsible for ("At some point, I had to say, best, last, and final offer," she laughed.) But woven throughout their horse-trading of video games versus Xbox membership versus Uber Eats, etc. was a deeper message. As Dominique told us, "We are a family of faith, and there's a scripture that we're often talking to the kids about that says, 'A good man leaveth an inheritance for his children's children.' So, during the very tense negotiations with the 14-year-old, one of the things I was really homing in on with him was, 'I want you, son, to be more than a consumer. Money is a tool.'"

Seeking wisdom, not perfection

It's not easy to look within. It can be challenging—but ultimately enlightening and sometimes life-changing—to ask yourself the question: am I the grown-up that I want my child to be? And do I think about, interact with, and feel about my wealth the way I hope my child will? If your answers to these questions are "not really" or "not yet," it's worth reflecting deeply on why that's not the case and what you might want to change as a result. As parenting coach Bonnie Harris says, "Parenting is engaging in a process of self-discovery so that we may develop the confidence to support and guide our children in ways that fully accept who they are." This is particularly true in the realm of inheritance.

To be clear, it's not necessary or even feasible to emerge from this process of self-discovery with perfection—with all inner wealth conflicts resolved, skills learned, and faults corrected. In fact, just the opposite. We find that parents who are honest with themselves and with their children about areas they have struggled with as a result of wealth can be even more effective than those who try to portray invincibility. These parents empathize with their children and model not only vulnerability but also that they have traveled the same journey and continue to put in the effort to improve themselves, improve their relationship to wealth, and conquer any lingering fears. Your having the courage to grow and learn will inspire your children to do the same. Share with them what you are learning about yourself.

Now is the time

If you've read this chapter but have decided to put its questions aside and come back to them at a later date because your children are too young (or not yet here), we would argue that now is the time. The perfect time to do the type of deep self-reflection and learning necessary to be a proactive and intentional parent is before you need it, before the exhaustion of the new baby phase, the three-ring circus of the toddler phase, or the fully scheduled school phase. In short, the time to think about these issues is now, when you can think! It's far easier to triage the constant decision-making required of parents if you have already done the hard work of articulating your values, reflecting on your own inner conflicts, and committing to an approach that is aligned with your goals in advance.

But if you're putting these questions aside for another reason—that you think they are irrelevant because your children are older and you feel that the die is cast—I'll share that some of the most meaningful work I feel I do is when I help parents go through this process when their children are in their teens or 20s. Those of us who work in this field know that many of the saddest examples of parents hoping for one outcome but enabling another with misaligned behavior manifests when children are this age, as these are the ages when the impact of wealth can most derail a child's decision-making and life trajectory. This also tends to be when it's most important for parents to be on the same page, as children of this age understand how to leverage parenting disagreements to their advantage. Finally, if going through this process when your children are older reveals decisions either you or your partner regret, even these revelations can ultimately serve your parenting—not only do you have an opportunity to course-correct, but more importantly, you have an opportunity to share your fallibility with your child. It's remarkable how children respond to vulnerability, particularly when they are at an age when they are trying to get out from under the shadow of a parent who otherwise may seem quite successful.

Regardless of the age of your children, commit to engaging with this work and becoming the parent you hope to be. I know that in reality, few parents make the time to do this. If this is you, and if you find that this chapter—and these questions—keep falling to the bottom of your to-do list, seek help. Just like a physical trainer can motivate you to do the exercise you know is imperative for your health, a parenting coach or (well-informed) wealth advisor can inspire you to make the same life-enhancing commitment to this exercise.

CHAPTER NINE

Breaking Free

We saw in the previous chapter that parenthood can prompt in an inheritor and their partner a desire to be more intentional about the purpose of their wealth. Our interviewees shared that parenthood can prompt something else as well—a desire to break free. This was particularly true of our interviewees who had found it challenging to assert their own identity amid the gravitational pull of their origin family's wealth management infrastructure and influences (e.g., enabling support, family office protocols, collective family decision-making, etc.). Now parents themselves, these inheritors and their partners envisioned how these same influences might play out in the lives of their children, or impair their ability to parent as they chose, and felt an urgent need to make a change.

In fact, we saw a breaking point emerge for any parent (even those without this personal history) when they sensed their wishes for how to parent amid wealth—on issues such as when to tell their children about the family wealth, when to provide them with distributions, or how involved the family office should be in their lives—begin to diverge from others in the family system, including trustees, wealth advisors, the family office, or other family members. Parents who faced this disconnect and sensed no willingness for the broader system to change often reached the conclusion that they must break free—or at least break loose—of these relationships in order to parent as they saw best.

We saw the need to break free manifest in our interviewees for another reason as well. For many, exercising agency in their wealth management relationships was the next and necessary step in the identity journey begun in Section One. In keeping with the question we asked last chapter, "Am I the grown-up I want to be?" (for yourself, for your children), the wealth management arena stood out for many of our interviewees as a remaining area where they felt they were not. They were still in a passive, subordinate (in other words, childlike) role. This chapter is about how our interviewees claimed agency in these relationships—either by replacing them or changing them—and about the possibilities that opened up for them when they (finally) felt that their wealth management ecosystem aligned with their values.

What it feels like to break free

As you'll hear from our interviewees, this process of breaking free can take years, even decades. And it can be so emotionally difficult as to at times feel paralyzing. But it's worth it. The relief, excitement, hope, and newfound sense of wholeness we heard in the voices of our inheritors who finally felt free—to lead an authentic life, parent in a manner consistent with their values, and work with an advisor who understood *their* goals—was palpable.

Before we hear our interviewees' stories, though, we wanted to note a recurring pattern we saw in our interviews—our inheritor interviewees often credited their partner with opening their eyes to a new perspective (a sense that there might be a reasonable solution other than whatever the family defined as the norm) and then having the determination, persistence, and courage to enable the couple together to step out to find this new solution. As our interviewee Tim puts it,

"When you grow up in a culture, it's harder to find the resilience, or the strength, or the understanding even to kind of pull back and say, huh, maybe this isn't right. I think it's the benefit of having a spouse—that they help you kind of look outside of what you've grown up in and can empower you in ways that you never would have." It's poignant that, in a multigenerational wealth setting, this fact pattern might contribute to an inheritor's partner being viewed by the wealth-owning family as an instigator—in reality, though, they are simply reminding the inheritor of their own basic human need to experience self-definition and autonomy, and then imbuing them with the confidence and fortitude necessary to go out and find it.

Fundamentally, we saw that this process of breaking free was about thinking for yourself versus accepting as a given all that the inherited family wealth system mandated. And while this breaking free didn't need to be absolute or forever, it did need to be effective—it had to create a realignment, a reprioritization, that allowed the inheritor and their partner to claim their agency and shape the system sufficiently so that this agency could be expressed.

So, in which areas of the wealth management ecosystem did our interviewees feel it was most important to break free? In short, any and all areas that had a meaningful impact on their life. We'll take them one by one and see not only how our interviewees effected a change but also what it felt like when they eventually found new solutions that reflected their authentic selves.

Breaking free from the family trustee

Helen remembers hearing as she grew up the special tone of reverence her mother would reserve for the trust company that managed the family's inherited wealth. The company had been investing the assets inherited by Helen's mother's generation for more than 30 years, had grown the assets substantially, and was now the sole advisor for 15 family members. "It was almost as if the money was theirs," Helen says.

Embedded in the relationship was an unquestioned family assumption that the trust company knew best. And a certain degree of "old-school" (and patriarchal) elusiveness. Helen remembers the time her mother, "who is painfully fearful of numbers," asked the lead trustee, "So, how much money do I have?" and he replied "Oh, Jeanine, you don't want to know."

In keeping with the family assumption that the trust company was infallible, Helen spent her early 20s dutifully following along, dressing up whenever she had to go to their offices to ask for a distribution (she remembers, "It was always a little bit scary, and I think they kind of wanted it that way"), attending the family meetings held at the trust company offices—in which invariably a family member would open the session by praising the company's investment performance and stewardship—and even signing the prenuptial agreement the trustees informed her would be required when she married her husband, Stefan.

But when Helen and Stefan became parents, the two of them began to question this arrangement. Helen says, "I did not want my kids to go through what I went through at all." As Stefan remembers it, Helen "started thinking about her own experience, and wondering, 'What will this do to our kids?' And decided we have to do something about this. We were like, wow this is our family. This is our kids."

They started by setting up meetings with the trustees for just the two of them (versus with the rest of the family), hoping they could learn more this way and exert more agency. But, Stefan says, "We never gained any traction. They were always ready to meet with us, but they weren't going to divulge anything. They weren't going to help us from that point of view."

The breaking point came several years later when the trustees informed them that they had set up trusts for the benefit of their children. As Stefan remembers, "They had done this behind my back and behind Helen's back. Not asking what we want for our kids or how we'd want them managed. Nothing like that." He continued, "That really made me feel like my role as a father was completely undermined." Helen remembers Stefan saying at the time, "It's not that I don't want our kids to have any money. But *I* want to decide how we're going to give them money."

The couple decided they needed to make a change. Thus began a five-year process of various logistical hurdles including hiring a family wealth consultant, a new attorney, and ultimately a new wealth advisor and trustee. But harder than the logistical steps was the emotional process. There was the termination meeting itself in which the head trustee said, "I can't believe it, I can't believe it, after all we've done for you." There were the calls from family members informing Helen that the trustees were hurt and the intimations that she should no longer attend the family meetings held at their offices. And there was the guilt Helen herself felt because of the "teeny part of me that feels like it is their money because they made it—they invested it in such a way to make it grow." All in all, she remembers this period of separation as "so hard, so hard. It's just so hard to get out of."

But now, ten years on, Helen and Stefan's only regret is that they didn't make this change earlier. She and Stefan describe their new advisory team as their partners. "I feel like we're just sort of holding hands and walking forward towards a common goal," Helen says, "which is education and understanding, with the finances behind us. Moving forward and bringing positivity and goodness." And they have buckled down with their new team to begin to plan proactively for the impact their wealth will have on their children. All in all, they feel that the change "really set us free."

Breaking loose from the family office

Our interviewees Alice and Tim have spent recent years reflecting on the impact Tim's multigenerational family office has had in their lives and whether they would like the same for their teenagers. As Alice puts it, "We're thinking about the learned helplessness that the situation has brought to our lives, which we've fought hard against, and reject for our kids. It's not healthy. It's not good for them."

Both Alice and Tim feel that their quest to forge their own identity in life was affected by the (albeit well-intentioned) influence of the family office—the requests to serve in governance and due diligence roles, the offer of services that obviated their need to master "adulting skills," and the free distribution of wealth and accompanying message that work was not necessary. As a result, they have concluded they want something different for their children. As Tim puts it, "It's easy to inherit or fall into a system like we did. We got married and this system was created, and you're just kind of floating along, and the next thing you know, your identity is wrapped up in it. But if you look at what that means and the obstacles that puts up for your kids to create their own sense of identity—whoa, wait a minute. I wouldn't wish this on anybody."

How to effect this transition is what they are discussing now. The fact that their children are rapidly reaching the age of eligibility for distributions of family wealth has awakened in the couple an urgent need to exercise their agency as parents if they want to avoid repeating the past. While the question has crossed their mind about whether they should remain with the family office in the long-term (as Alice puts it, "What are the benefits of it, and are they necessary?"), they are focused in the immediate term on working within the system to influence the magnitude of the distributions and to limit the life assistance the family office offers their children.

They feel like they're making some headway, partially because of how strongly they have advocated for their position, and partially because the family office head has demonstrated flexibility and has grown over time, as Tim puts it, "more comfortable helping us make choices that are independent of other family members and for the benefit of what we think is important to us."

They also think their children's own efforts have made a difference. All three have held summer jobs and family office executives "see how proud they are of making their own money." As a result, they are now working to ensure that distributions are structured in a way that won't disrupt this process.

Embedded in Tim and Alice's story, and particularly in their desire to draw the line on how much the family office helps their children, is a lesson to the wealth advising industry. In the last decade, the industry has made a welcome shift, broadening its focus from just the money (investment returns and wealth transfer strategies, etc.) to the well-being of the wealth-owning family and particularly the "next gen." There is a double-edged sword in this shift, though.

While it's true that the industry's efforts to preserve wealth will be largely irrelevant if they leave a younger generation feeling entitled, enabled, or adrift, the solution to this problem is rarely a cadre of (well-meaning) advisors and family office executives enveloping a young person and focusing intently on helping them to develop their personal potential. What most young people need is the space to do that on their own. They desperately need a chance to invest in themselves without their eventual success, accomplishments, even drive itself, being able to be tied back to (and therefore attributed to) their family. Ironically, it may be that the best thing our industry can do to "prepare the next generation" is to envision how these young people would prepare themselves for life if we weren't there and then do everything in our power to allow them to do that.

Finding a new advisor

Our interviewee Lucy, whom we met in Section One, shared with us that a "really important milestone" in her "developmental arc" of integrating self with wealth was replacing the wealth advisor she had inherited from her parents with one that cared about and encouraged her to articulate *her* goals.

Lucy explained that when her father died, making her the unexpected beneficiary of a $20 million trust, she began to work with the wealth advisory team her father had hired years earlier to manage the family's wealth. Lucy's relationship with the team was perfunctory. "I would get quarterly calls," Lucy recalls, where the advisor would say, "'Hey, I just want to let you know the S&P was down two, you're only down one, we're doing great.'" Lucy remembers, "And I would be like, 'great,' I don't even know what that means, you know what I mean? That was it." She explains that at that point in her life, "I didn't know that it could be different. I didn't know that it should be different. I didn't know that I should want anything else. I was like, I'm supposed to take these calls every three months, and be like, 'thanks for letting me know.'"

This went on for a decade until about four years ago, Lucy's best friend from childhood joined a comprehensive, holistic wealth management firm (not ours, by the way!) and described to Lucy what they offer. Lucy remembers saying to her husband, "This sounds really good. We're not getting this now." The couple decided to explore moving some of their assets and remembers the first meeting with the new firm in which the team (diplomatically) inquired why Lucy and her husband were considering keeping a portion of their assets with an advisor who clearly wasn't focused on their goals. "I mean that was just like mind blowing for us," Lucy said. "We were like, wait, what are our goals? And it was so helpful because we never ever had that conversation, because we inherited the team that managed the money. And so, hiring the new firm was really one of the steps, one of the important milestones of me having more agency and authority around engaging with wealth and making decisions."

Lucy's description of how her parent's advisor related to her is sadly a familiar tale. Authors Jay Hughes, Susan Massenzio, and Keith Whitaker speak to this dynamic in their book *The Voice of the Rising Generation*: "You may wonder, 'Who is truly standing for me and not just for my money?'... Most advisers to families with significant wealth or businesses also operate within the gravitational pull of that same black hole. That is why 95 percent of you, the rising generation, leave your parents' advisers as soon as you receive gifts and 98 percent of you leave your parents' advisers once your parents have died."[97]

Whether those percentages (sourced from a 2011 study) are still that high, the underlying message is valid, that many inheritors ultimately leave their parents' advisor because they don't feel recognized as their own people, separate from the larger family wealth system. If you wonder if this is you and whether you should make a change, ask yourself if your family's wealth advisor treats you as being in charge of your own life? Do they ask you about your goals, versus just convey to you your family's goals? In short, do you feel like you have agency in the relationship and that this advisor is "standing for you"? If not, maybe it's time to make a change. It might turn out, as it did for Lucy, to be a necessary stepping-stone along the journey of integrating self and wealth.

And as you contemplate a change, remember what Lucy ultimately found. Her new advisor focused their conversations not on investment returns but on Lucy's goals and on how she could harness her wealth to have greater impact in the areas of her life she found important.

Too many young inheritors have been made to feel that they are somehow ill-equipped to manage an inheritance unless they are interested in the investment part of the meetings with their wealth advisor (or master specialized financial skills like picking money managers, assessing portfolio risk, and sourcing private investment deals). In reality, having skilled professionals who can handle these tasks for you is one of the reasons to hire a wealth advisor, and the majority of clients of firms like ours delegate these responsibilities so that they can be free to engage fully in the areas of their lives that matter to them. So instead of trying to master investment knowledge (or feeling bad that you haven't and have no interest in doing so), focus on choosing a professional advisor you can trust to stand for you and having an accountability process in place (like an articulated list of goals—and not just investment goals!—and periodic reporting against those goals) to reaffirm this trust on an ongoing basis.

Redefining family togetherness

One final note on Lucy's story—when I mentioned to her the 95% statistic about inheritors leaving their parents' advisor, she said, "I'm actually surprised the number is so high, because there is so much inertia. So much inertia." She said that when her new advisor delicately asked her why she had remained with the former advisor for so long, she responded, "I was like 'For so many reasons!' What if I make the wrong decision, right? My siblings are still all-in there. So if my husband and I make a change, there's going to be some difference in the ledger, either positive or negative. Like, how am I going to explain that to my children?" Lucy's fear about how her decision to leave her parents' advisor would forever be compared to the rest of the family's decision to remain demonstrates how challenging it can be to break from the family norm.

Reinforcing this is the oft repeated refrain within the wealth advising industry that "together is better." Our industry presents staying together as normal—much of the family wealth advising industry revolves around the institutions and mechanisms of togetherness (governance, councils, retreats). While these tools emerged from the family business or "enterprise" arena, where they are often beneficial, they are now applied with a broad brush to the entire landscape of family *wealth*, even though there is far less need for family coordination when inherited assets are in the form of an investment portfolio.

Compounding this, there is a pull to *create* structures that necessitate togetherness, even when none is required. This may be due partly to economics (the industry is more scalable when families aggregate assets and more in demand when families seek help to work together effectively), but less cynically, may simply be the result of well-meaning advisors doing their best to serve their "G1" clients, who typically derive a sense of meaning and fulfillment from seeing the rest of the family (i.e., their children) work together to manage the family's wealth.

But, often these "children," now adults themselves with their own nuclear families as their first priority, feel differently. Our interviewee Tim told us, "Historically, and especially in our family, when you have wealth managers trying to figure out how to pass the wealth on from one generation to the next, they create all these structures, all these trusts that are combined, so it's generational versus individual. You're just setting up systems where everyone is forced to stay together.... Sometimes it's two generations, sometimes it's five generations, but eventually, you've got people who are stuck together and don't know anything about each other or don't like each other."

A number of our interviewees echoed Tim sentiments. And explained that their impetus to pull away from this enforced togetherness became strongest when their parenting preferences began to diverge from others they felt locked together with. Stefan told us that part of his and Helen's decision to leave the family trustee was due to the enabling culture the trustee fostered in the family and that other family members' parenting styles reinforced. Seeing how family members "had been very negatively affected by their access to money—

living in a parallel universe where there's no accountability, no obligation to earn a living or be part of society, just drifting aimlessly through life," they now saw the pattern repeating in the next generation. As Stefan puts it, "We could see a parallel in Helen's cousins and how they were treating their kids who are five to ten years older than ours." He concludes, "That's a whole other reason Helen and I went so far as to break away."

In truth, it's normal for parenting preferences to diverge across family members (just as divergences emerge among siblings or cousins in geography, career choice, and political persuasion). The challenge is when the enmeshment fostered by the wealth advising industry and family wealth management structures makes it impossible to exercise your own parenting preferences or to do so without looking like you are rejecting a family norm or passing judgment on other family members' parenting choices.

And as we discussed earlier, the drive to go your own way goes even beyond parenting preferences to a deeper, more fundamental need to align wealth (and its attendant ecosystem and advisory relationships) with self. It is a drive that is not only normal, but that manifests in each successive generation. Throughout my interviewees, regardless of the interviewee's age or the number of generations from wealth creation, I heard a common theme—a natural generational pull to go your own way, carve out your own path in life, and be free from the constraints and structures put in place by those who've come before.

Tim and Alice reflected poignantly on how the very family office they have made steps to break loose from was itself created in his mother's generation in a bid to carve out a path separate from the rest of her family. "Freedom," Alice said. "That was the word. Freedom from the other cousins, which is so interesting. So, here we are 30 years later, thinking about the same thing, but just the next spiral, the next generation."

So, if breaking away is normal, why don't we treat it that way (rather than stigmatizing it as a failure or a breakdown in family governance)? And how might we redefine family togetherness to accommodate this norm? What if, rather than our industry creating wealth management structures that glued family members together, we set as a goal to enable each nuclear family to design a wealth management ecosystem that afforded them as much autonomy from other family members as possible, and then found other ways to foster the type of togetherness that most families enjoy?

In short, what if we stopped conflating successful wealth preservation with families remaining together? After all, you don't need convoluted structures tying family members together to responsibly manage inherited assets, and you don't need assets at all (or wealth management structures) to share loving, rewarding, life-enhancing relationships with family. In fact, it's often just the opposite—we often see that it's not until individuals are allowed to go their own way that friction is relieved, family relationships improve, and family members *choose* to spend time together or even work jointly on areas of shared interest (e.g., philanthropy). Collective efforts that arise once everyone is free to go their own way feel different because all the players are there because they *want* to be.

If after reading this section, you are now contemplating breaking free, but fear that your family relationships will be forever impaired, take heart in the words of clinical psychologist and family wealth consultant Jamie Weiner: "Family connections are hard to break. And often good to break. Breaking away is painful but leads to growth.... Breaking need not cause a permanent ending of relationships, but it does change the family dynamics.... A family that undergoes the torque and strain of breaking away can also reshape and strengthen their relationships."[98] In other words, families that allow their members to strike out for autonomy can then enjoy real togetherness, an authentic togetherness, where everyone is allowed to be themselves.

Redefining "stewardship"

The phrase "prepare the next generation to be good stewards of wealth" has become commonplace, often used by advisors as a shorthand to convey to their wealth-generating clients that they have programs and other offerings designed to train these clients' children how to preserve the assets they will eventually inherit.

But how does it feel to be the young inheritor who is the object of this phrase? Charlotte Beyer said it best in her book *Wealth Management Unwrapped* when she titled the section devoted to this topic, "When I grow up I want to be a steward (said no one ever)."[99] Charlotte's humor cuts to the core of what is wrong with the concept of preparing an inheritor for stewardship. Stewardship should not be the goal in itself. It's true that stewardship often manifests when an inheritor forges their own path to a self-driven life. But ironically, setting it out as the primary goal can derail that path. As Charles Lowenhaupt writes, "Becoming a 'family wealth steward' is not a road to freedom; instead the family wealth steward is enslaved in the infrastructure of family wealth. The culture of stewardship takes away that freedom to pursue self-actualization and leaves a person incapable of becoming all he or she can become."[100]

Beyond the point that stewardship should not be an end in itself, we find that the connotations of the word (preserving, protecting) don't comport with what the inheritors we spoke with most wrestled with when thinking about the assets they will inherit. They were focused on how to harness their inherited wealth to live a life of meaning, purpose, and contribution to the broader world, how best to communicate about their wealth to set their own children up for a healthy integration of self and wealth, and how to decide, ultimately, when to say enough—in other words, how much and how best to question the very assumption that dynastic accumulation and growth of assets should be the goal. We'll illustrate these one by one.

How to harness wealth

Our interviewee Justin described to us how one of the things he most appreciates about the peer group he has joined is that it's given him a place he can talk with other inheritors about their responsibilities to the world as a result of their position—"to feel this sense of community amongst other people who are asking the same questions, and are feeling the same things, who are independent thinkers," he says. "A lot of us are sort of like, 'Wait, hold on a second. Let's stop everything. Why are we getting this money? Who is it for? How do we use this? What's the responsibility?'" He says there is a palpable sense within the group that, "We have to rethink this [conventional expectations of stewardship and wealth preservation], because we're living in a world where a lot of people are really hurting. So, you know, what can we do to be helpful and really make sure that we have an impact."

Justin acknowledges that "It's not a very traditional approach to wealth and family wealth," and talks about how grateful and honored he is that his parents have left the decision of what to do with his inheritance up to him. "They didn't say things like, you have to use it for this, this, and this. Or you can't give it all away. They were just like, hey, this is yours, it's a lot of responsibility. Think about it and, you know, if you want to talk about it, we're here for you."

Justin says this freedom has only increased the sense of gravity with which he approaches the question of how best to use his inheritance. "When you give people trust and responsibility, they want to deliver. I want to make my parents proud. I want to feel proud of the work that I'm doing." So far he says he's on track. "I feel really good about how I'm using the wealth to engage in philanthropic endeavors. I feel more whole in my identity because it is true to me as a person."

How to communicate about wealth

An area we saw our interviewees wrestle with as they began to construct a wealth management ecosystem that was their own was the question of how they would communicate about their wealth to their children. The question of what to say and when can be especially vexing to the inheritor partner if they remember the experience of learning about their own inheritance as painful.

But having lived through an experience you found suboptimal can also be an advantage. You understand how your children might feel. And you have a much better sense of what you'd like to avoid. Our interviewee Penelope, whose father founded a successful furniture manufacturing business, told us, "We grew up without really having a number in our heads or a clear understanding of what we had access to or what we would someday have to manage. And I'm almost 50, and I'm still not in charge of that." She says that the part that is hardest is that "How I look at myself as an adult is tied up in 'Do you not trust me enough to handle this responsibility?'"

This is the part she's most determined to change for her own children. She says that she and her husband have agreed that "we are going to have to do this completely differently for our girls so that they aren't paralyzed like that. I want them to understand. We are going to need to empower them and make sure that they know what they're working with and that they know how to handle themselves and that they trust themselves."

When to say "enough"

Our interviewees Scarlett and Elliot, whom we met in chapter 6, told us about a conversation with her father about his plans to use a wealth transfer technique to set funds aside for their child when Scarlett was expecting. "My dad called me," Scarlett says, "and he was, rightfully, so excited and enthusiastic about this chunk of money that he was going to be able to give our child. And was saying he was going to set this trust up and isn't this great. And I said, 'Yes, and thank you very much, and I'm very appreciative, but this is also something I'd need to talk to Elliot about.'"

Scarlett remembers that there was a long pause and her father asked, "What's that mean?" What she meant was that, while she appreciated the motivation behind her father's gift, she expected to be consulted, and to have a chance to discuss it with her husband, the child's father, before the decision was made.

"We're the unit now, and that needs to be sacred," Scarlett said. "Nor are we preoccupied with the handing down of wealth through the generations." Elliot chimes in, "Yeah, I think both of us want our child or children to have opportunity and be comfortable, but not so comfortable that they never have to struggle or fight for anything on their own. And not have any sense that they need to provide for themselves or, you know, do something productive with their life."

While it wasn't the easiest discussion with her father, Scarlett said that fundamentally it was important for her and Elliot "to really draw a line around our unit and not make it about my family coming in and dictating how they feel about money. I think it's just so important to carve out your own philosophies about it. And I do think it's important to be explicit."

We heard in both Scarlett's and Justin's stories that neither prioritized the goal of increasing how much their future children would inherit. There were goals they valued more—for Justin it was the chance to use his wealth to beneficially impact the world, and for Scarlett it was prioritizing her marital unit and exerting agency in her parenting preferences. But also, both fundamentally questioned whether dynastic accumulation of wealth was a worthy (or even ethical) goal.

Readers wondering whether this line of thinking might be the ideological province of only millennials (or inheritors) might find it surprising that, more than a century ago, industrialist Andrew Carnegie expressed a similar view in his seminal *The Gospel of Wealth*: "Why should men leave great fortunes to their children? If this is done from affection, is it not misguided affection? Observation teaches that, generally speaking, it is not well for the children that they should be so burdened. Neither is it well for the State.... Wise men will soon conclude that, for the best interests of the members of their families, and of the State, such bequests are an improper use of their means."[101]

Regardless of where you come down on the question of how much wealth you should leave to your children, part of the process of breaking free is to own the answer to this question yourself. It is now your turn to decide—and to ensure that whatever you decide is consistent with your values, your parenting goals, and your hopes for how your children will one day describe how wealth has impacted them.

"Next gen" no more

What we've heard in our interviewees' stories in this chapter is the difference between stewardship—as it is broadly understood—and ownership. It's the difference between a passive backseat ride toward someone else's vision and a driver's seat, hands-on-the-wheel steering toward your own—informed by the acknowledgment of the power (and responsibilities, burdens, risks, etc.) of the vehicle under your control. Doing this well (even getting into the driver's seat at all) often necessitates breaking away from the structures, decisions, and dreams of those who've come before you and striking out on your own. Even if you ultimately decide you want to drive to the same destination, you won't know for sure until you're behind the wheel—and finally think of yourself as a "next gen" no more.

And if amidst the inevitable hurdles you encounter as you make your way from the backseat up to the front you begin to feel your resolve flagging, be buoyed by the words (rallying cry) of our interviewee Abby: "I think there's a lot of infantilizing of adults, of younger adults, you know, the inheritors, the 'next gen.' Like, why are you a next gen, you're 40 years old, this is crazy. You know, why is this space totally infantilizing grown people?" She continues, "I think that my grandmother was making so many choices all the way up until she died for, like, the whole family. I think being the holder of the money creates these different dynamics around independence. But at any stage in your life, you do have the wisdom to make choices for yourself."

We agree. Exercising choice is the first step in exerting agency. And it's the first step in being able to take sufficient ownership over your wealth to truly make it your own.

Chapter Ten

....

Fully Engaged

In his book, *Spiritual Evolution*, psychiatrist George Vaillant, who spent 30 years at the helm of Harvard's Study of Adult Development (one of longest studies ever conducted of adult life, beginning with participants in 1938 and now grown to include more than 1,300 of their children), writes, "successful human development involves, first, absorbing love, next, reciprocally sharing love, and finally, giving love unselfishly away."[102]

Writer and theologian Frederick Buechner covers a similar terrain, but layers in the wrinkle of how wealth intersects with this developmental arc: "The trouble with being rich is that, since you can solve with your checkbook virtually all of the practical problems that bedevil ordinary people, you are left in your leisure with nothing but the great human problems to contend with: how to be happy, how to love and be loved, how to find meaning and purpose in your life."[103]

We agree with both of them—that this developmental arc is necessary, that love is at its core, and that the opportunity of wealth can paradoxically make it harder. This is the landscape we have aimed to travel in this book. Hopefully if you've read this far, you feel better equipped to travel it yourself. Perhaps you're even well on your way, having dispelled with any shame you might have felt as an inheritor, feeling buoyed by the life partner at your side, and beginning to look outward to how you might channel your wealth into contribution, meaning, and purpose.

Our interviewees shared with us how this arc played out for them, and how it was iterative—that the love of a partner not only lightened the load (as our interviewee Duncan said, reflecting back on almost 40 years of marriage to Beatrice, "It's easier to go through life in a team than it is alone") but also bolstered their sense of self sufficiently that they could begin to look outside themselves.

Helen told us that she credits her husband Stefan's support and persistence with imbuing her with the courage to finally step away from the enabling family wealth culture she inherited, telling us, "I have to applaud Stefan—none of this would have happened without him." And then she shares the internal transformation that has manifested since. "It is absolutely so liberating and invigorating," she says, "and it really has done so much for me as a person." She tells us that she finally feels acceptance. "I'm not sure I can articulate this properly," she says, "but I guess being okay with having money. Really being okay with it. It took me so long, but I did." And she feels energized and engaged by how she and Stefan might work together to harness their wealth: "Our whole ability to understand and plan for our philanthropy has blossomed in a way that makes me really, really happy. That is very meaningful to me."

Our interviewee Lucy described a similar transformation that has unfolded for her as she emerged from the isolation she felt around her wealth in her 20s to the integration she feels now 20 years on, in a supportive partnership with her husband and leading the organization she founded to empower affluent white women to use their purchasing power to help close the racial wealth gap. She tells us, "It is truly the highest and best use. I have found this perfect marrying of my capacity to persuade others, to build partnerships, and really build a new conversation about white wealth." And when I ask her if finding this "highest and best use" has led to more acceptance of her wealth, she answers, "Oh yeah. Because it's like, great, look at what I have to work with. Look at what impact I can make on the world if I can integrate my values with my wealth. I can die feeling like I've lived a good life." She adds, "That was very dramatic. But you know what I mean? I think one of my deepest fears is what if I get to the end and I look back and I'm like, I wasted it. I wasted an opportunity or a thousand opportunities."

We can hear in both Helen's and Lucy's voices relief, jubilation, urgency—or as Lynne Twist puts it in *The Soul of Money*, "the rush of energy unleashed" when money is brought into alignment with "the fulfillment of soul" and used to "express our humanity—our highest ideals and our most soulful commitments and values."[104] At long last, and after many twists and turns, they each have integrated their sense of self with the presence of inherited wealth in their lives and are well on their way to the vision of a life well-lived that both Vaillant and Buechner described.

My hope with writing the book is that many more will feel as they do. If you're not there yet, if you feel like you're still at the beginning of your journey and that shame, fear, distrust, or insecurity are holding you back, take heart in the words of Lucy, Helen, and our other interviewees. Believe them when they say this can be done, that you can feel this way too. And know that when you get there, you will have earned it. After all, no inheritance—money, influence, or otherwise—can give you confidence in yourself, a sense of purpose, and trust and joy in the loving partner by your side. When you achieve these things—the things that turn out to matter most in life—you'll know that you (and your partner) have yourselves to thank.

Section Four

Appendices

Relationship Movies that Will Make You Think (and Hope)

Themes we've explored:

Movies, in chronological order:	Forging a sense of self amid wealth and/or family expectations	Role of significant other in bolstering this sense of self	Navigating disparate backgrounds	Seeking broader family acceptance
It Happened One Night (1934)	x	x	x	x
Holiday (1938)	x	x	x	x
The Philadelphia Story (1940)	x	x	x	
Roman Holiday (1953)	x	x		
Guess Who's Coming to Dinner (1967)			x	x
Love Story (1970)	x	x	x	x
Moonstruck (1987)	x	x		
Coming to America (1988)	x	x	x	x
Mystic Pizza (1988)	x	x	x	x
My Big Fat Greek Wedding (2002)	x	x	x	x
Crazy Rich Asians (2018)	x	x	x	x

Recommended Reading

Section One

Life Is What You Make It: Find Your Own Path to Fulfillment
by Peter Buffett

Man's Search for Meaning
by Viktor E. Frankl

The Legacy of Inherited Wealth: Interviews with Heirs
by Katherine Gibson and Barbara Blouin

The Voice of the Rising Generation: Family Wealth and Wisdom
by James E. Hughes Jr., Susan E. Massenzio, and Keith Whitaker

The Defining Decade: Why Your Twenties Matter—And How to Make the Most of Them Now
by Meg Jay

The Myth of the Silver Spoon: Navigating Family Wealth and Creating an Impactful Life
by Kristin Keffeler

Inherited Wealth: Opportunities and Dilemmas
by John L. Levy

Classified: How to Stop Hiding Your Privilege and Use It for Social Change!
   by Karen Pittelman and Resource Generation

The Inheritor's Sherpa: A Life-Summiting Guide for Inheritors
   by Myra Salzer

Living Richly: Seizing the Potential of Inherited Wealth
   by Myra Salzer and Greg I. Hamilton

The Ultimate Gift: A Novel
   by Jim Stovall

The Quest for Legitimacy
   by Jamie Weiner

Beyond Gold: True Wealth for Inheritors
   by Thayer Cheatham Willis

Dennis T. Jaffe and James A. Grubman, "Acquirers' and Inheritors' Dilemma: Discovering Life Purpose and Building Personal Identity in the Presence of Wealth," The Journal of Wealth Management Fall 2007, 10 (2) 20-44; DOI: https://doi.org/10.3905/jwm.2007.690946

Section Two

How to Love
   by Thích Nhất Hanh

The Generous Prenup: How to Support Your Marriage and Avoid the Pitfalls
   by Laurie Israel

The Heart of Money: A Couple's Guide to Creating True Financial Intimacy
   by Deborah Price

Section Three

The Gospel of Wealth
   by Andrew Carnegie

Raised Healthy, Wealthy & Wise
   by Coventry Edwards-Pitt

Generation Impact: How Next Gen Donors Are Revolutionizing Giving
   by Sharna Goldseker and Michael Moody

In Three Generations: A Story About Family, Wealth, and Beating the Odds
   by Kristen Heaney

Family Compact Among Generations
   by James E. Hughes Jr.

The Wise Inheritor's Guide to Freedom from Wealth
   by Charles A. Lowenhaupt

The Soul of Money: Transforming Your Relationship with Money and Life
   by Lynne Twist

Scott Peppet, "How would you know whether someone has (fully? sufficiently?) integrated financial wealth in a healthy way?" https://scottpeppet.com/articles/for-family-members/how-would-you-know-whether-someone-has-fully-sufficiently-integrated-financial-wealth-in-a-healthy-way/

Endnotes

Chapter One

[1] In their book, *Cross Cultures: How Global Families Negotiate Change across Generations* (2016), wealth consultants and psychologists Jim Grubman, PhD, and Dennis Jaffe, PhD, define three global cultures— Individualist culture (typically known as "Western"), Collective Harmony culture (typically known as "Eastern"), and Honor culture (reflected in diverse geographies, including Latin America, the Middle East, India, Africa, and Southern Europe). The authors explore how varying priorities and value systems of these cultures intersect with generational change in the family business and wealth management landscape.

[2] This is perhaps primarily true in a Western individualistic cultural model, as described by authors Dennis Jaffe and Jim Grubman in their book *Cross Cultures*.

[3] Meg Jay, *The Defining Decade: Why Your Twenties Matter—And How to Make the Most of Them Now* (New York: Twelve Books, 2012) xiv.

[4] Dennis Jaffe and Jim Grubman, "Acquirers' and Inheritors' Dilemma," Fall 2007, *The Journal of Wealth Management*, 3, 11. See https://clearingcustody.fidelity.com/app/proxy/content?literatureURL=/9895146.PDF.

[5] John Sedgwick, *Rich Kids* (New York: William Morrow and Company, 1985), 106–107. In Jaffe and Grubman, "Acquirers' and Inheritors' Dilemma," Fall 2007, *The Journal of Wealth Management*, 31.

[6] Zoë Beery, "The Rich Kids Who Want to Tear Down Capitalism," November 27, 2020, *The New York Times*, https://www.nytimes.com/2020/11/27/style/trust-fund-activism-resouce-generation.html.

[7] Eileen Rockefeller, *Being a Rockefeller, Becoming Myself: A Memoir* (New York: Blue Rider Press, 2013), 2.

[8] James E. Hughes, Susan E. Massenzio, and Keith Whitaker, *The Voice of the Rising Generation: Family Wealth and Wisdom* (Hoboken, NJ: Wiley Publishing, 2014), 17.

[9] James E. Hughes, Susan E. Massenzio, and Keith Whitaker, *The Cycle of the Gift: Family Wealth and Wisdom* (New York: Bloomberg Press, 2012), xxviii.

[10] Thích Nhất Hanh, *How to Love* (Berkeley, CA: Parallax Press, 2014), 17.

[11] Myra Salzer, *The Inheritor's Sherpa: The Life-Summiting Guide for Inheritors* (Boulder, CO: The Wealth Conservancy, 2005), 97.

[12] Coventry Edwards-Pit, *Raised Healthy, Wealthy & Wise* (2014), 22–32.

[13] Abraham Maslow, "A Theory of Human Motivation" in *Psychological Review*, vol. 50, 370–396, https://psychclassics.yorku.ca/Maslow/motivation.htm. In his later writings, Maslow articulated a higher need, self-transcendence—akin to altruism or spiritual needs—in which an individual is motivated by something outside of and beyond the self. Maslow's later writings viewed self-actualization as a necessary step to achieving this self-transcendence. See endnote 14 for more.

[14] Scott Barry Kaufman, *Transcend: The New Science of Self-Actualization* (New York: TarcherPerigree, 2021). Kaufman expands on Maslow's theory and builds on Maslow's later writings, which viewed self-actualization as a step on an ultimate path to transcendence of the self, or selflessness.

[15] Jaffe and Grubman, "Acquirers' and Inheritors' Dilemma," Fall 2007, *The Journal of Wealth Management*, 21, https://clearingcustody.fidelity.com/app/proxy/content?literatureURL=/9895146.PDF. Quoting Deanne Stone, *Family Issues*. Washington, DC: Council on Foundations, 1997, 55.

[16] Kelly Williams Brown, *Adulting: How to Become a Grown-up in 468 Easy(ish) Steps* (New York: Grand Central Publishing, 2013), 240.

[17] Peter Buffett, *Life Is What You Make It: Find Your Own Path to Fulfillment* (New York: Crown Publishing Group, 2011), 129.

[18] James E. Hughes, *Family: The Compact Among Generations* (New York: Bloomberg Press, 2007), 223–224.

[19] Meg Jay, *The Defining Decade*, 147.

20 Viktor Frankl, *Man's Search for Meaning* (Boston, MA: Beacon Press, 1946), 158.
21 Salzer, *The Inheritor's Sherpa*, 10.
22 Heather Havrileski, "I Am Rich and Worthless," April 17, 2019, "Ask Polly" advice column, *The Cut* (published by *New York* magazine), https://www.thecut.com/2019/04/ask-polly-i-am-rich-and-worthless.html.
23 Ralph Waldo Emerson, "Self-Reliance," in *Essays: First Series* (Boston: Houghton, Mifflin Company, 1841), 44, https://books.google.com/books?id=XIw5AQAAMAAJ&q=envy+is+ignorance#v=snippet&q=envy%20is%20ignorance&f=false.
24 Eleanor Roosevelt, *You Learn by Living: Eleven Keys for a More Fulfilling Life* (Louisville, KY: Westminster John Knox Press, 1983), 29.
25 Joshua Fields Millburn and Ryan Nicodemus, *Minimalism: Live a Meaningful Life* ([no location]: Asymmetrical Press, 2011), 107.
26 Heather Havrileski, "I Am Rich and Worthless," April 17, 2019, "Ask Polly" (advice column), *The Cut* (published by *New York* magazine), https://www.thecut.com/2019/04/ask-polly-i-am-rich-and-worthless.html.
27 Ibid., 4–5.
28 Buffett, *Life Is What You Make It*, 207–208.

Chapter Two

29 Joanie Bronfman, *The Experience of Inherited Wealth: A Social and Psychological Perspective*; PhD dissertation, Brandeis University, 1987, 108.
30 Rainier Zitelmann, interview, "What People Really Think About The Wealthy," June 26, 2020, *Family Wealth Report*, 4–5, https://www.familywealthreport.com/article.php?id=187774.
31 Karen Pittelman and Resource Generation, *Classified: How to Stop Hiding Your Privilege and Use It for Social Change* (New York: Soft Skull Press, 2006), p. 16.
32 Erving Goffman, *Stigma: Notes on the Management of Spoiled Identity* (New York: Touchstone Publishing [imprint of Simon & Schuster], 1963).
33 Eileen Rockefeller, *Being a Rockefeller*, p. 1.

[34] Jaffe and Grubman, "Acquirers' and Inheritors' Dilemma," Fall 2007, *The Journal of Wealth Management*, 14.
[35] Paul Schervish, Platon Coutsoukis, and Ethan Lewis, *Gospels of Wealth*. In Jaffe and Grubman, "Acquirers' and Inheritors' Dilemma," Fall 2007, *The Journal of Wealth Management*, 38, https://clearingcustody.fidelity.com/app/proxy/content?literatureURL=/9895146.PDF.
[36] Charles W. Collier, *Wealth in Families* (Boston: Harvard University Press, 2006), 19.
[37] Ibid.
[38] Paul Schervish, Platon Coutsoukis, and Ethan Lewis, *Gospels of Wealth* (New York: Praeger Publishing, 1994), 11.
[39] Brené Brown, *Dare to Lead: Brave Work, Tough Conversations*, Whole Hearts (New York: Random House, 2018), https://brenebrown.com/art/dare-to-lead-when-we-have-the-courage-to-walk-into-our-story-and-own-it/.
[40] Sally Jenkins, "On paper, Tom Brady was unremarkable; on the field, he grew into a legend," February 1, 2022, *Washington Post*, https://www.washingtonpost.com/sports/2022/02/01/jenkins-brady-retirement/.
[41] James Grubman, *Strangers in Paradise: How Families Adapt to Wealth across Generations* ([no location]: Familywealth Consulting, 2013), 7.
[42] Salzer, *The Inheritor's Sherpa*, 97.
[43] Buffett, *Life Is What You Make It*, 247–248.

Chapter Three

[44] Meg Jay, *The Defining Decade*, 69, 72.
[45] Frankl, *Man's Search for Meaning*, 37.
[46] Barbara Blouin and Katherine Gibson, *For Love and/or Money: The Impact of Inherited Wealth on Relationships*, revised edition (Trio Press, 1997), 5.
[47] Salzer, *The Inheritor's Sherpa*, 116.
[48] Thayer Willis, *Navigating the Dark Side of Wealth: A Life Guide for Inheritors* ([no location]: New Concord Press, 2002), 70.

[49] Alexandra Solomon, In Christine Gross Loh, "The First Lesson of Marriage 101: There Are No Soul Mates," February 12, 2014, *The Atlantic*, 5, https://www.theatlantic.com/education/archive/2014/02/the-first-lesson-of-marriage-101-there-are-no-soul-mates/283712/.
[50] Salzer, *The Inheritor's Sherpa*, 109–110.
[51] Thích Nhất Hanh, *How to Love*, 22.
[52] Massimo Pigliucci, *Answers for Aristotle: How Science and Philosophy Can Lead Us to a More Meaningful Life* (New York: Basic Books, 2012), 179.
[53] Thomas Lewis, M.D., Fari Amini, M.D., and Richard Lannon, M.D., *A General Theory of Love* (New York: Random House, 2000), 144.
[54] Ibid., 208–209.
[55] Salzer, *The Inheritor's Sherpa*, 111–112.
[56] Thích Nhất Hanh, *How to Love*, 50.

Chapter Four

[57] Derek Thompson, "How America's Marriage Crisis Makes Income Inequality So Much Worse," October 1, 2013, *The Atlantic*, https://www.theatlantic.com/business/archive/2013/10/how-americas-marriage-crisis-makes-income-inequality-so-much-worse/280056/.
[58] John M. Gottman and Nan Silver, *The Seven Principles for Making Marriage Work: A Practical Guide* (New York: Harmony Books, 2015), 26.
[59] Gary Chapman, *Things I Wish I'd Known Before We Got Married* ([no location]: Northfield Publishing, 2010), 85.
[60] In Helaine Olen, "Opinion: The common wisdom about managing money in relationships is wrong," March 29, 2022, *The Washington Post*, https://www.washingtonpost.com/opinions/2022/03/29/managing-money-relationships-advice-typically-wrong-new-paper-finds/.
[61] Laurie Israel, *The Generous Prenup: How to Support Your Marriage and Avoid the Pitfalls* (Brookline, MA: 2018), 9.
[62] Laurie Israel, "The Art of the Prenup—Use Sparingly," 2007, Israel Van Kooy Law, LLC. Laurie Israel writes: "In other words, it is my belief that having a prenuptial agreement, in many cases, makes it more likely (perhaps much more likely) that a divorce will ultimately occur. Put another

way, by reducing the risk, the gain (of having a lifetime marriage) is also reduced." See https://ivkdlaw.com/the-firm/our-articles/prenuptial-agreements-and-lawyering/the-art-of-the-prenup-%e2%80%94-use-sparingly/.

[63] Tom McCullough and Keith Whitaker, *Wealth of Wisdom: The Top 50 Questions Wealthy Families Ask* (Hoboken, NJ: Wiley Publishing, 2018), 64.

[64] James E. Hughes, Susan E. Massenzio, and Keith Whitaker, *The Cycle of the Gift: Family Wealth and Wisdom* (New York: Bloomberg Press, 2012), 93.

CHAPTER FIVE

[65] Kahlil Gibran, "On Children," *The Prophet* (New York: Alfred A. Knopf Publishing, 1923), https://poets.org/poem/children-1.

[66] Charles A. Lowenhaupt, *The Wise Inheritor's Guide to Freedom from Wealth: Making Family Wealth Work for You* (New York: Praeger Publishing, 2018), 78.

[67] Laurie Israel, "Ten Things I Hate about Prenuptial Agreements," April 30, 2021, https://www.laurieisrael.com/ten-things-i-hate-about-prenuptial-agreements/.

[68] Laurie Israel, "Why Prenups Are Bad for Your Marital Health," October 6, 2012, Mediate University, https://www.mediate.com/why-prenups-are-bad-for-your-marital-health/.

[69] Laurie Israel, "The Benefits of Prenuptial Agreement Mediation," January 26, 2022, https://www.laurieisrael.com/the-benefits-of-prenuptial-agreement-mediation/.

[70] Emily Bouchard and Emily Chase Smith, *Beginners Guide to Purposeful Prenups: Three Essential Elements for a Successful Prenup Conversation* (Irvine, CA: Redwood Publishing, 2018), 8.

Chapter Six

[71] Jennifer Petriglieri, "The Key to Bliss for a Dual-Career Couple? A Contract," October 4, 2019, *The Wall Street Journal*, https://www.wsj.com/articles/the-key-to-bliss-for-a-dual-career-couple-a-contract-11570186805.

[72] Coventry Edwards-Pitt, *Raised Healthy, Wealthy & Wise* (2014), 129.

[73] John Gottman and Julie Schwartz Gottman, *Eight Dates: Essential Conversations for a Lifetime of Love* (New York: Workman Publishing Company, 2019), 117.

[74] James E. Hughes, Joanie Bronfman, Jacqueline Merrill, "Reflections on Fiscal Unequals," 2000 (originally published in *The Chase Journal*, Volume IV, Issue 4), 2, https://static1.squarespace.com/static/562bfb3ce4b022641da90dbb/t/56c0b62359827e22c042ffd/1455470115277/FiscalUnequals.pdf.

[75] Ibid., 6.

[76] Michele Mikeska, "When She Has the Money," 2019, dissertation; includes a beta study of six couples, a paper titled "When She Has the Money: Challenging Ancient Conventions and Supporting the New Normal: from Fiscal Unequals to Financial Diversity" by Kristin Keffeler, Will Hughes, and Adrienne Iglehart (2021); and an ongoing continuation of the study interviewing couples in this situation by wealth consultant and psychologist Dr. Jamie Traeger-Muney (who joined with Kristin and Michele). The purpose of the ongoing study is to expand on this initial work, codify research and best practices to help these couples flourish, and continue to erode the taboo many couples feel discussing this topic. For more information on the study or if you'd like to contribute your personal experiences with this situation to the study, see: https://wealthlegacygroup.org/financially-diverse-couples-research-project/; also, see Joe Reilly's interview in *Family Wealth Report* with Kristin Keffeler (titled HNW Family's Wealth Dynamics: Who's Really in Charge, June 18, 2019) for more information on the study and a fuller explication of this topic and its impact on broader family relationships: https://www.familywealthreport.com/article.php?id=183960.

[77] Hughes, et al., "Reflections on Fiscal Unequals," 11.

[78] Ibid., 14.
[79] Petriglieri, "The Key to Bliss," October 4, 2019, *The Wall Street Journal*.
[80] Hughes, et al., "Reflections on Fiscal Unequals," 18.
[81] Ibid., 13–18.

Chapter Seven

[82] Chapman, *Things I Wish I'd Known*, 101.
[83] Lowenhaupt, *The Wise Inheritor's Guide*, 87.
[84] James E. Hughes, *Family: The Compact Among Generations* (New York: Bloomberg Press, 2007) 21–22.
[85] Ibid., 130–131.
[86] Ellen Miley Perry, *A Wealth of Possibilities: Navigating Family, Money, and Legacy* (Ely, UK: Egremont Press, 2012) 81.
[87] Lowenhaupt, *The Wise Inheritor's Guide*, 91.
[88] Ibid., 88.
[89] Eileen Rockefeller, *Being a Rockefeller*, 177–178.
[90] Stephanie Brun de Pontet, Craig E. Aronoff, Drew S. Mendoza, and John L. Ward, *Siblings and the Family Business: Making It Work for Business, the Family, and the Future* (New York: Palgrave Macmillan, 2012), 46.

Chapter Eight

[91] John L. Levy, *Inherited Wealth: Opportunities and Dilemmas* (Charleston, SC: BookSurge Publishing, 2012), 39–40.
[92] Willis, *Navigating the Dark Side of Wealth*, 79.
[93] Kristin Keffeler, *The Myth of the Silver Spoon: Navigating Family Wealth and Creating an Impactful Life* (Hoboken, NJ: Wiley Publishing, 2022), 185.
[94] Lynne Twist, *The Soul of Money: Transforming Your Relationship with Money and Life* (New York: W. W. Norton and Company, 2017), 241.

95 Jaffe and Grubman, "Acquirers' and Inheritors' Dilemma," Fall 2007, *The Journal of Wealth Management*, 18. See https://clearingcustody.fidelity.com/app/proxy/content?literatureURL=/9895146.PDF.
96 Levy, *Inherited Wealth*, 29.

CHAPTER NINE

97 Hughes, et al., *The Voice of the Rising Generation*, 26, referencing Doolin, Preisser, and Williams, "Engaging and Retaining Families," In *Investments and Wealth Monitor*, September/October 2011, 10–16.
98 Jamie Weiner; *The Quest for Legitimacy: How Children of Prominent Families Discover Their Unique Place in the World* (Hoboken, NJ: Wiley Publishing, 2022), 65–66.
99 Charlotte B. Beyer, *Wealth Management Unwrapped* (Hoboken, NJ: Wiley Publishing, 2017), 100.
100 Lowenhaupt, *The Wise Inheritor's Guide*, 135.
101 Andrew Carnegie, *The Gospel of Wealth and Other Timely Essays* (New York: The Century Company, 1901), 9. See https://books.google.com/books?id=q5ALvRp61wgC&printsec=titlepage&dq=Carnegie+onCuba&lr=&sou...#v=onepage&q&f=false.

CHAPTER TEN

102 George Vaillant, *Spiritual Evolution: How We Are Wired for Faith, Hope, and Love* (New York: Harmony Books, 2009), 101. In Scott Barry Kaufman, *Transcend: The New Science of Self-Actualization* (New York: TarcherPerigree, 2021), 119.
103 Originally published in Buechner's *Wishful Thinking* and later in *Beyond Words* and quoted on page 133 of Kristen Heaney's wonderful book, *in Three Generations*.
104 Twist, *The Soul of Money*, 40, 17, xxvii.

Notes

Notes

Notes